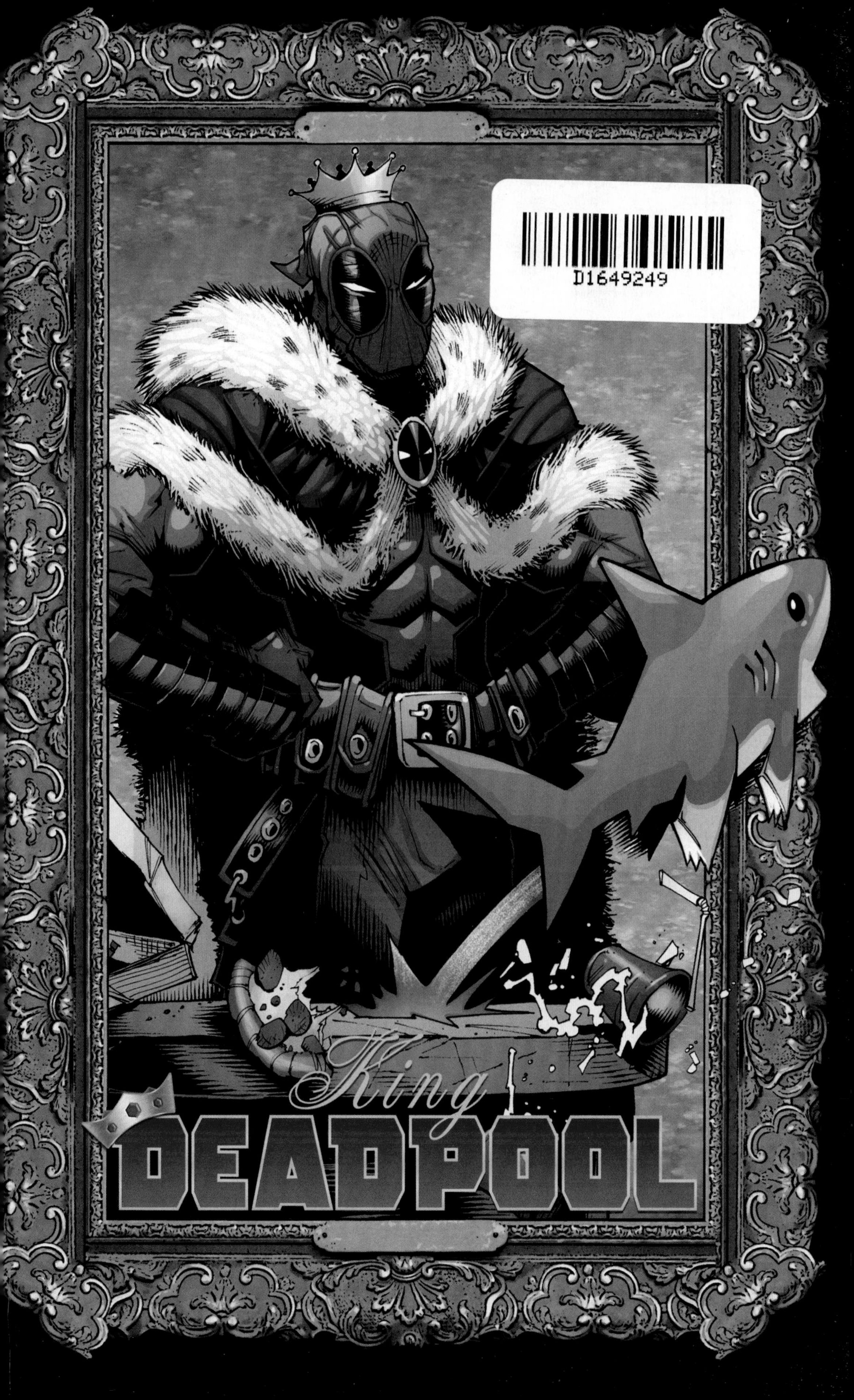
King
DEADPOOL

CHOSEN TO TAKE PART IN A TOP-SECRET GOVERNMENT PROGRAM, WADE WILSON WAS BESTOWED WITH THE ABILITY TO HEAL FROM ANY WOUND. HE BECAME A MERCENARY. THEN, FOR A WHILE, HE TRIED TO BE A HERO.

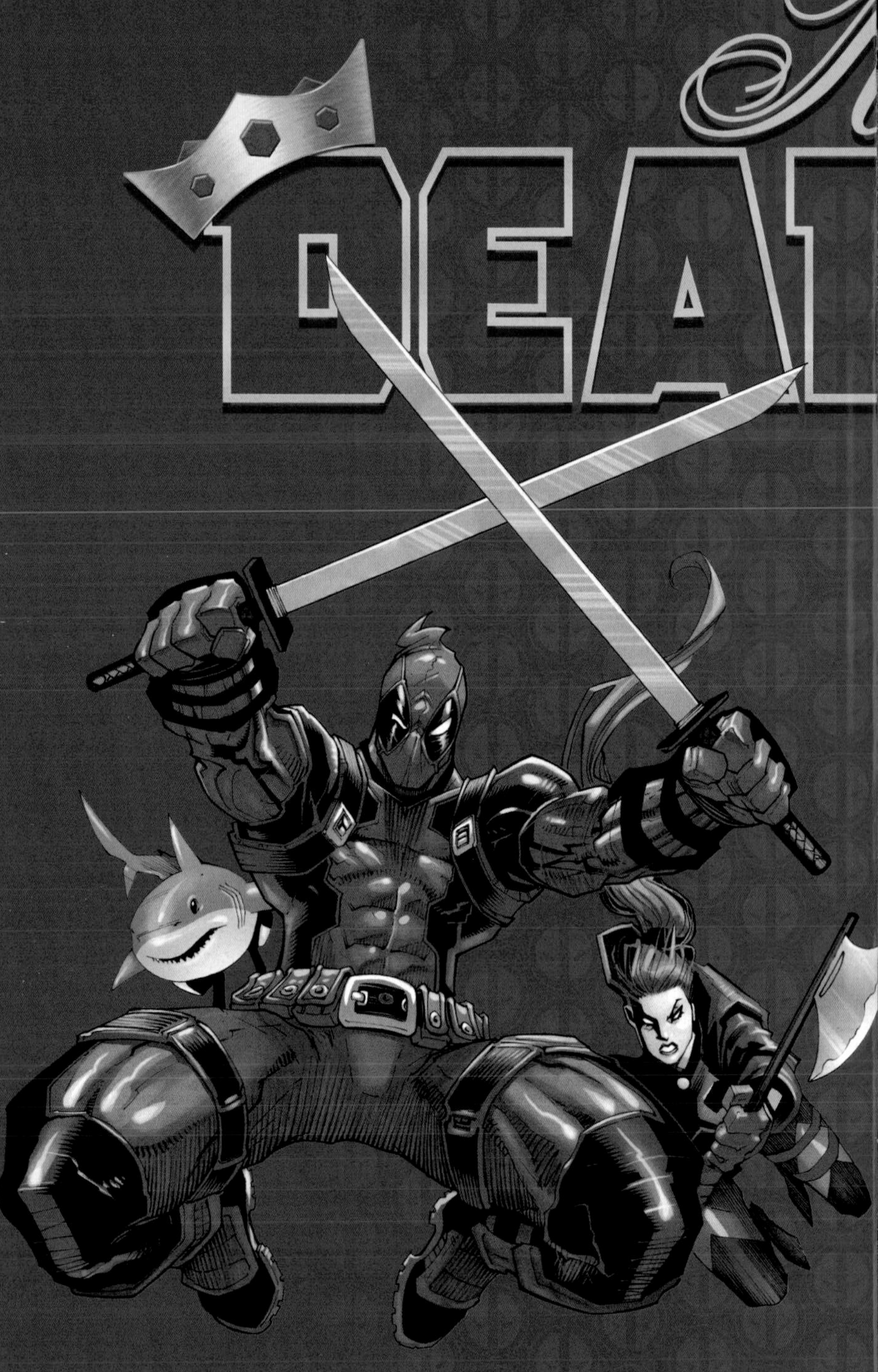

KING DEADPOOL VOL. 2. Contains material originally published in magazine form as DEADPOOL (2019) #7-10. First printing 2021. ISBN 978-1-302-92104-0. Published by MARVEL WORLDWIDE, INC., a subsidiary of MARVEL ENTERTAINMENT, LLC. OFFICE OF PUBLICATION: 1290 Avenue of the Americas, New York, NY 10104. **Printed in Canada.** KEVIN FEIGE, Chief Creative Officer; DAN BUCKLEY, President, Marvel Entertainment; JOE QUESADA, EVP & Creative Director; DAVID BOGART, Associate Publisher & SVP of Talent Affairs; TOM BREVOORT, VP, Executive Editor; NICK LOWE, Executive Editor, VP of Content, Digital Publishing; DAVID GABRIEL, VP of Print & Digital Publishing; JEFF YOUNGQUIST, VP of Production & Special Projects; ALEX MORALES, Director of Publishing Operations; DAN EDINGTON, Managing Editor; RICKEY PURDIN, Director of Talent Relations; JENNIFER GRÜNWALD, Senior Editor, Special Projects; SUSAN CRESPI, Production Manager; STAN LEE, Chairman Emeritus. For information regarding advertising in Marvel Comics or on Marvel.com, please contact Vit DeBellis, Custom Solutions & Integrated Advertising Manager, at vdebellis@marvel.com. For Marvel subscription inquiries, please call 888-511-5480. **Manufactured between 3/12/2021 and 4/13/2021 by SOLISCO PRINTERS, SCOTT, QC, CANADA.**

10 9 8 7 6 5 4 3 2 1

IT... WELL, IT WENT PRETTY BADLY. SO BADLY THAT
WADE DECIDED TO GO BACK TO BEING A CLASSIC
CHAOS AGENT, THE MERC WITH THE MOUTH, THE
REGENERATIN' DEGENERATE KNOWN AS...

KELLY THOMPSON
WRITER

GERARDO SANDOVAL
PENCILER

VICTOR NAVA (#7-10) &
GERARDO SANDOVAL (#7-8, #10)
INKERS

CHRIS SOTOMAYOR
COLOR ARTIST

VC'S JOE SABINO
LETTERER

CHRIS BACHALO (#7-9) WITH AL VEY (#7-8) &
TIM TOWNSEND (#9); AND GERARDO SANDOVAL &
CHRIS SOTOMAYOR (#10)
COVER ART

SALENA MAHINA
LOGO

LINDSEY COHICK &
SHANNON ANDREWS
BALLESTEROS
ASSISTANT EDITORS

JAKE THOMAS
EDITOR

DEADPOOL CREATED BY ROB LIEFELD & FABIAN NICIEZA

COLLECTION EDITOR JENNIFER GRÜNWALD
ASSISTANT EDITOR DANIEL KIRCHHOFFER
ASSISTANT MANAGING EDITOR MAIA LOY
ASSISTANT MANAGING EDITOR LISA MONTALBANO
VP PRODUCTION & SPECIAL PROJECTS JEFF YOUNGQUIST
BOOK DESIGNERS STACIE ZUCKER WITH SALENA MAHINA AND CARLOS LAO
SVP PRINT, SALES & MARKETING DAVID GABRIEL
EDITOR IN CHIEF C.B. CEBULSKI

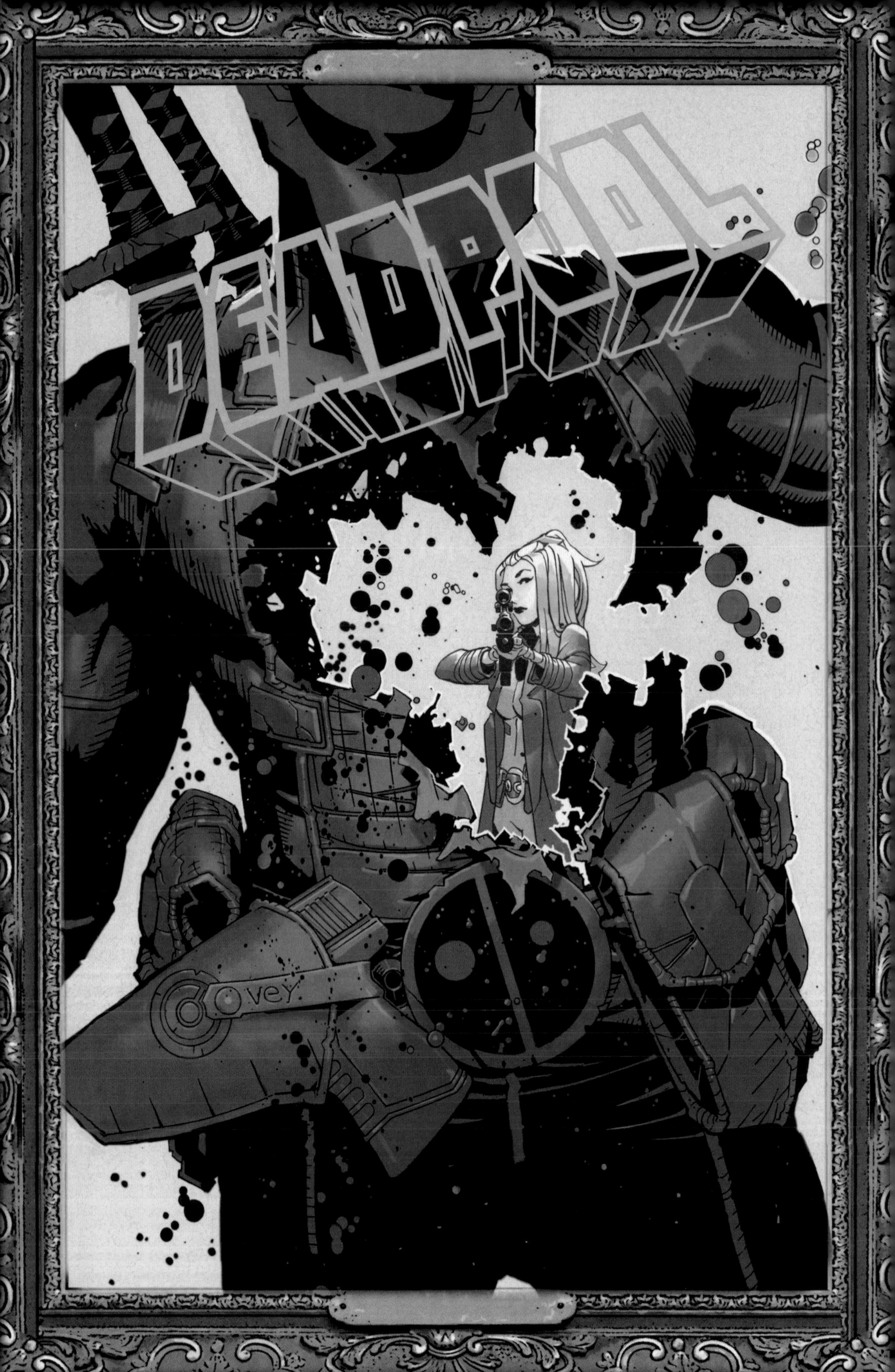
DEADPOOL

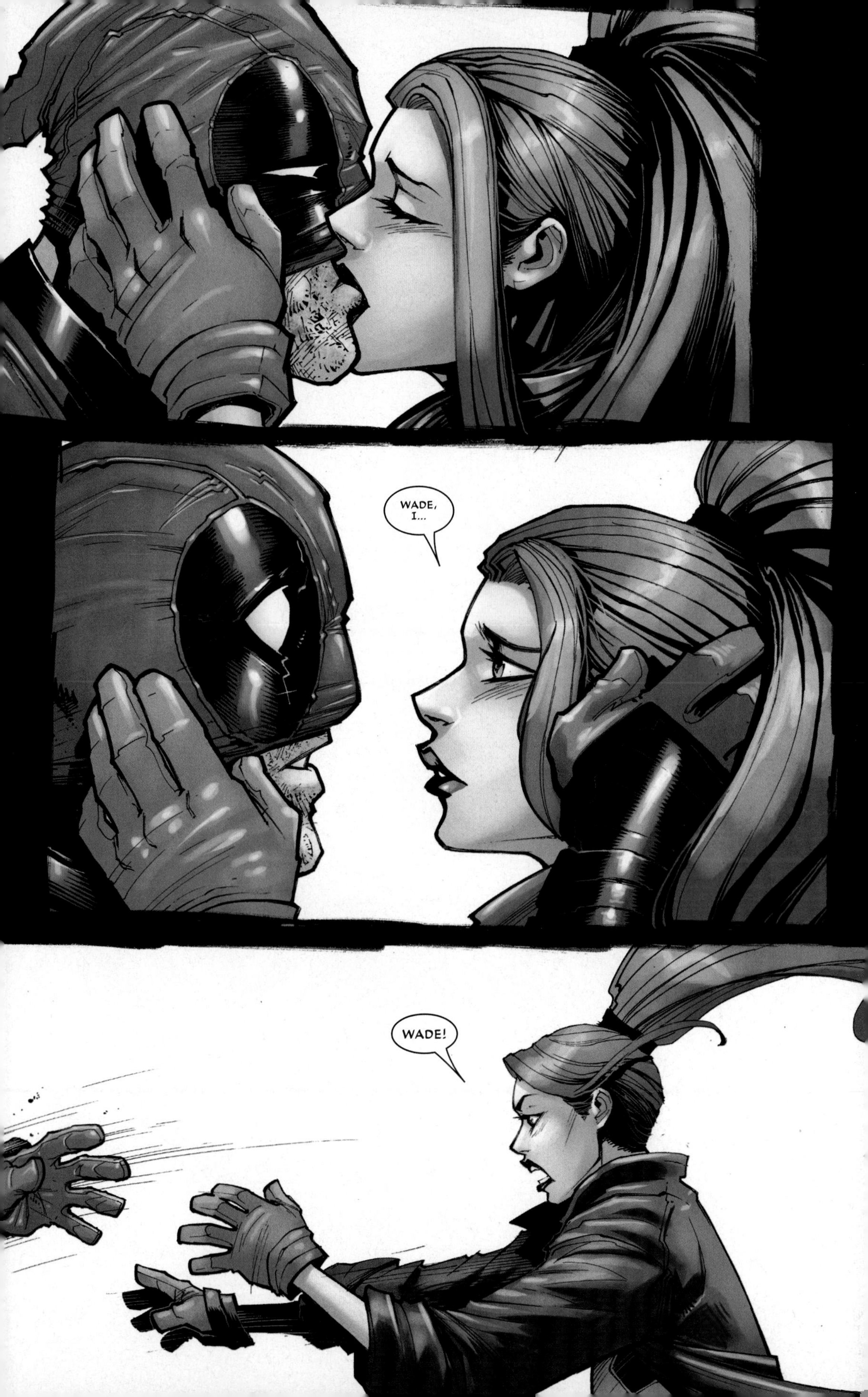
WADE, I...
WADE!

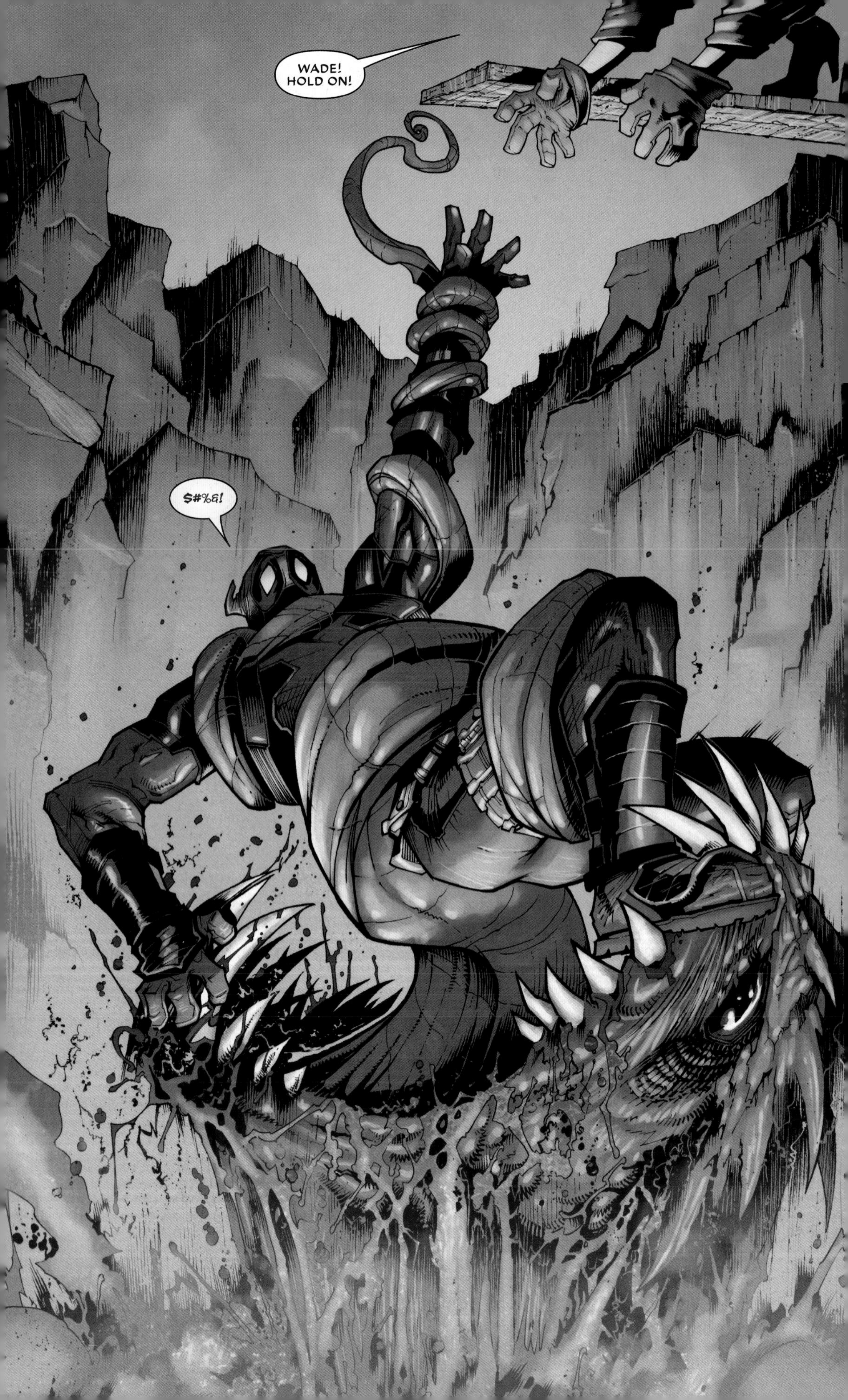
WADE! HOLD ON!
$#%&!

When monsters took over Staten Island thanks to a centuries-old legal claim, Deadpool was hired to slay the Monster King. Wade killed the king, which, according to monster law, made HIM the new king of the monsters!

Being king turned out to be a lot less fun than it seemed. Deadpool's reign began with numerous bureaucratic complaints, a hostile Royal Guard Corps, the appearance of monster hunter Elsa Bloodstone, and tense relations with the neighboring boroughs. But after saving his monster citizens from a killing spree by Kraven the Hunter, Deadpool gained the trust of his royal subjects, as well as the loyalty of his royal guards.

Of course, nothing in Deadpool's life ever stays hunky-dory for long. Like a bad penny, Elsa turned up with some dire news: the bloodstone embedded in her palm is killing her, and she needs Wade's help to stop it — before it's too late!

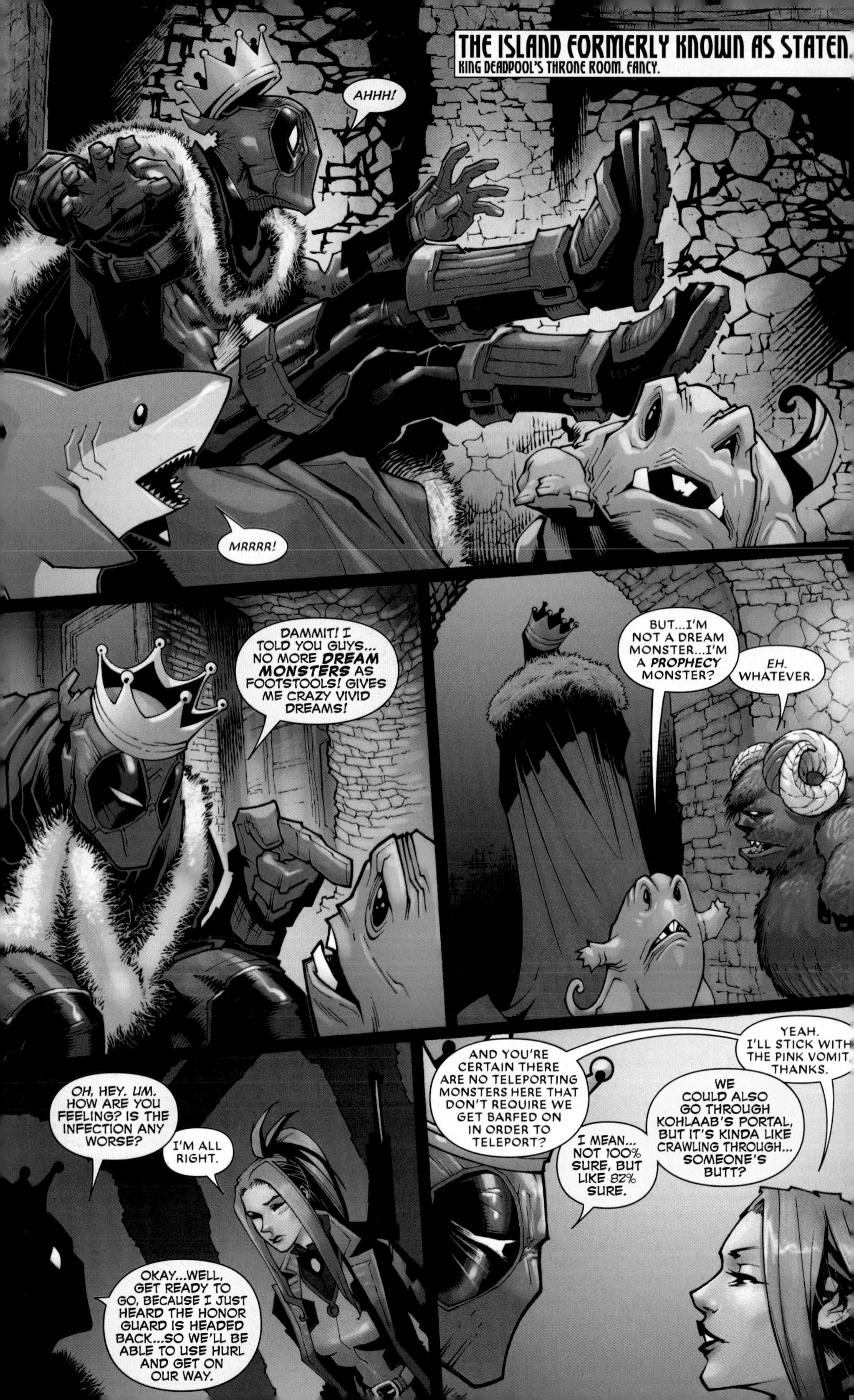
THE ISLAND FORMERLY KNOWN AS STATEN.
KING DEADPOOL'S THRONE ROOM. FANCY.
AHHH!
MRRRR!
DAMMIT! I TOLD YOU GUYS... NO MORE DREAM MONSTERS AS FOOTSTOOLS! GIVES ME CRAZY VIVID DREAMS!
BUT...I'M NOT A DREAM MONSTER...I'M A PROPHECY MONSTER?
EH. WHATEVER.
OH, HEY. UM. HOW ARE YOU FEELING? IS THE INFECTION ANY WORSE?
I'M ALL RIGHT.
OKAY...WELL, GET READY TO GO, BECAUSE I JUST HEARD THE HONOR GUARD IS HEADED BACK...SO WE'LL BE ABLE TO USE HURL AND GET ON OUR WAY.
AND YOU'RE CERTAIN THERE ARE NO TELEPORTING MONSTERS HERE THAT DON'T REQUIRE WE GET BARFED ON IN ORDER TO TELEPORT?
I MEAN... NOT 100% SURE, BUT LIKE 82% SURE.
WE COULD ALSO GO THROUGH KOHLAAB'S PORTAL, BUT IT'S KINDA LIKE CRAWLING THROUGH... SOMEONE'S BUTT?
YEAH. I'LL STICK WITH THE PINK VOMIT, THANKS.

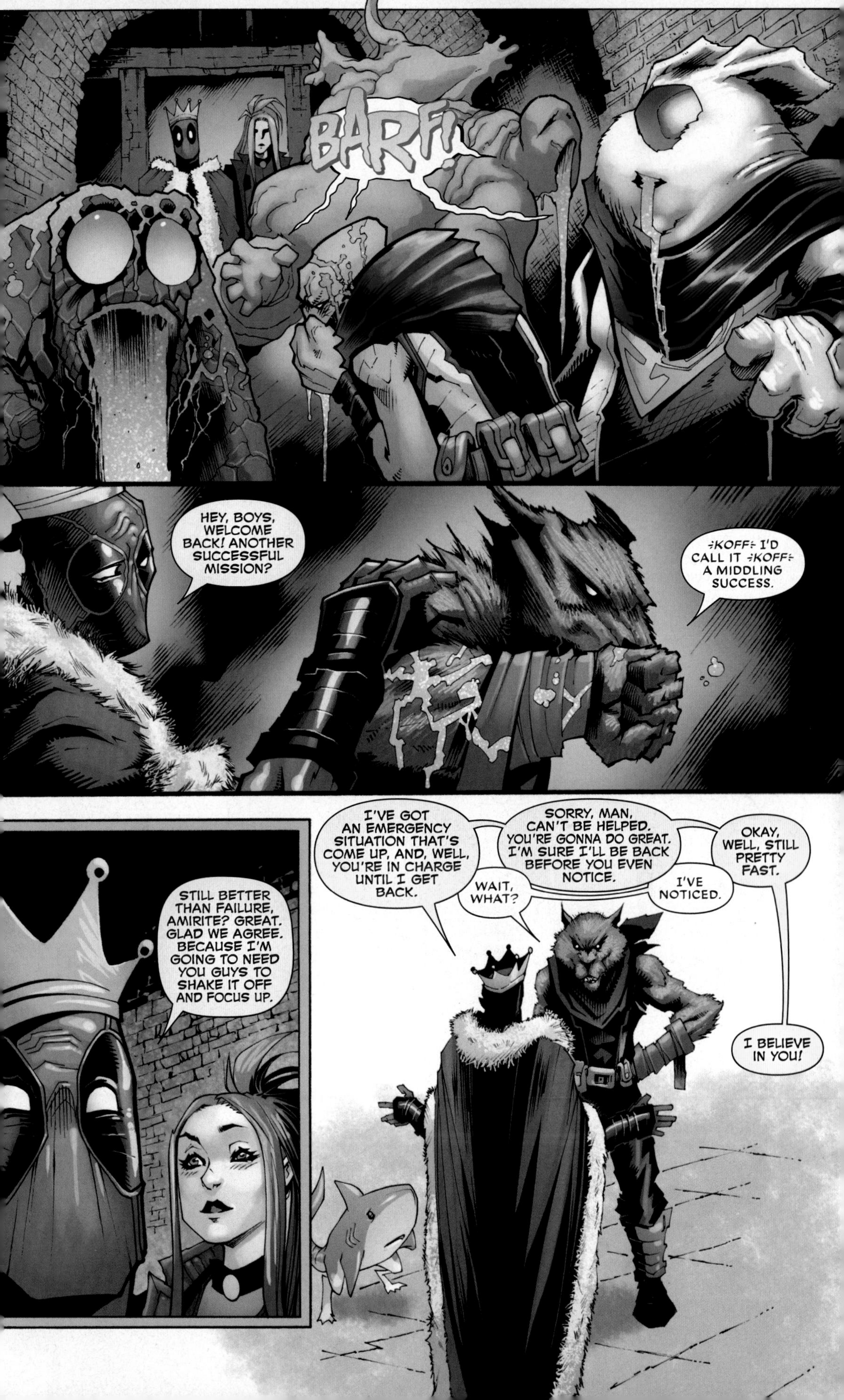
BARF!
HEY, BOYS, WELCOME BACK! ANOTHER SUCCESSFUL MISSION?
÷KOFF÷ I'D CALL IT ÷KOFF÷ A MIDDLING SUCCESS.
STILL BETTER THAN FAILURE, AMIRITE? GREAT. GLAD WE AGREE. BECAUSE I'M GOING TO NEED YOU GUYS TO SHAKE IT OFF AND FOCUS UP.
I'VE GOT AN EMERGENCY SITUATION THAT'S COME UP, AND, WELL, YOU'RE IN CHARGE UNTIL I GET BACK.
WAIT, WHAT?
SORRY, MAN, CAN'T BE HELPED. YOU'RE GONNA DO GREAT. I'M SURE I'LL BE BACK BEFORE YOU EVEN NOTICE.
I'VE NOTICED.
OKAY, WELL, STILL PRETTY FAST.
I BELIEVE IN YOU!

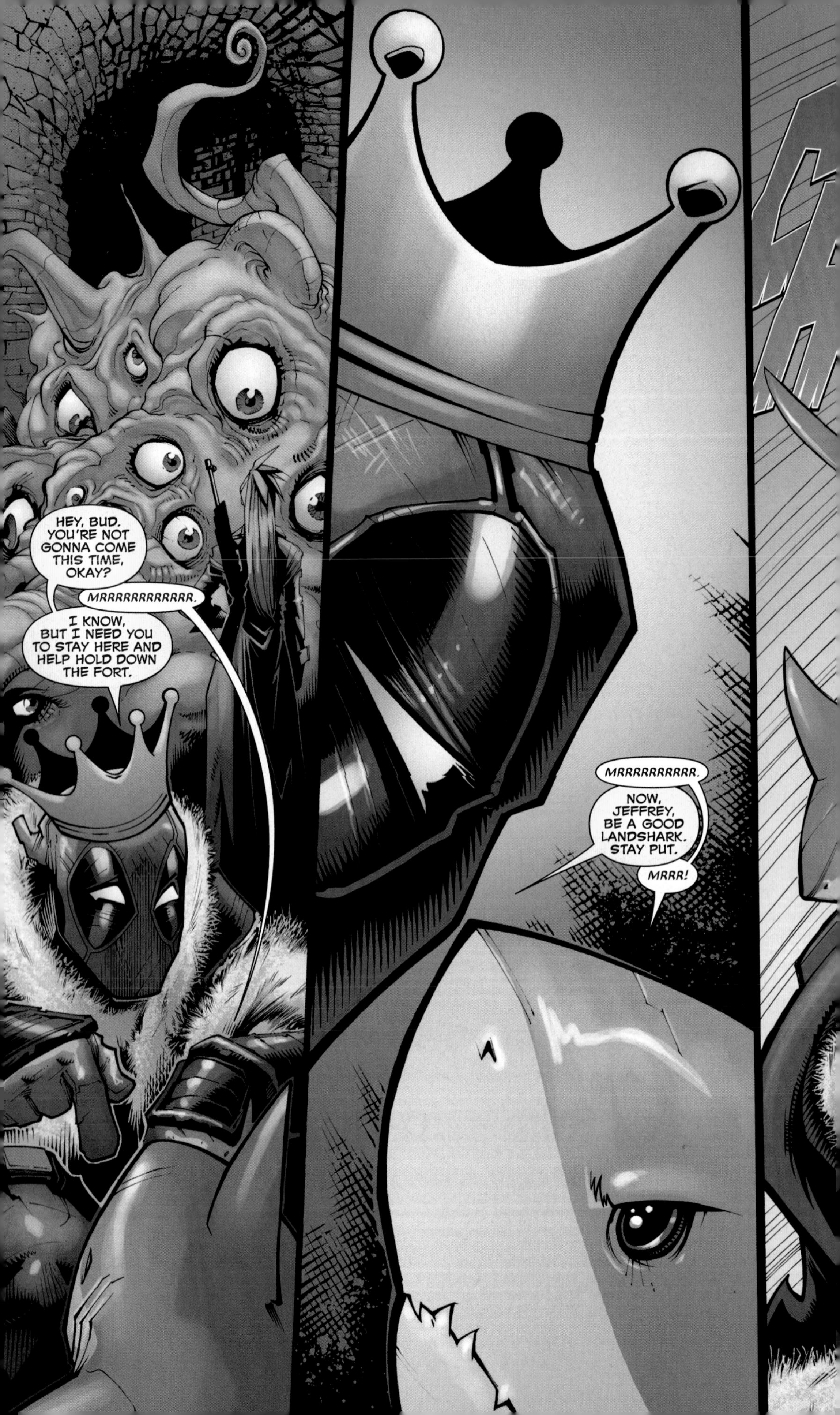
HEY, BUD. YOU'RE NOT GONNA COME THIS TIME, OKAY?
MRRRRRRRRRRRR.
I KNOW, BUT I NEED YOU TO STAY HERE AND HELP HOLD DOWN THE FORT.
MRRRRRRRRRR.
NOW, JEFFREY, BE A GOOD LANDSHARK. STAY PUT.
MRRR!

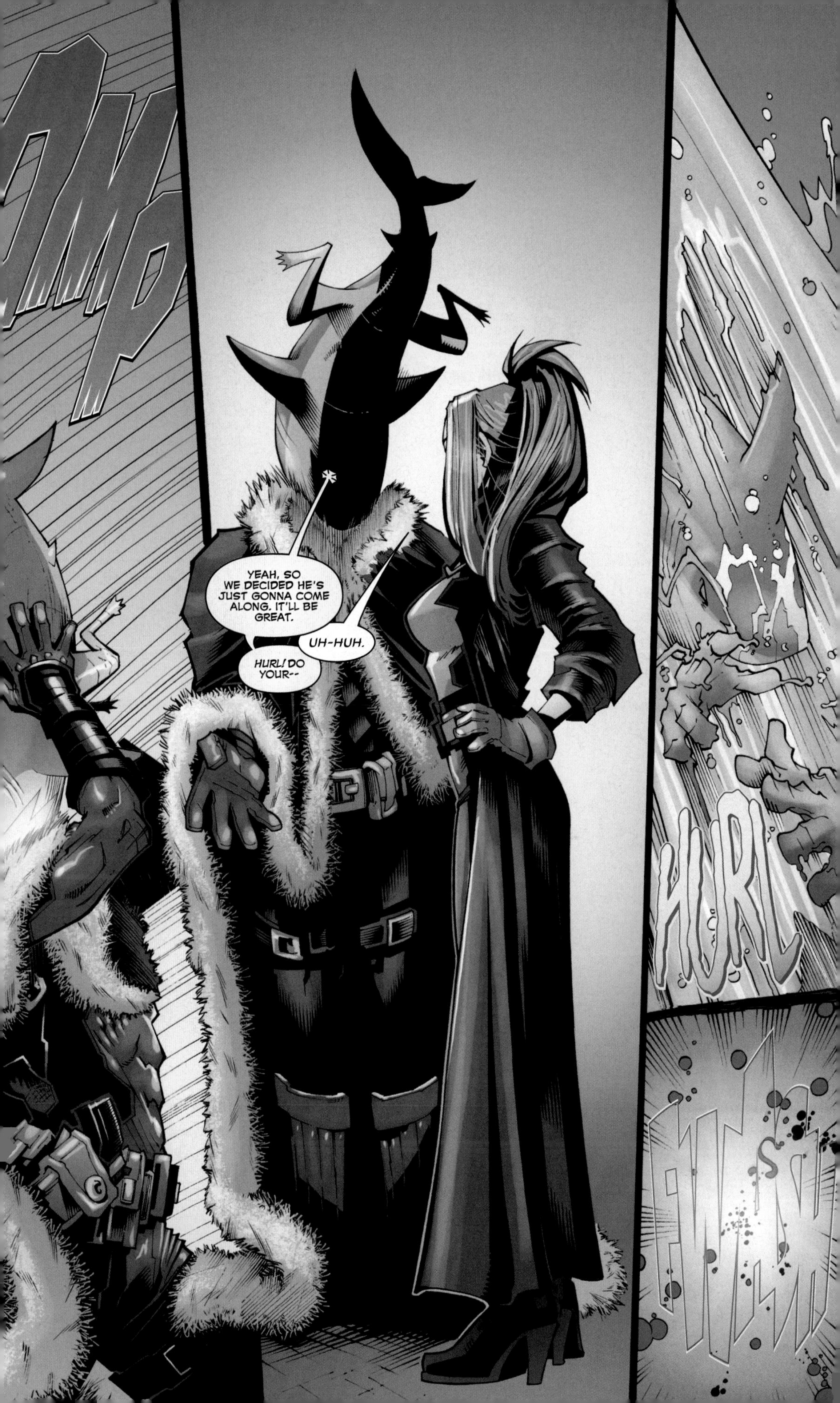

YEAH, SO WE DECIDED HE'S JUST GONNA COME ALONG. IT'LL BE GREAT.
UH-HUH.
HURL! DO YOUR--
HURL

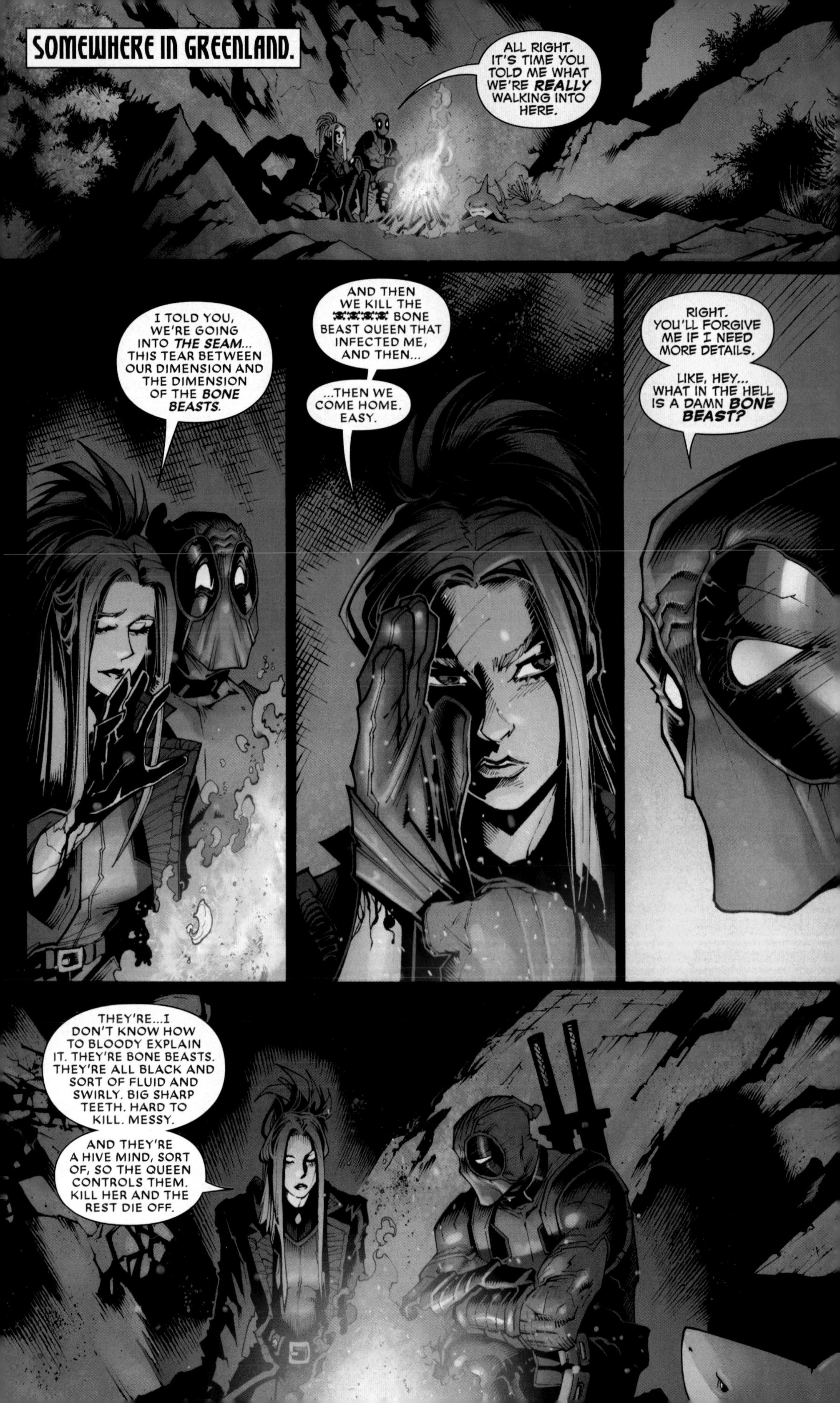

SOMEWHERE IN GREENLAND.
ALL RIGHT. IT'S TIME YOU TOLD ME WHAT WE'RE REALLY WALKING INTO HERE.
I TOLD YOU, WE'RE GOING INTO THE SEAM... THIS TEAR BETWEEN OUR DIMENSION AND THE DIMENSION OF THE BONE BEASTS.
AND THEN WE KILL THE ☠☠☠☠ BONE BEAST QUEEN THAT INFECTED ME, AND THEN...
...THEN WE COME HOME. EASY.
RIGHT. YOU'LL FORGIVE ME IF I NEED MORE DETAILS.
LIKE, HEY... WHAT IN THE HELL IS A DAMN BONE BEAST?
THEY'RE...I DON'T KNOW HOW TO BLOODY EXPLAIN IT. THEY'RE BONE BEASTS. THEY'RE ALL BLACK AND SORT OF FLUID AND SWIRLY. BIG SHARP TEETH. HARD TO KILL. MESSY.
AND THEY'RE A HIVE MIND, SORT OF, SO THE QUEEN CONTROLS THEM. KILL HER AND THE REST DIE OFF.

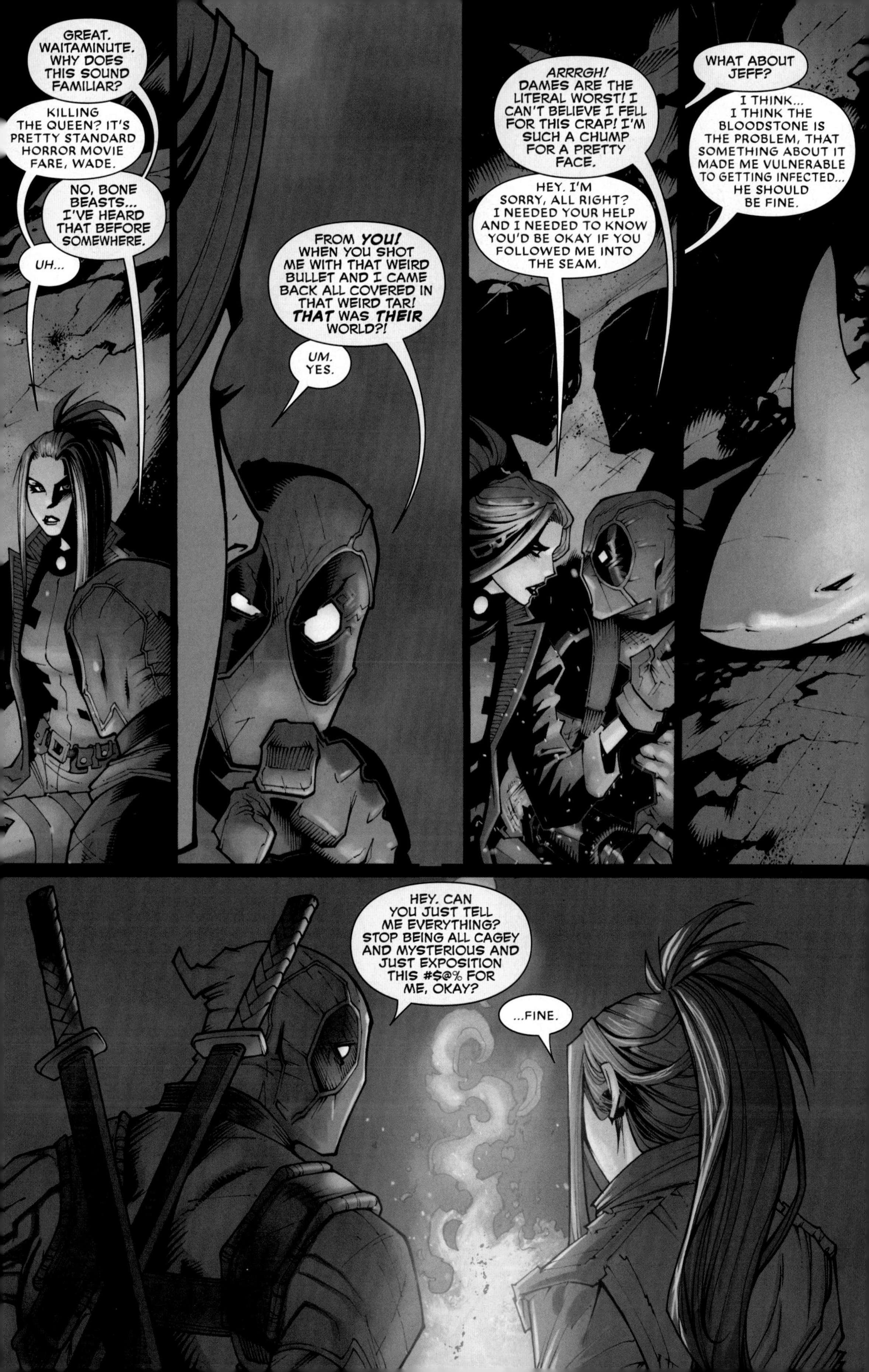
GREAT. WAITAMINUTE. WHY DOES THIS SOUND FAMILIAR?
KILLING THE QUEEN? IT'S PRETTY STANDARD HORROR MOVIE FARE, WADE.
NO, BONE BEASTS... I'VE HEARD THAT BEFORE SOMEWHERE.
UH...
FROM YOU! WHEN YOU SHOT ME WITH THAT WEIRD BULLET AND I CAME BACK ALL COVERED IN THAT WEIRD TAR! THAT WAS THEIR WORLD?!
UM. YES.
ARRRGH! DAMES ARE THE LITERAL WORST! I CAN'T BELIEVE I FELL FOR THIS CRAP! I'M SUCH A CHUMP FOR A PRETTY FACE.
HEY. I'M SORRY, ALL RIGHT? I NEEDED YOUR HELP AND I NEEDED TO KNOW YOU'D BE OKAY IF YOU FOLLOWED ME INTO THE SEAM.
WHAT ABOUT JEFF?
I THINK... I THINK THE BLOODSTONE IS THE PROBLEM, THAT SOMETHING ABOUT IT MADE ME VULNERABLE TO GETTING INFECTED... HE SHOULD BE FINE.
HEY. CAN YOU JUST TELL ME EVERYTHING? STOP BEING ALL CAGEY AND MYSTERIOUS AND JUST EXPOSITION THIS #$@% FOR ME, OKAY?
...FINE.

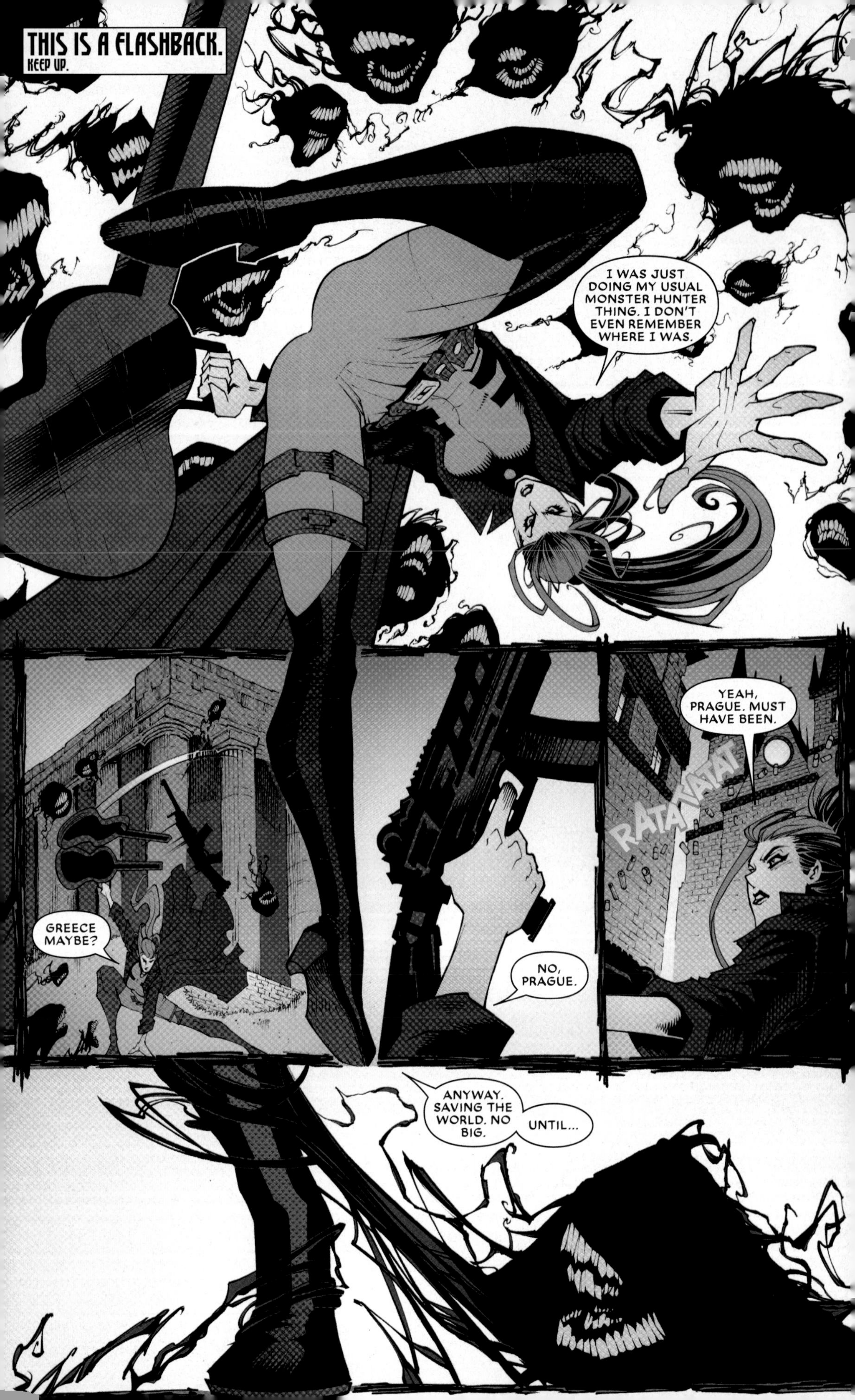
THIS IS A FLASHBACK.
KEEP UP.
I WAS JUST DOING MY USUAL MONSTER HUNTER THING. I DON'T EVEN REMEMBER WHERE I WAS.
GREECE MAYBE?
NO, PRAGUE.
YEAH, PRAGUE. MUST HAVE BEEN.
RATATATAT
ANYWAY. SAVING THE WORLD. NO BIG.
UNTIL...

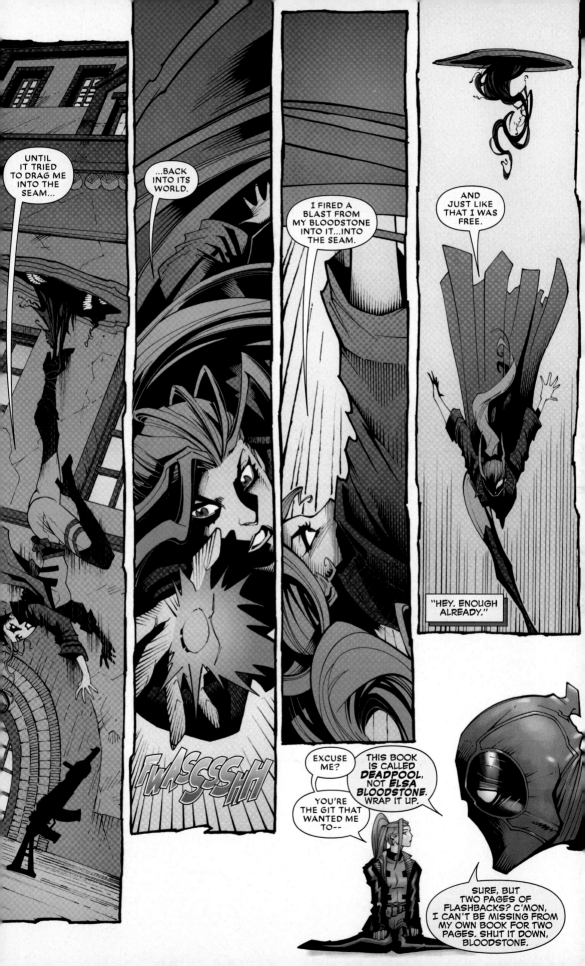

UNTIL IT TRIED TO DRAG ME INTO THE SEAM...

...BACK INTO ITS WORLD.

I FIRED A BLAST FROM MY BLOODSTONE INTO IT...INTO THE SEAM.

AND JUST LIKE THAT I WAS FREE.

"HEY. ENOUGH ALREADY."

FWASSSSHH

EXCUSE ME?

THIS BOOK IS CALLED *DEADPOOL,* NOT *ELSA BLOODSTONE.* WRAP IT UP.

YOU'RE THE GIT THAT WANTED ME TO--

SURE, BUT TWO PAGES OF FLASHBACKS? C'MON, I CAN'T BE MISSING FROM MY OWN BOOK FOR TWO PAGES. SHUT IT DOWN, BLOODSTONE.

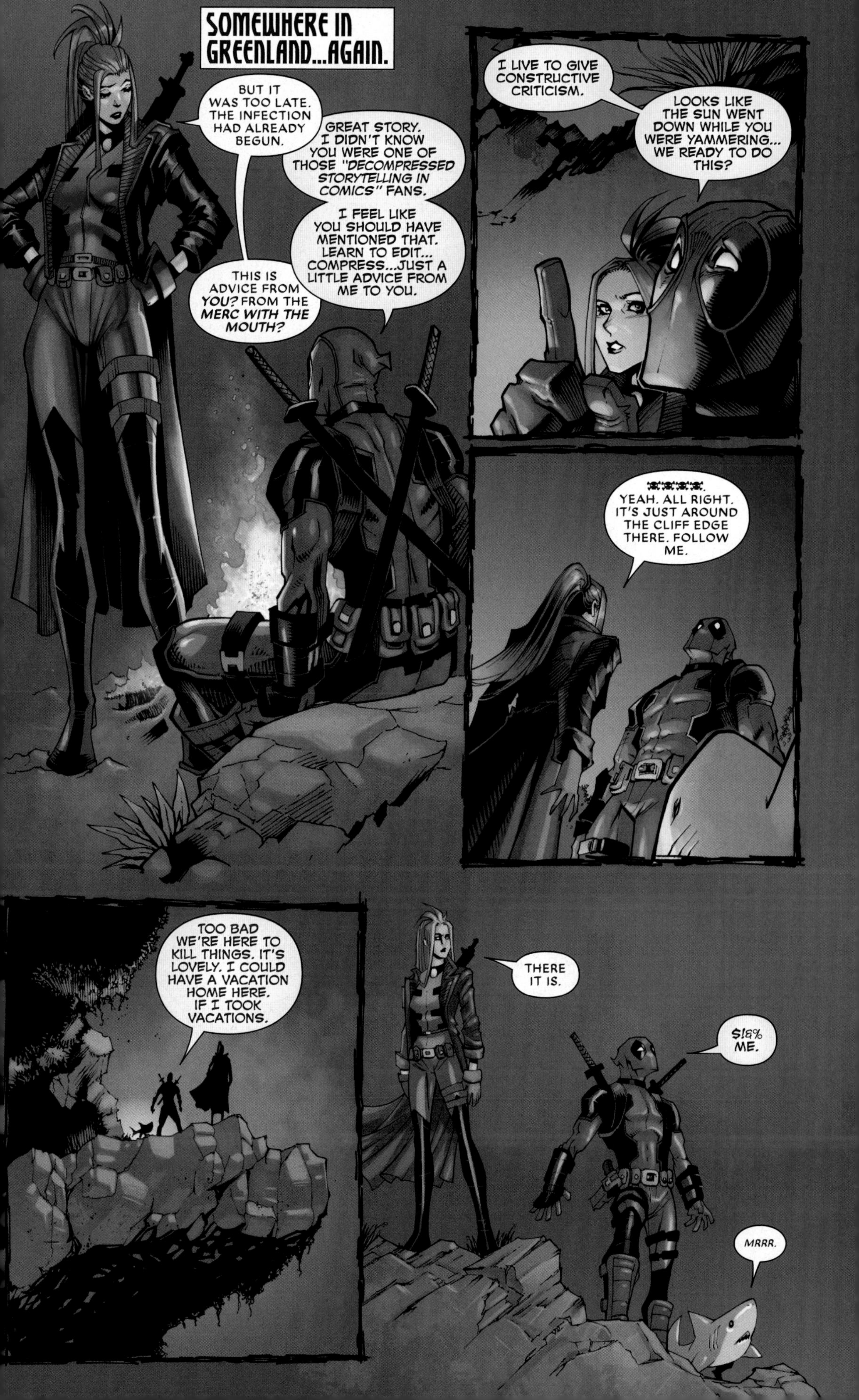

SOMEWHERE IN GREENLAND...AGAIN.
BUT IT WAS TOO LATE. THE INFECTION HAD ALREADY BEGUN.
GREAT STORY. I DIDN'T KNOW YOU WERE ONE OF THOSE "DECOMPRESSED STORYTELLING IN COMICS" FANS.
I FEEL LIKE YOU SHOULD HAVE MENTIONED THAT. LEARN TO EDIT... COMPRESS...JUST A LITTLE ADVICE FROM ME TO YOU.
THIS IS ADVICE FROM YOU? FROM THE MERC WITH THE MOUTH?
I LIVE TO GIVE CONSTRUCTIVE CRITICISM.
LOOKS LIKE THE SUN WENT DOWN WHILE YOU WERE YAMMERING... WE READY TO DO THIS?
YEAH. ALL RIGHT. IT'S JUST AROUND THE CLIFF EDGE THERE. FOLLOW ME.
TOO BAD WE'RE HERE TO KILL THINGS. IT'S LOVELY. I COULD HAVE A VACATION HOME HERE. IF I TOOK VACATIONS.
THERE IT IS.
$!&% ME.
MRRR.

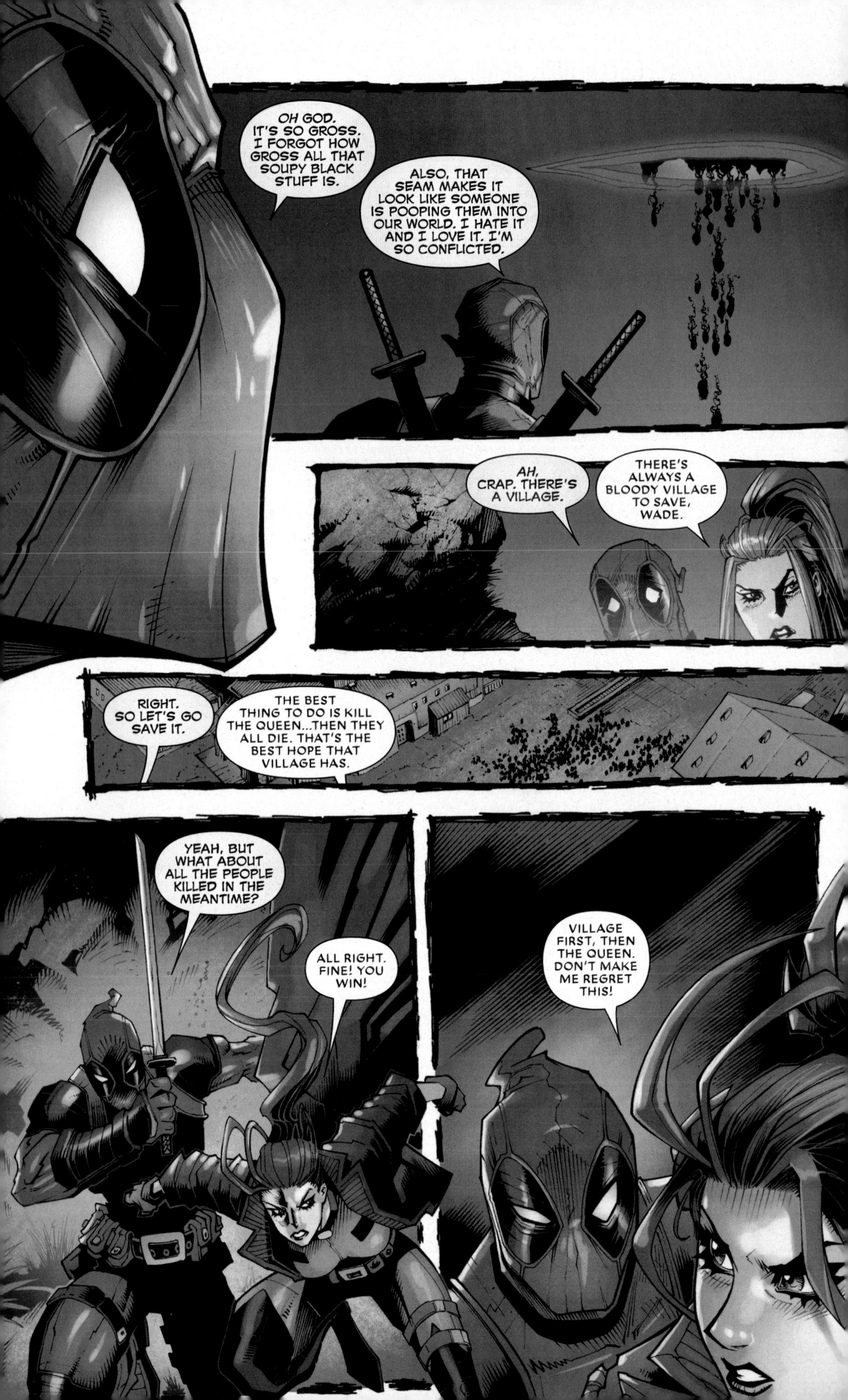
OH GOD. IT'S SO GROSS. I FORGOT HOW GROSS ALL THAT SOUPY BLACK STUFF IS.
ALSO, THAT SEAM MAKES IT LOOK LIKE SOMEONE IS POOPING THEM INTO OUR WORLD. I HATE IT AND I LOVE IT. I'M SO CONFLICTED.
AH, CRAP. THERE'S A VILLAGE.
THERE'S ALWAYS A BLOODY VILLAGE TO SAVE, WADE.
RIGHT. SO LET'S GO SAVE IT.
THE BEST THING TO DO IS KILL THE QUEEN...THEN THEY ALL DIE. THAT'S THE BEST HOPE THAT VILLAGE HAS.
YEAH, BUT WHAT ABOUT ALL THE PEOPLE KILLED IN THE MEANTIME?
ALL RIGHT. FINE! YOU WIN!
VILLAGE FIRST, THEN THE QUEEN. DON'T MAKE ME REGRET THIS!

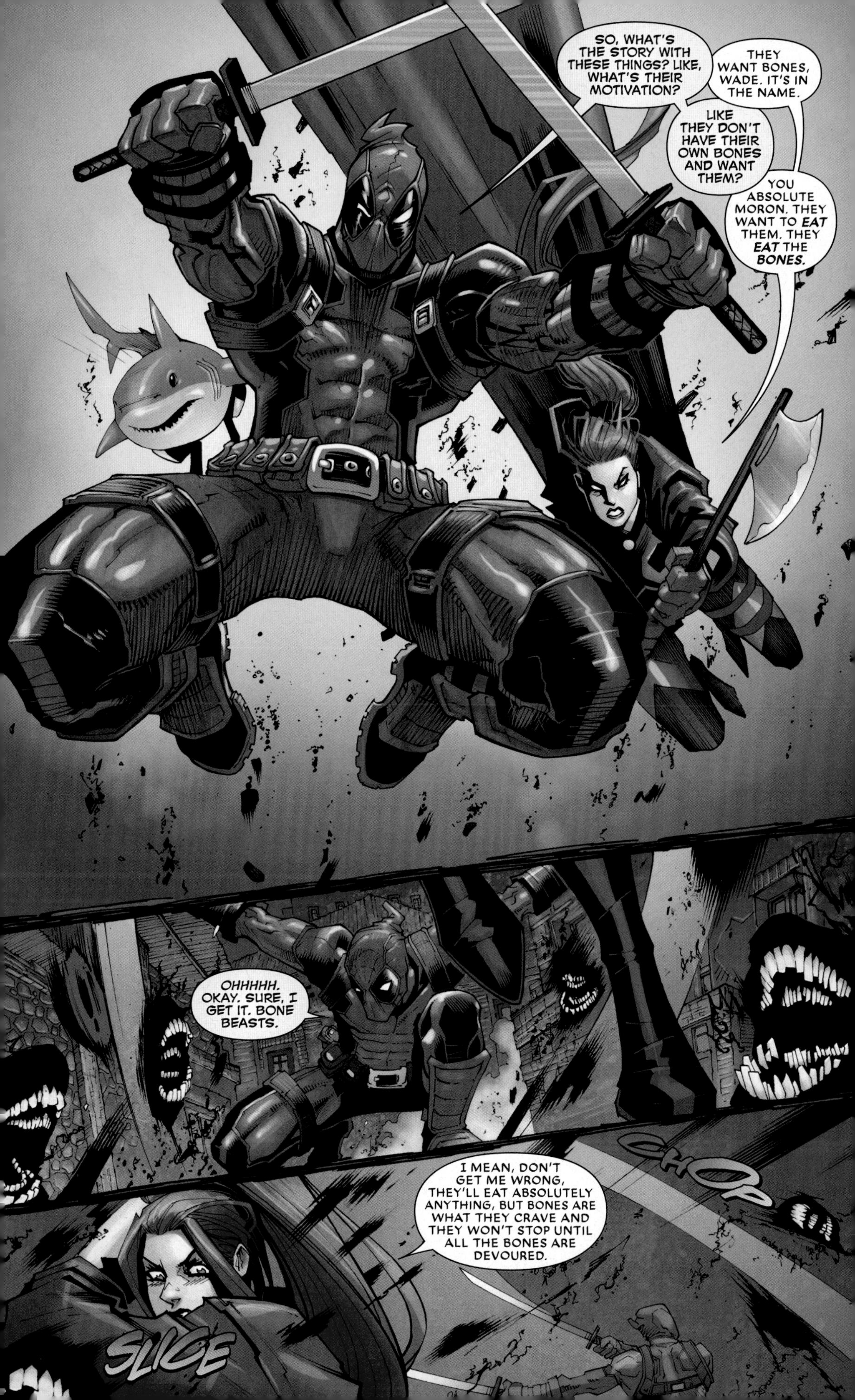
SO, WHAT'S THE STORY WITH THESE THINGS? LIKE, WHAT'S THEIR MOTIVATION?
THEY WANT BONES, WADE. IT'S IN THE NAME.
LIKE THEY DON'T HAVE THEIR OWN BONES AND WANT THEM?
YOU ABSOLUTE MORON. THEY WANT TO *EAT* THEM. THEY *EAT* THE *BONES.*
OHHHHH. OKAY. SURE, I GET IT. BONE BEASTS.
CHOP
I MEAN, DON'T GET ME WRONG, THEY'LL EAT ABSOLUTELY ANYTHING, BUT BONES ARE WHAT THEY CRAVE AND THEY WON'T STOP UNTIL ALL THE BONES ARE DEVOURED.
SLICE

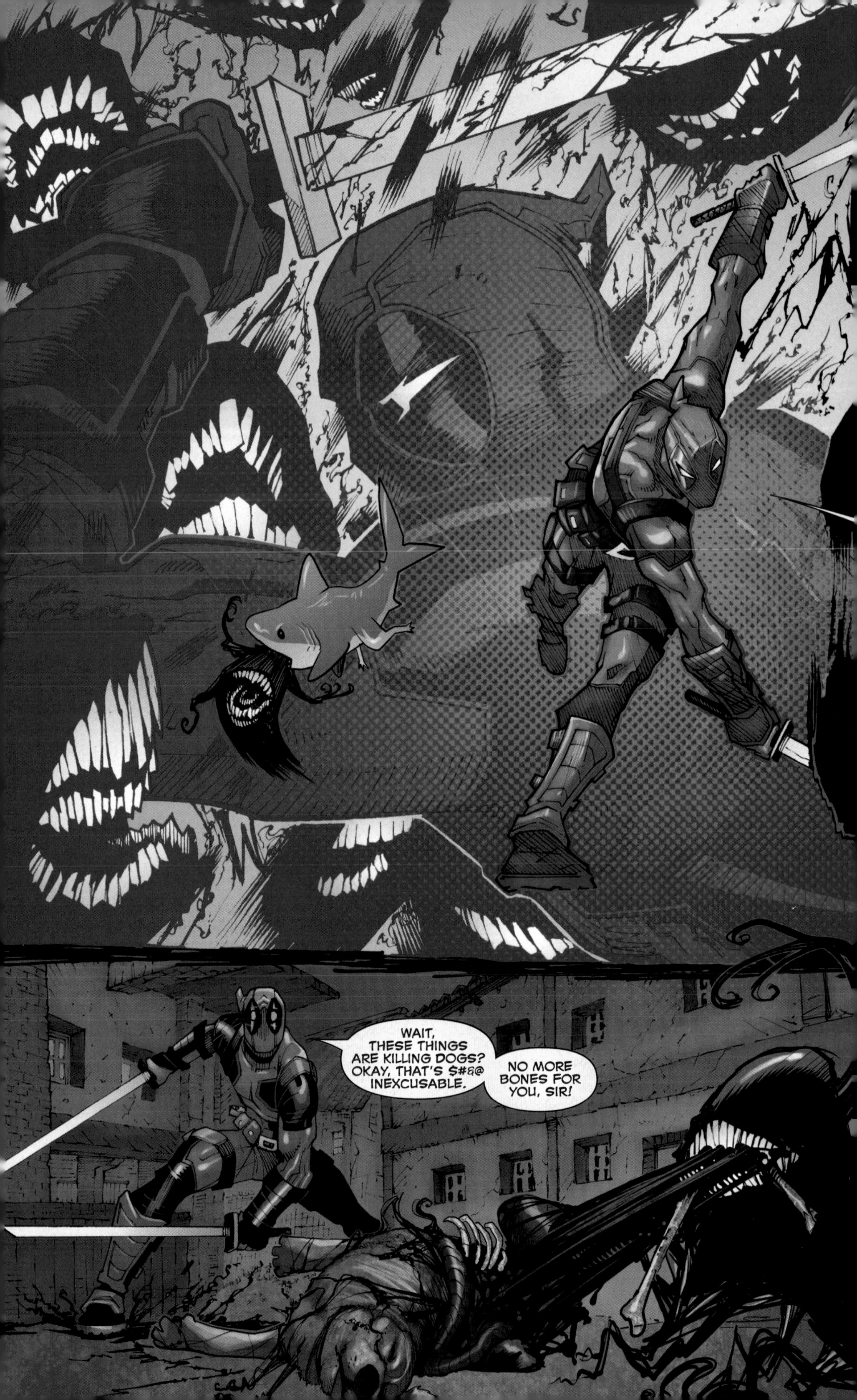
WAIT, THESE THINGS ARE KILLING DOGS? OKAY, THAT'S $#&@ INEXCUSABLE.
NO MORE BONES FOR YOU, SIR!

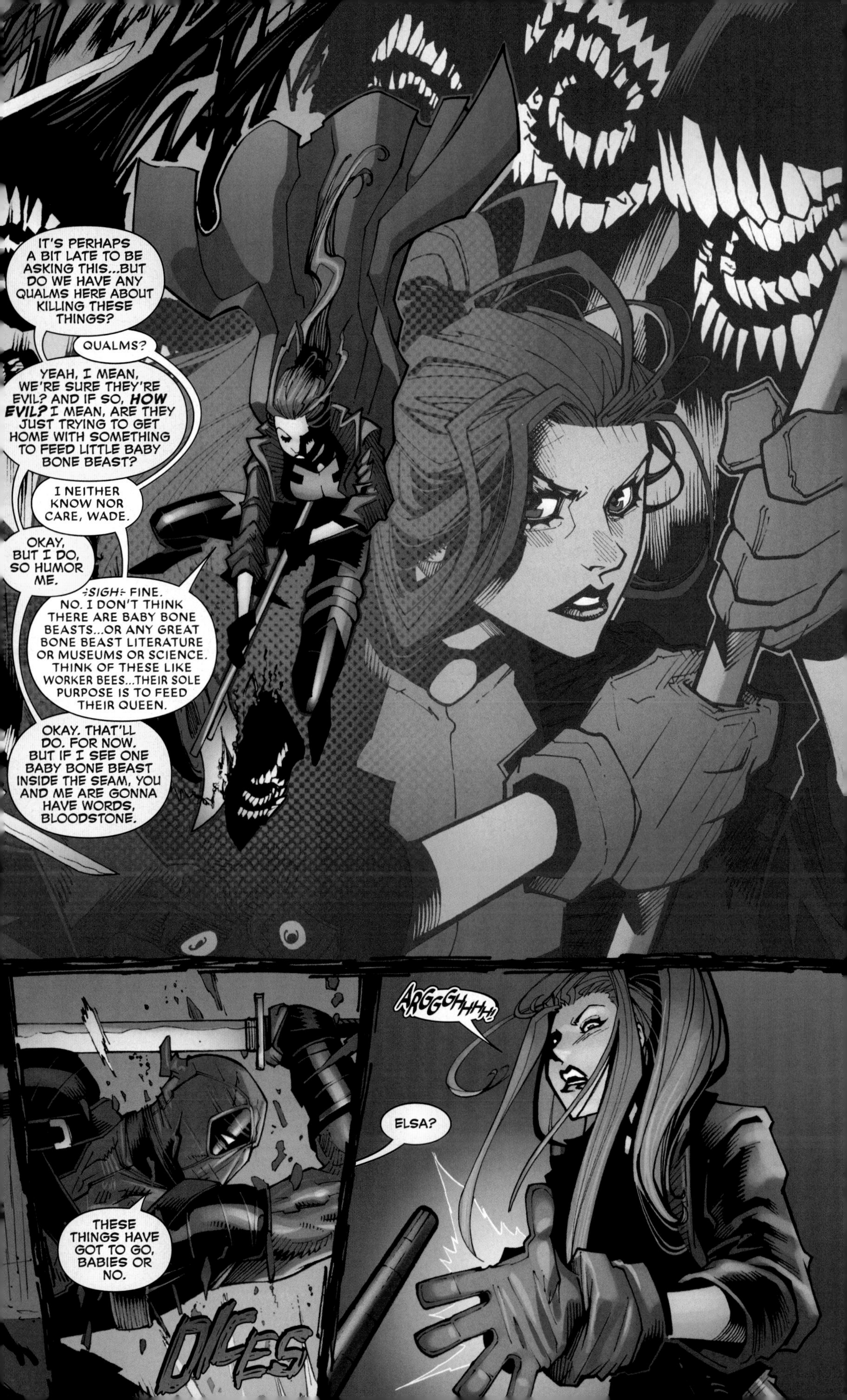
IT'S PERHAPS A BIT LATE TO BE ASKING THIS...BUT DO WE HAVE ANY QUALMS HERE ABOUT KILLING THESE THINGS?
QUALMS?
YEAH, I MEAN, WE'RE SURE THEY'RE EVIL? AND IF SO, HOW EVIL? I MEAN, ARE THEY JUST TRYING TO GET HOME WITH SOMETHING TO FEED LITTLE BABY BONE BEAST?
I NEITHER KNOW NOR CARE, WADE.
OKAY, BUT I DO, SO HUMOR ME.
-SIGH- FINE. NO. I DON'T THINK THERE ARE BABY BONE BEASTS...OR ANY GREAT BONE BEAST LITERATURE OR MUSEUMS OR SCIENCE. THINK OF THESE LIKE WORKER BEES...THEIR SOLE PURPOSE IS TO FEED THEIR QUEEN.
OKAY. THAT'LL DO. FOR NOW. BUT IF I SEE ONE BABY BONE BEAST INSIDE THE SEAM, YOU AND ME ARE GONNA HAVE WORDS, BLOODSTONE.
THESE THINGS HAVE GOT TO GO, BABIES OR NO.
DICES
ARGGGHHHH!
ELSA?

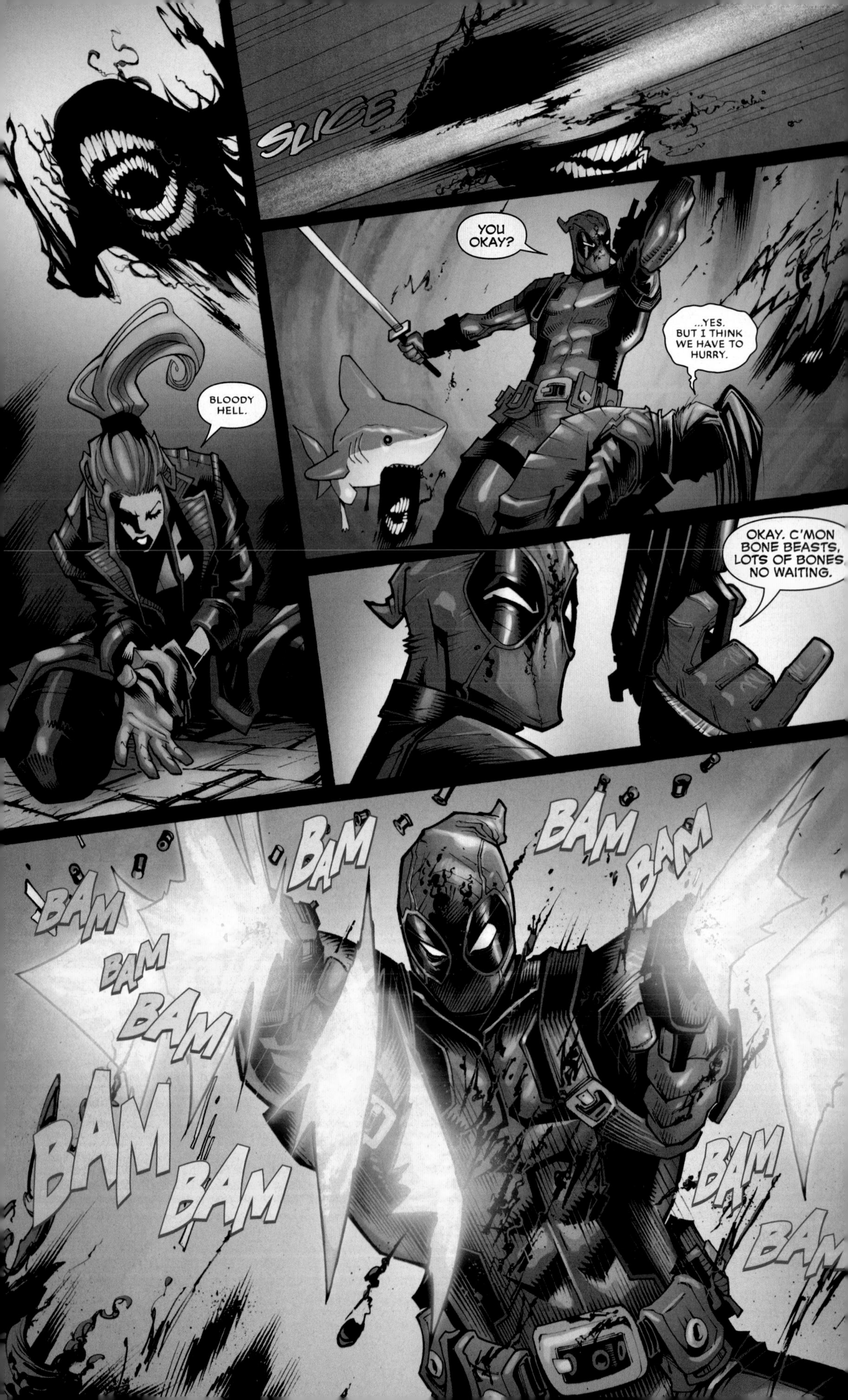
SLICE
YOU OKAY?
BLOODY HELL.
...YES. BUT I THINK WE HAVE TO HURRY.
OKAY. C'MON BONE BEASTS, LOTS OF BONES NO WAITING.
BAM
BAM
BAM
BAM
BAM
BAM
BAM
BAM
BAM
BAM

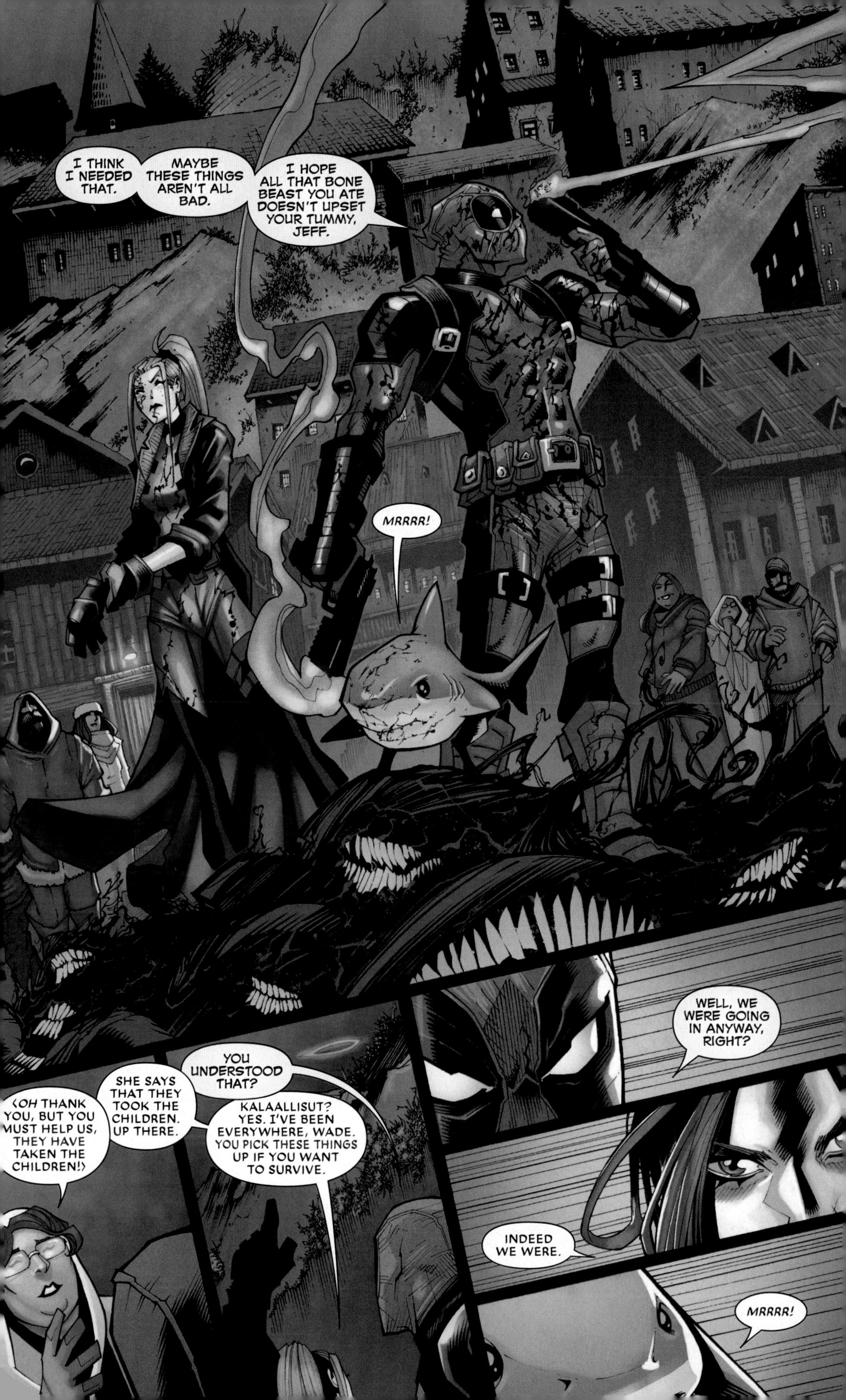
I THINK I NEEDED THAT.
MAYBE THESE THINGS AREN'T ALL BAD.
I HOPE ALL THAT BONE BEAST YOU ATE DOESN'T UPSET YOUR TUMMY, JEFF.
MRRRR!
‹OH THANK YOU, BUT YOU MUST HELP US, THEY HAVE TAKEN THE CHILDREN!›
SHE SAYS THAT THEY TOOK THE CHILDREN. UP THERE.
YOU UNDERSTOOD THAT?
KALAALLISUT? YES. I'VE BEEN EVERYWHERE, WADE. YOU PICK THESE THINGS UP IF YOU WANT TO SURVIVE.
WELL, WE WERE GOING IN ANYWAY, RIGHT?
INDEED WE WERE.
MRRRR!

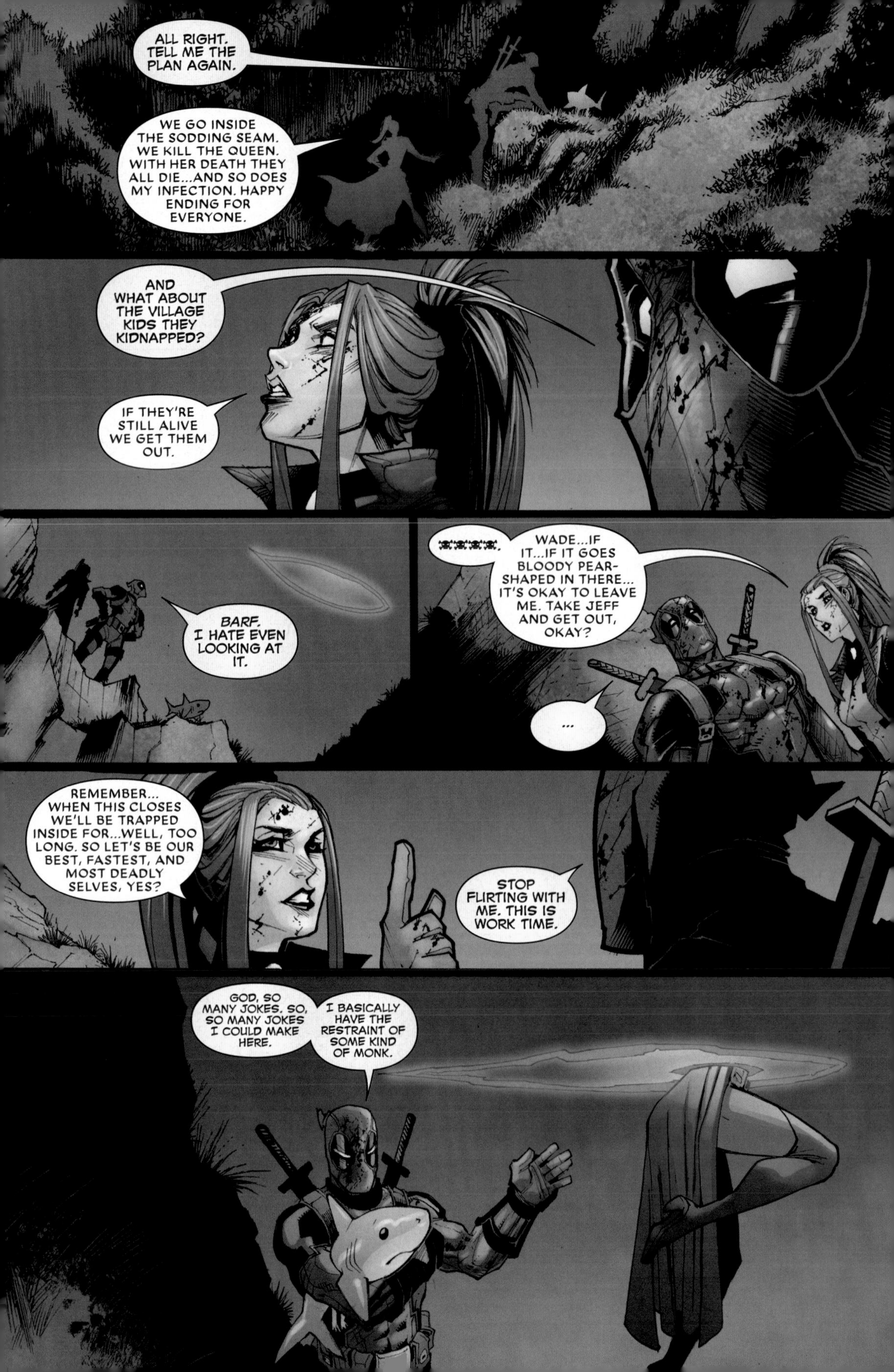
ALL RIGHT. TELL ME THE PLAN AGAIN.
WE GO INSIDE THE SODDING SEAM. WE KILL THE QUEEN. WITH HER DEATH THEY ALL DIE...AND SO DOES MY INFECTION. HAPPY ENDING FOR EVERYONE.
AND WHAT ABOUT THE VILLAGE KIDS THEY KIDNAPPED?
IF THEY'RE STILL ALIVE WE GET THEM OUT.
BARF. I HATE EVEN LOOKING AT IT.
WADE...IF IT...IF IT GOES BLOODY PEAR-SHAPED IN THERE... IT'S OKAY TO LEAVE ME. TAKE JEFF AND GET OUT, OKAY?
...
REMEMBER... WHEN THIS CLOSES WE'LL BE TRAPPED INSIDE FOR...WELL, TOO LONG. SO LET'S BE OUR BEST, FASTEST, AND MOST DEADLY SELVES, YES?
STOP FLIRTING WITH ME. THIS IS WORK TIME.
GOD, SO MANY JOKES. SO, SO MANY JOKES I COULD MAKE HERE.
I BASICALLY HAVE THE RESTRAINT OF SOME KIND OF MONK.

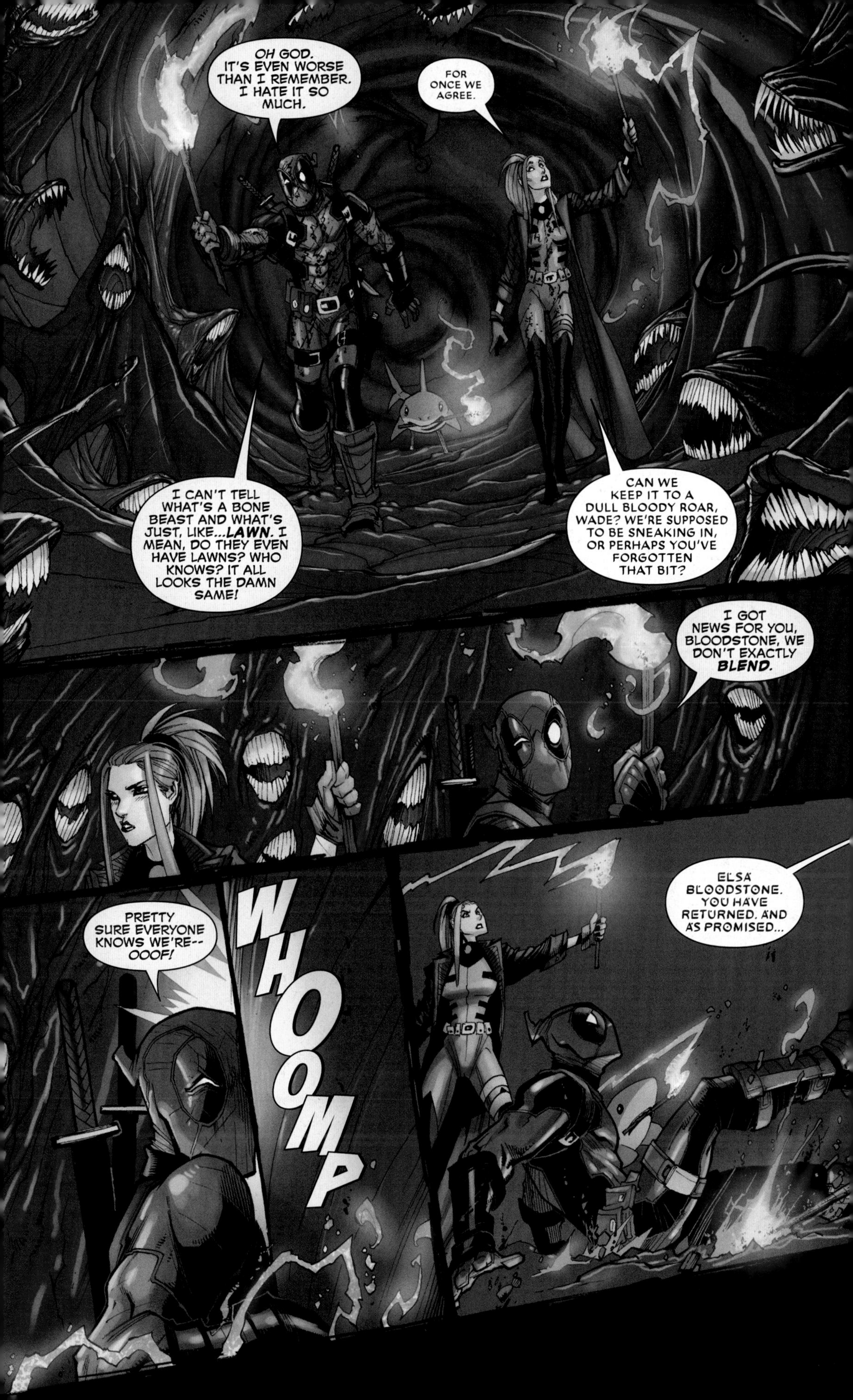
OH GOD. IT'S EVEN WORSE THAN I REMEMBER. I HATE IT SO MUCH.
FOR ONCE WE AGREE.
I CAN'T TELL WHAT'S A BONE BEAST AND WHAT'S JUST, LIKE...LAWN. I MEAN, DO THEY EVEN HAVE LAWNS? WHO KNOWS? IT ALL LOOKS THE DAMN SAME!
CAN WE KEEP IT TO A DULL BLOODY ROAR, WADE? WE'RE SUPPOSED TO BE SNEAKING IN, OR PERHAPS YOU'VE FORGOTTEN THAT BIT?
I GOT NEWS FOR YOU, BLOODSTONE, WE DON'T EXACTLY BLEND.
PRETTY SURE EVERYONE KNOWS WE'RE-- OOOF!
WHOOMP
ELSA BLOODSTONE. YOU HAVE RETURNED. AND AS PROMISED...

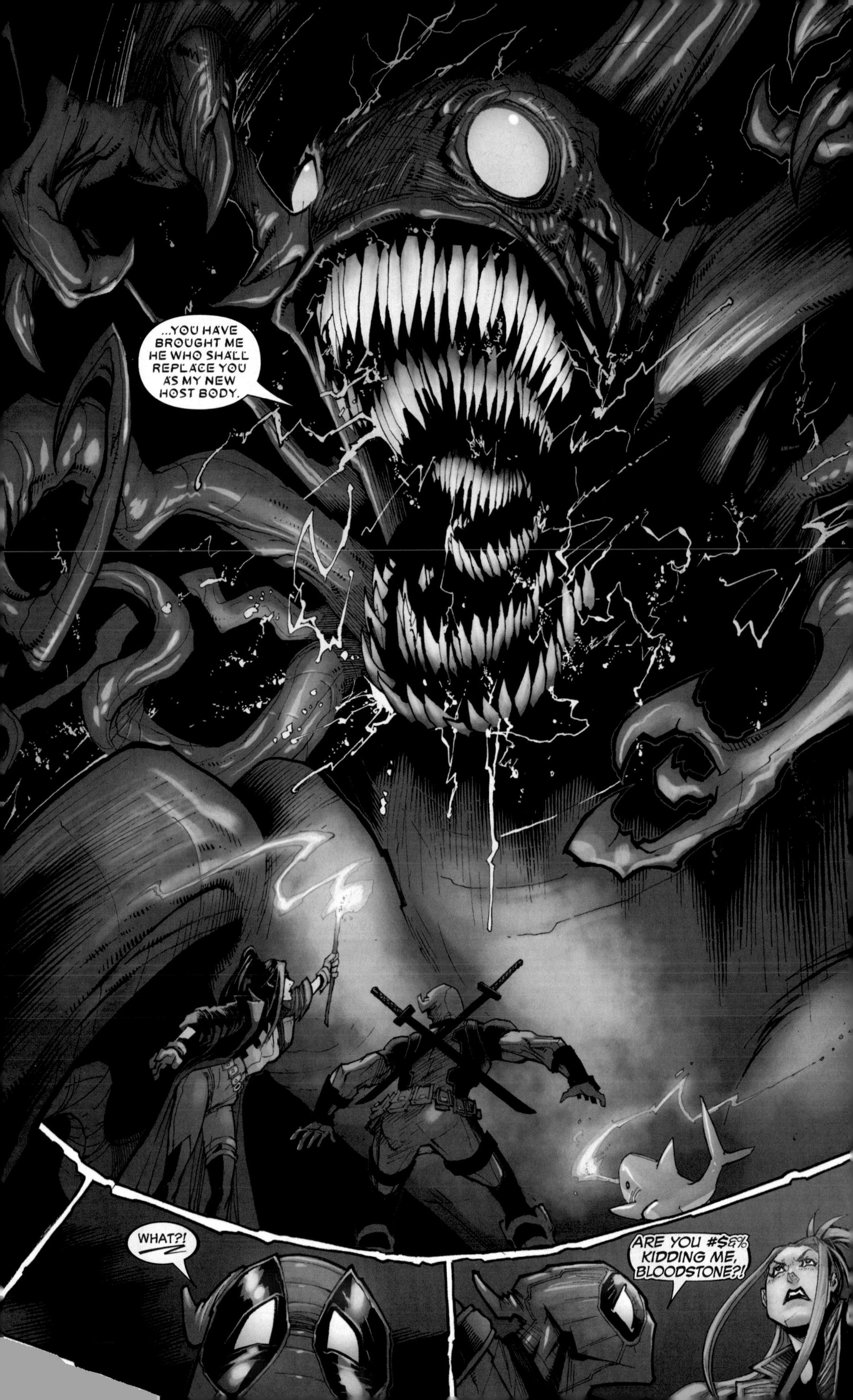
...YOU HAVE BROUGHT ME HE WHO SHALL REPLACE YOU AS MY NEW HOST BODY.
WHAT?!
ARE YOU #$&% KIDDING ME, BLOODSTONE?!

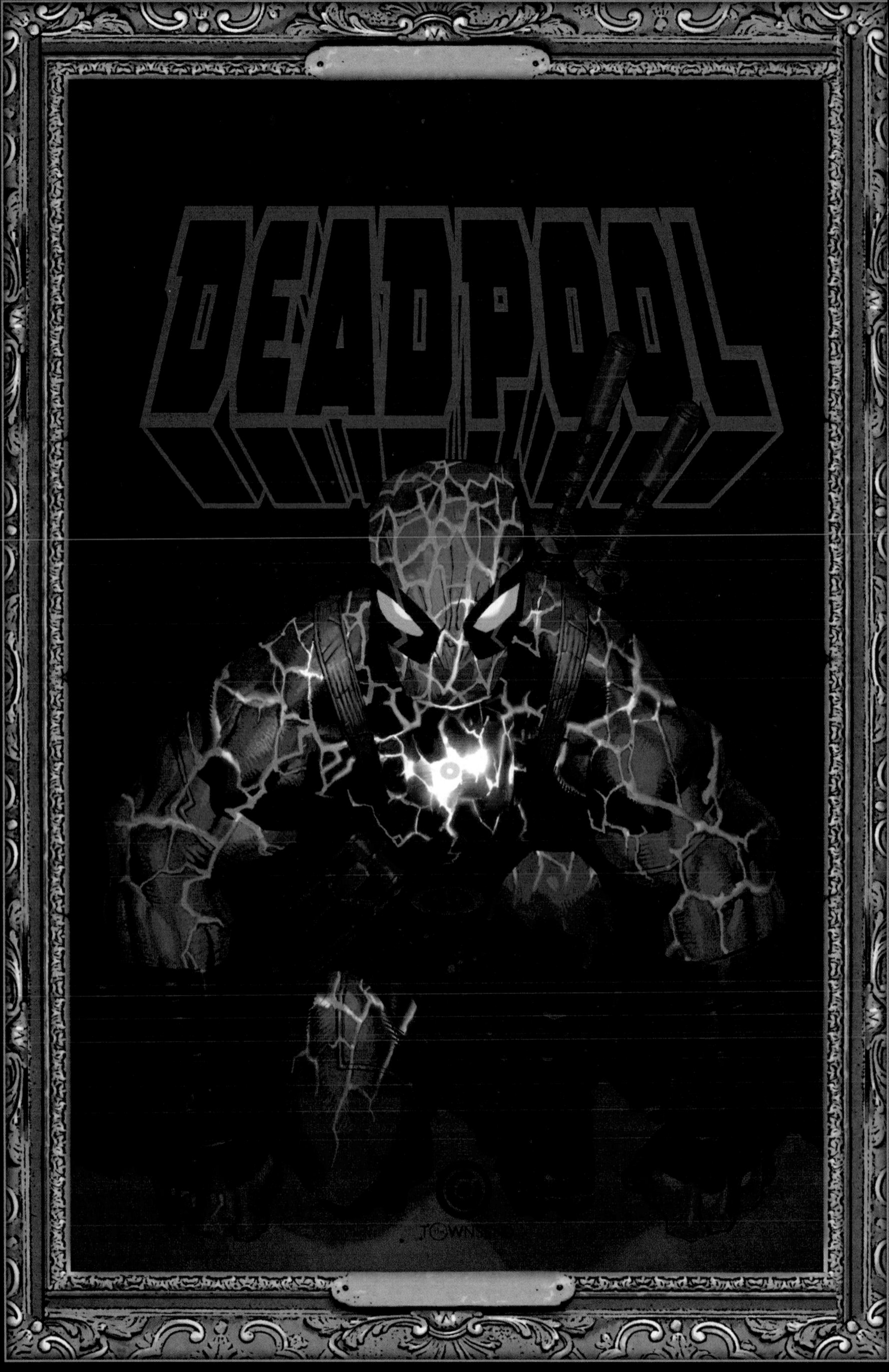
DEADPOOL

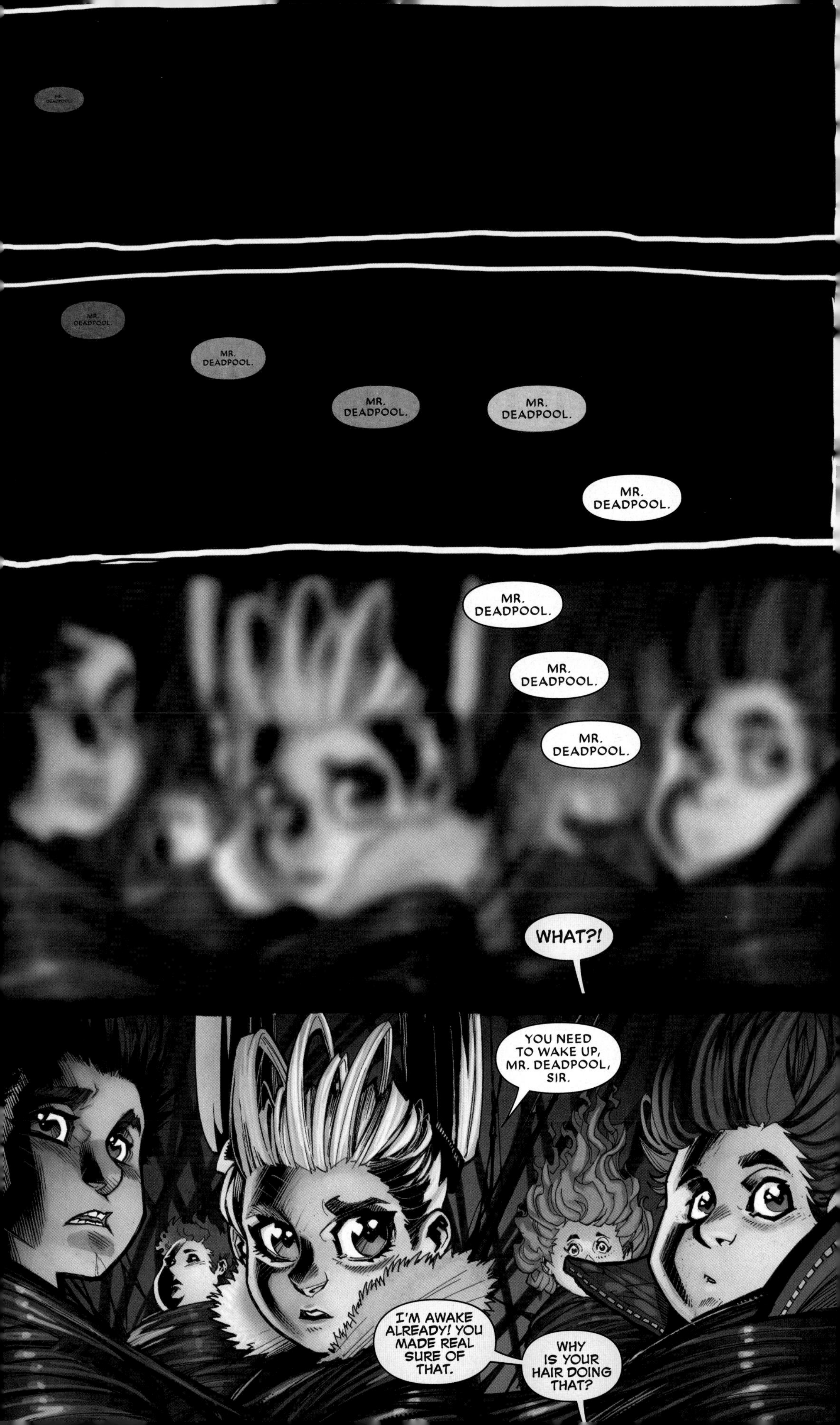
MR. DEADPOOL.
MR. DEADPOOL.
MR. DEADPOOL.
MR. DEADPOOL.
MR. DEADPOOL.
MR. DEADPOOL.
MR. DEADPOOL.
MR. DEADPOOL.
MR. DEADPOOL.
WHAT?!
YOU NEED TO WAKE UP, MR. DEADPOOL, SIR.
I'M AWAKE ALREADY! YOU MADE REAL SURE OF THAT.
WHY IS YOUR HAIR DOING THAT?

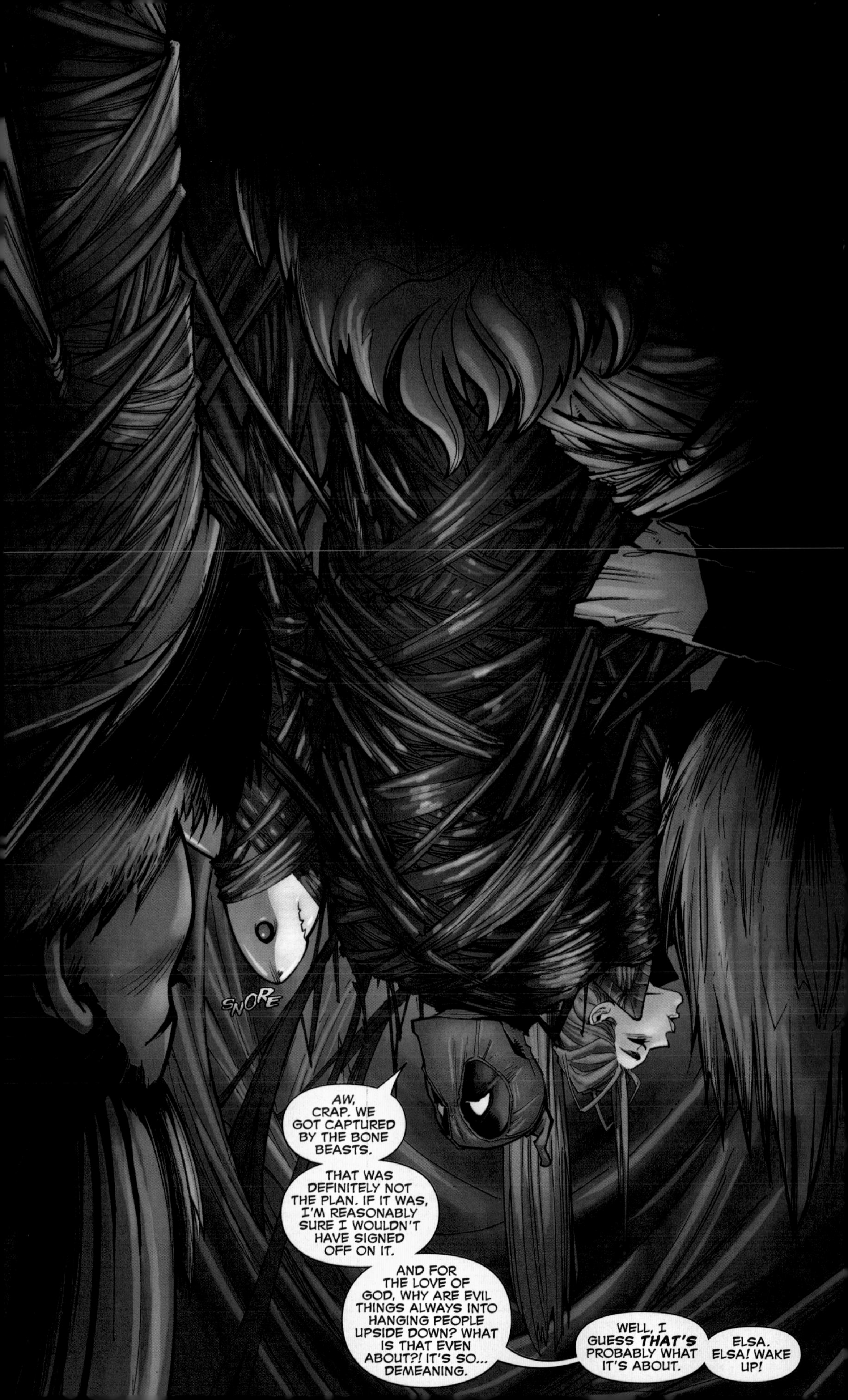
SNORE
AW, CRAP. WE GOT CAPTURED BY THE BONE BEASTS.
THAT WAS DEFINITELY NOT THE PLAN. IF IT WAS, I'M REASONABLY SURE I WOULDN'T HAVE SIGNED OFF ON IT.
AND FOR THE LOVE OF GOD, WHY ARE EVIL THINGS ALWAYS INTO HANGING PEOPLE UPSIDE DOWN? WHAT IS THAT EVEN ABOUT?! IT'S SO... DEMEANING.
WELL, I GUESS THAT'S PROBABLY WHAT IT'S ABOUT.
ELSA. ELSA! WAKE UP!

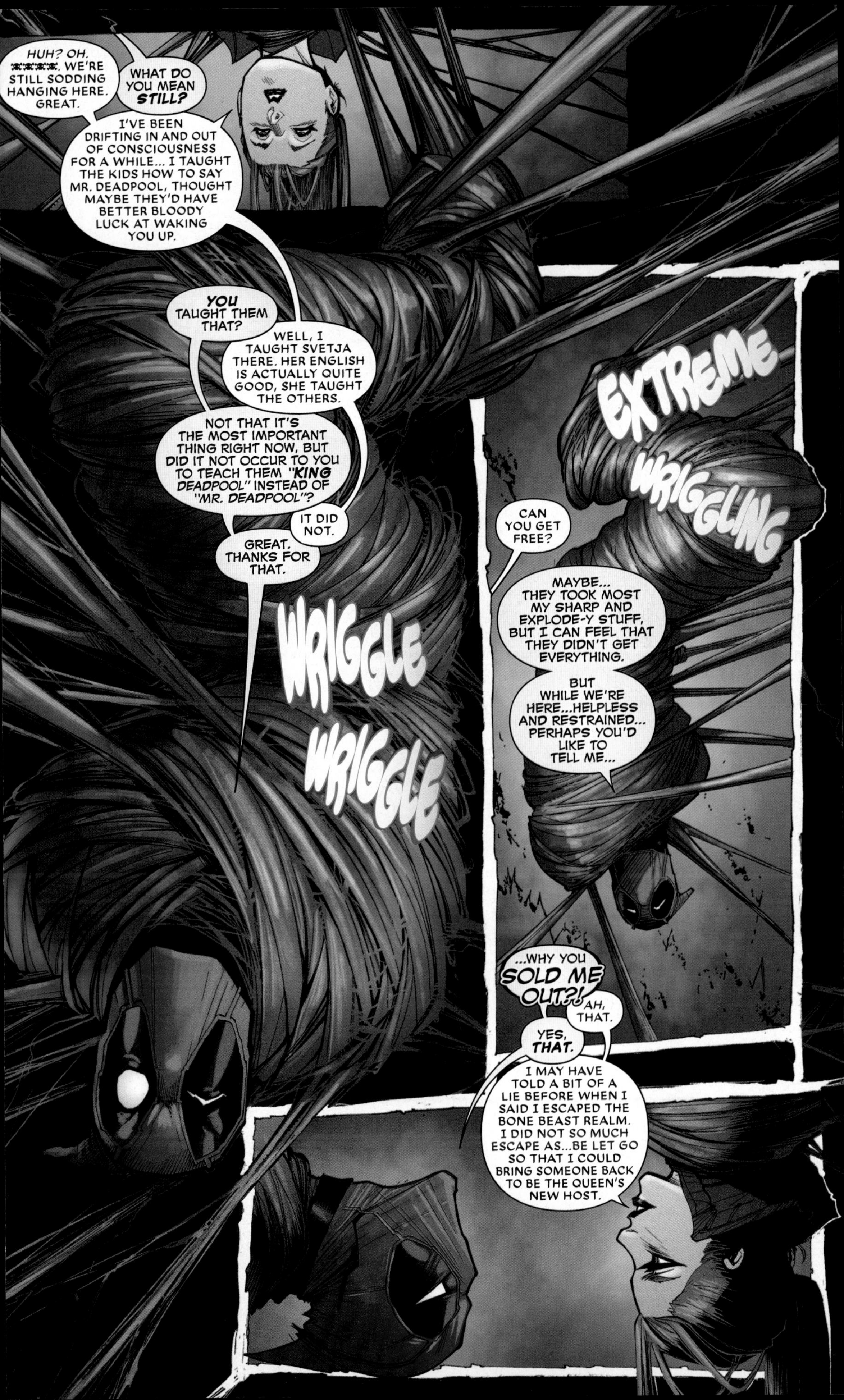
HUH? OH. ☠☠☠☠. WE'RE STILL SODDING HANGING HERE. GREAT.
WHAT DO YOU MEAN STILL?
I'VE BEEN DRIFTING IN AND OUT OF CONSCIOUSNESS FOR A WHILE... I TAUGHT THE KIDS HOW TO SAY MR. DEADPOOL, THOUGHT MAYBE THEY'D HAVE BETTER BLOODY LUCK AT WAKING YOU UP.
YOU TAUGHT THEM THAT?
WELL, I TAUGHT SVETJA THERE. HER ENGLISH IS ACTUALLY QUITE GOOD, SHE TAUGHT THE OTHERS.
NOT THAT IT'S THE MOST IMPORTANT THING RIGHT NOW, BUT DID IT NOT OCCUR TO YOU TO TEACH THEM "KING DEADPOOL" INSTEAD OF "MR. DEADPOOL"?
IT DID NOT.
GREAT. THANKS FOR THAT.
WRIGGLE WRIGGLE
EXTREME WRIGGLING
CAN YOU GET FREE?
MAYBE... THEY TOOK MOST MY SHARP AND EXPLODE-Y STUFF, BUT I CAN FEEL THAT THEY DIDN'T GET EVERYTHING.
BUT WHILE WE'RE HERE...HELPLESS AND RESTRAINED... PERHAPS YOU'D LIKE TO TELL ME...
...WHY YOU SOLD ME OUT?!
AH, THAT.
YES, THAT.
I MAY HAVE TOLD A BIT OF A LIE BEFORE WHEN I SAID I ESCAPED THE BONE BEAST REALM. I DID NOT SO MUCH ESCAPE AS...BE LET GO SO THAT I COULD BRING SOMEONE BACK TO BE THE QUEEN'S NEW HOST.

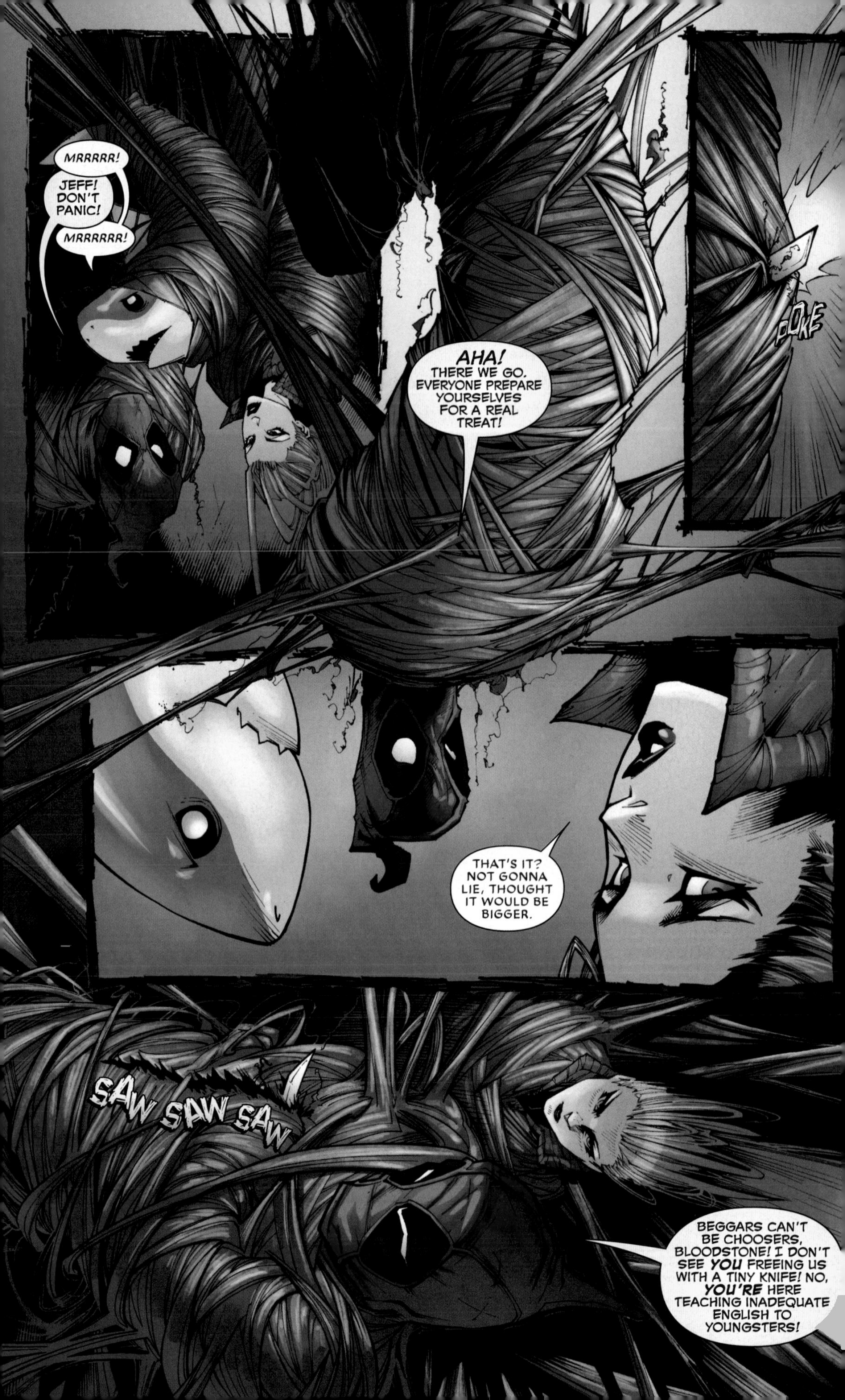
MRRRRR!
JEFF! DON'T PANIC!
MRRRRRR!
AHA! THERE WE GO. EVERYONE PREPARE YOURSELVES FOR A REAL TREAT!
POKE
THAT'S IT? NOT GONNA LIE, THOUGHT IT WOULD BE BIGGER.
SAW SAW SAW
BEGGARS CAN'T BE CHOOSERS, BLOODSTONE! I DON'T SEE YOU FREEING US WITH A TINY KNIFE! NO, YOU'RE HERE TEACHING INADEQUATE ENGLISH TO YOUNGSTERS!

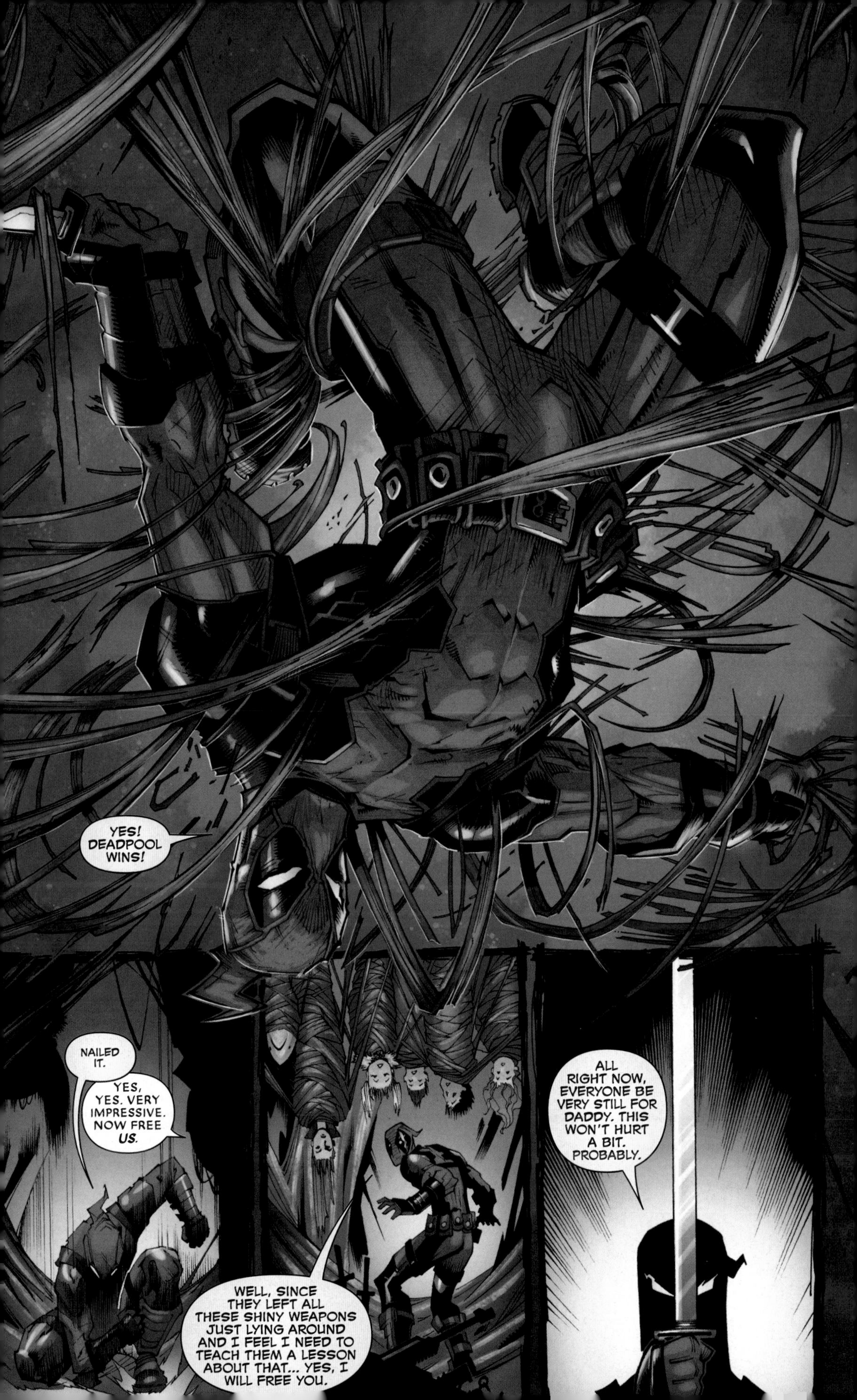
YES! DEADPOOL WINS!
NAILED IT.
YES, YES. VERY IMPRESSIVE. NOW FREE US.
WELL, SINCE THEY LEFT ALL THESE SHINY WEAPONS JUST LYING AROUND AND I FEEL I NEED TO TEACH THEM A LESSON ABOUT THAT... YES, I WILL FREE YOU.
ALL RIGHT NOW, EVERYONE BE VERY STILL FOR DADDY. THIS WON'T HURT A BIT. PROBABLY.

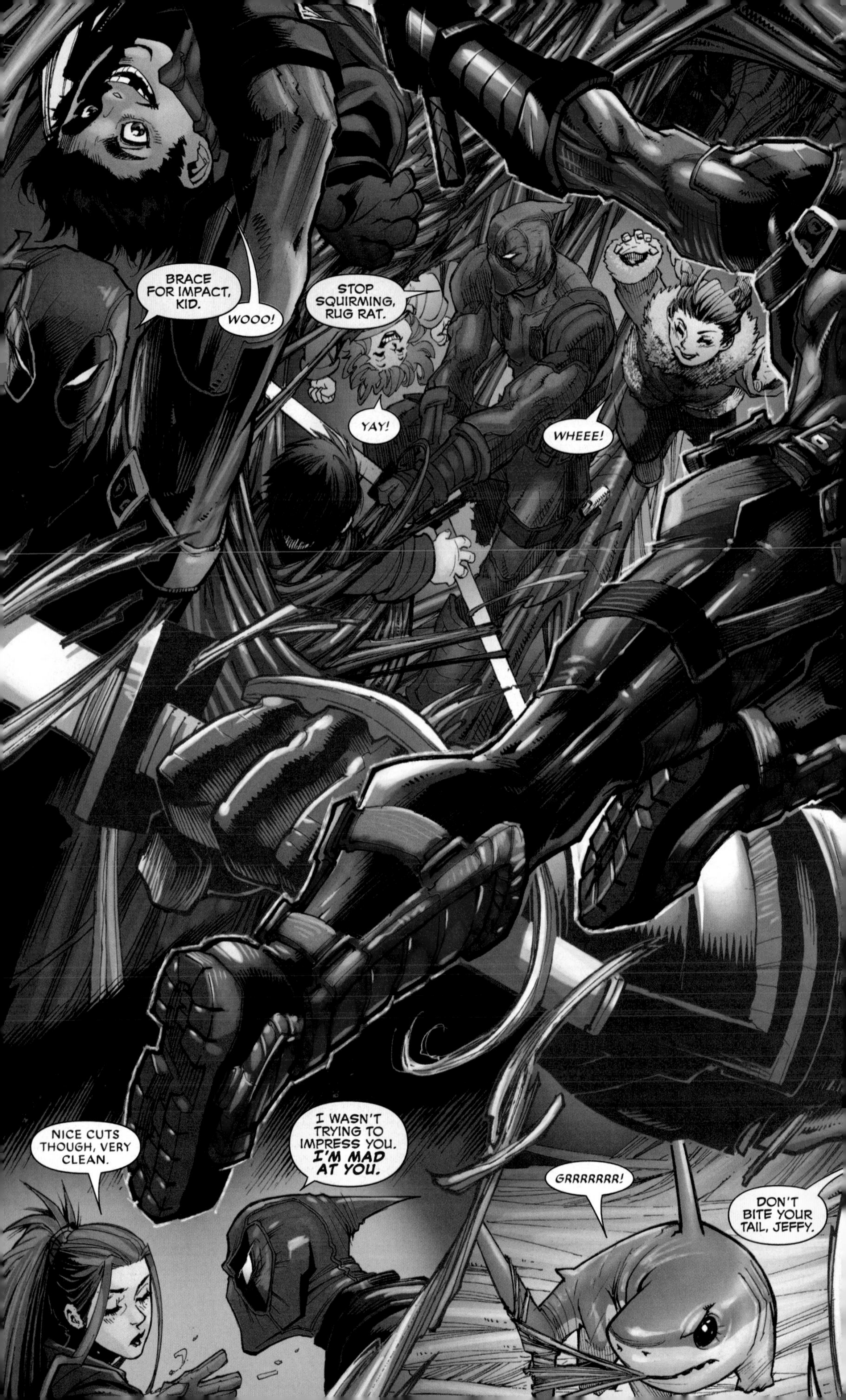

BRACE FOR IMPACT, KID.
WOOO!
STOP SQUIRMING, RUG RAT.
YAY!
WHEEE!
NICE CUTS THOUGH, VERY CLEAN.
I WASN'T TRYING TO IMPRESS YOU. I'M MAD AT YOU.
GRRRRRRR!
DON'T BITE YOUR TAIL, JEFFY.

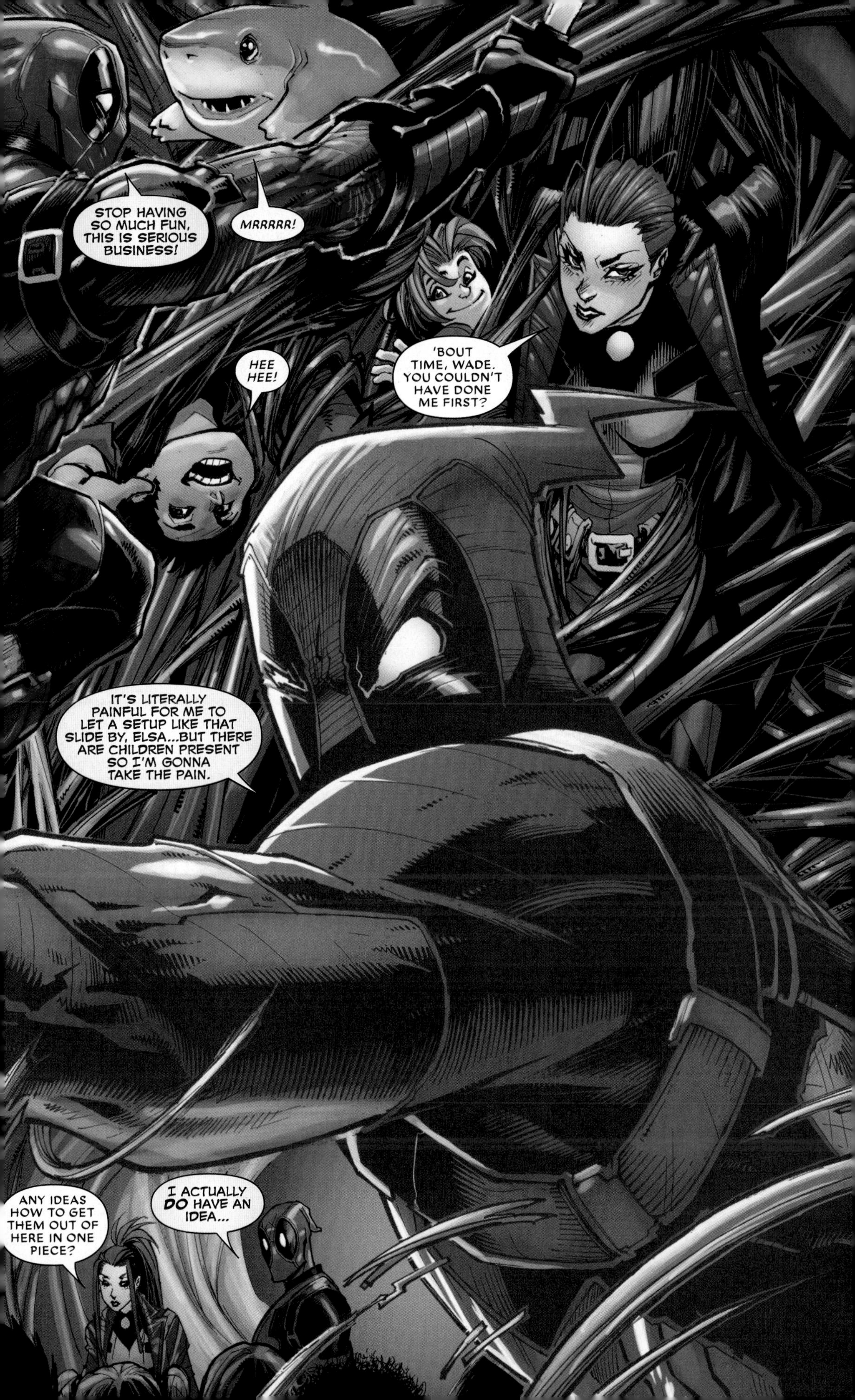
STOP HAVING SO MUCH FUN, THIS IS SERIOUS BUSINESS!
MRRRRR!
HEE HEE!
'BOUT TIME, WADE. YOU COULDN'T HAVE DONE ME FIRST?
IT'S LITERALLY PAINFUL FOR ME TO LET A SETUP LIKE THAT SLIDE BY, ELSA...BUT THERE ARE CHILDREN PRESENT SO I'M GONNA TAKE THE PAIN.
ANY IDEAS HOW TO GET THEM OUT OF HERE IN ONE PIECE?
I ACTUALLY DO HAVE AN IDEA...

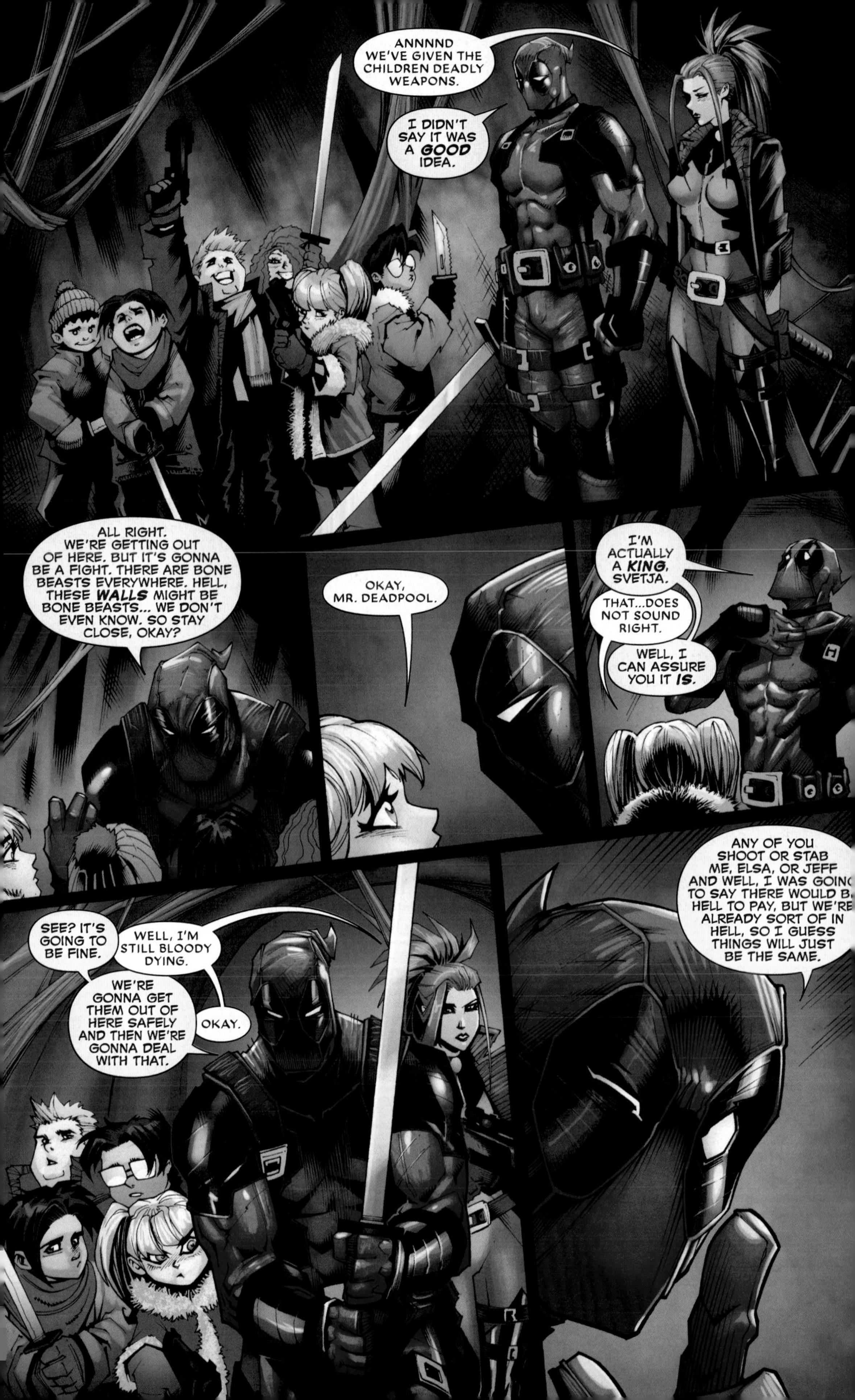
ANNNND WE'VE GIVEN THE CHILDREN DEADLY WEAPONS.
I DIDN'T SAY IT WAS A GOOD IDEA.
ALL RIGHT. WE'RE GETTING OUT OF HERE. BUT IT'S GONNA BE A FIGHT. THERE ARE BONE BEASTS EVERYWHERE. HELL, THESE WALLS MIGHT BE BONE BEASTS... WE DON'T EVEN KNOW. SO STAY CLOSE, OKAY?
OKAY, MR. DEADPOOL.
I'M ACTUALLY A KING, SVETJA.
THAT...DOES NOT SOUND RIGHT.
WELL, I CAN ASSURE YOU IT IS.
SEE? IT'S GOING TO BE FINE.
WELL, I'M STILL BLOODY DYING.
WE'RE GONNA GET THEM OUT OF HERE SAFELY AND THEN WE'RE GONNA DEAL WITH THAT.
OKAY.
ANY OF YOU SHOOT OR STAB ME, ELSA, OR JEFF AND WELL, I WAS GOING TO SAY THERE WOULD BE HELL TO PAY, BUT WE'RE ALREADY SORT OF IN HELL, SO I GUESS THINGS WILL JUST BE THE SAME.

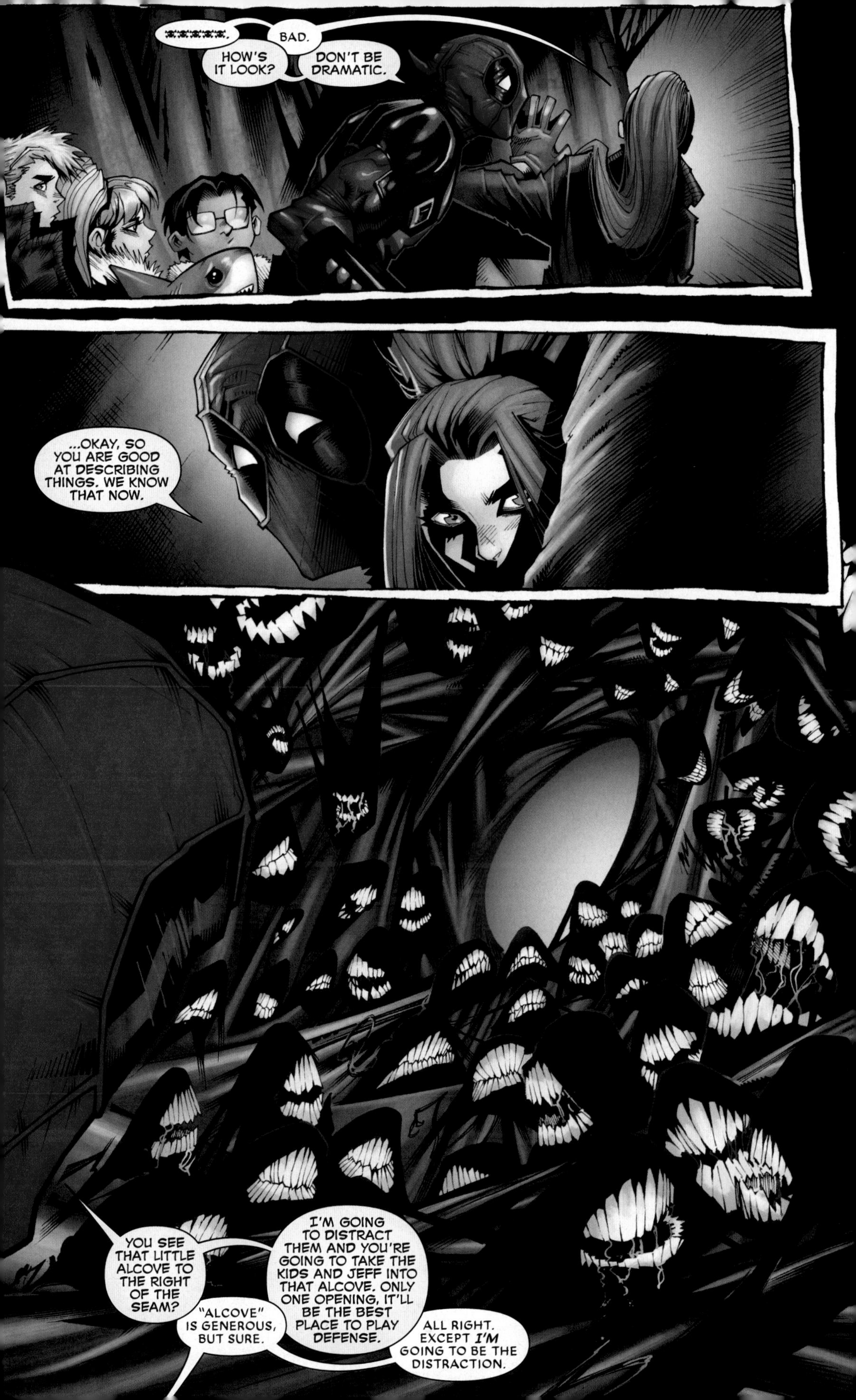
☠☠☠☠☠,
HOW'S IT LOOK?
BAD.
DON'T BE DRAMATIC.
...OKAY, SO YOU ARE GOOD AT DESCRIBING THINGS. WE KNOW THAT NOW.
YOU SEE THAT LITTLE ALCOVE TO THE RIGHT OF THE SEAM?
I'M GOING TO DISTRACT THEM AND YOU'RE GOING TO TAKE THE KIDS AND JEFF INTO THAT ALCOVE. ONLY ONE OPENING, IT'LL BE THE BEST PLACE TO PLAY DEFENSE.
"ALCOVE" IS GENEROUS, BUT SURE.
ALL RIGHT. EXCEPT *I'M* GOING TO BE THE DISTRACTION.

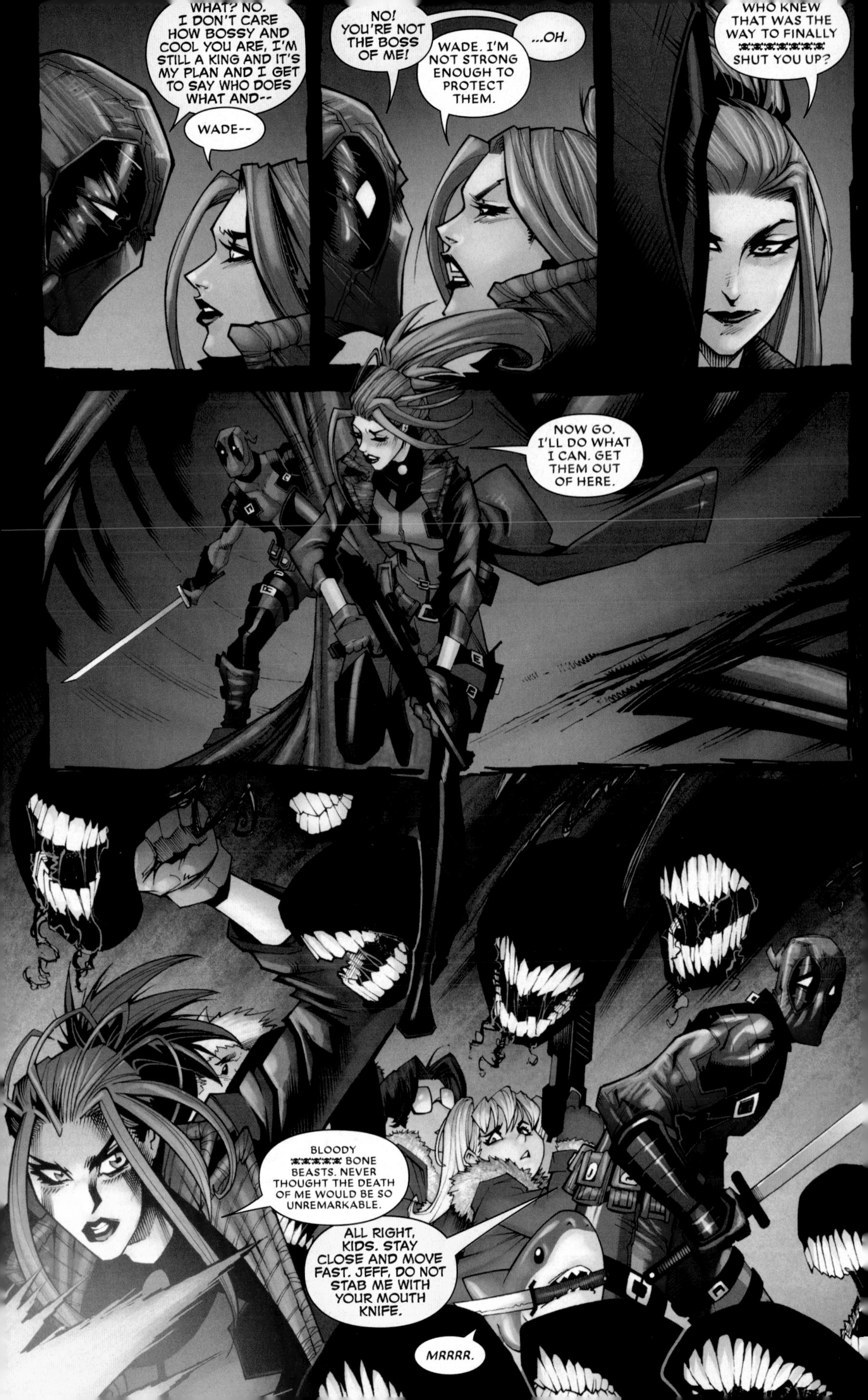
WHAT? NO. I DON'T CARE HOW BOSSY AND COOL YOU ARE, I'M STILL A KING AND IT'S MY PLAN AND I GET TO SAY WHO DOES WHAT AND--
WADE--
NO! YOU'RE NOT THE BOSS OF ME!
WADE. I'M NOT STRONG ENOUGH TO PROTECT THEM.
...OH.
WHO KNEW THAT WAS THE WAY TO FINALLY SHUT YOU UP?
NOW GO. I'LL DO WHAT I CAN. GET THEM OUT OF HERE.
BLOODY BONE BEASTS. NEVER THOUGHT THE DEATH OF ME WOULD BE SO UNREMARKABLE.
ALL RIGHT, KIDS. STAY CLOSE AND MOVE FAST. JEFF, DO NOT STAB ME WITH YOUR MOUTH KNIFE.
MRRRR.

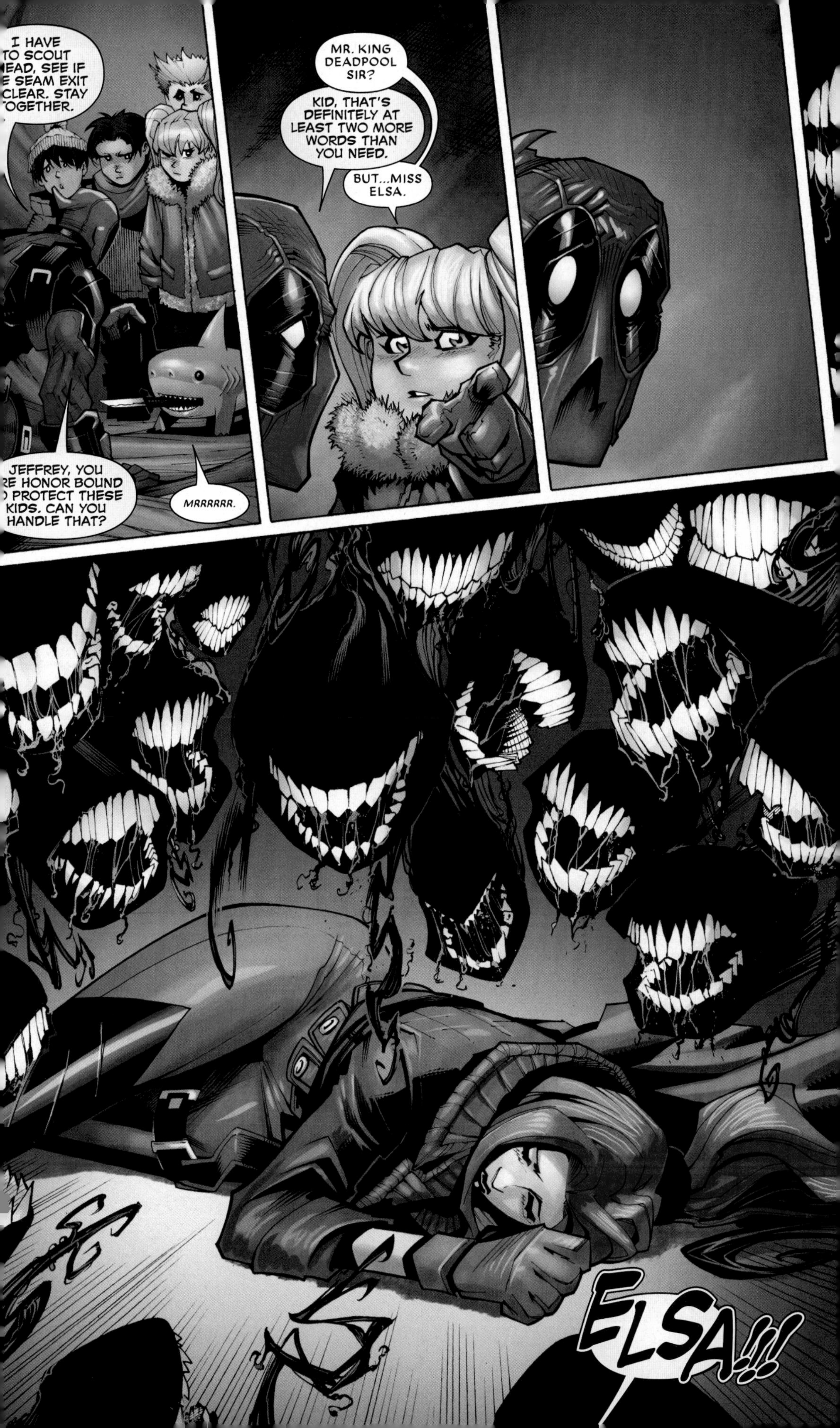

I HAVE TO SCOUT AHEAD, SEE IF THE SEAM EXIT IS CLEAR. STAY TOGETHER.
JEFFREY, YOU ARE HONOR BOUND TO PROTECT THESE KIDS. CAN YOU HANDLE THAT?
MRRRRRR.
MR. KING DEADPOOL SIR?
KID, THAT'S DEFINITELY AT LEAST TWO MORE WORDS THAN YOU NEED.
BUT...MISS ELSA.
ELSA!!!

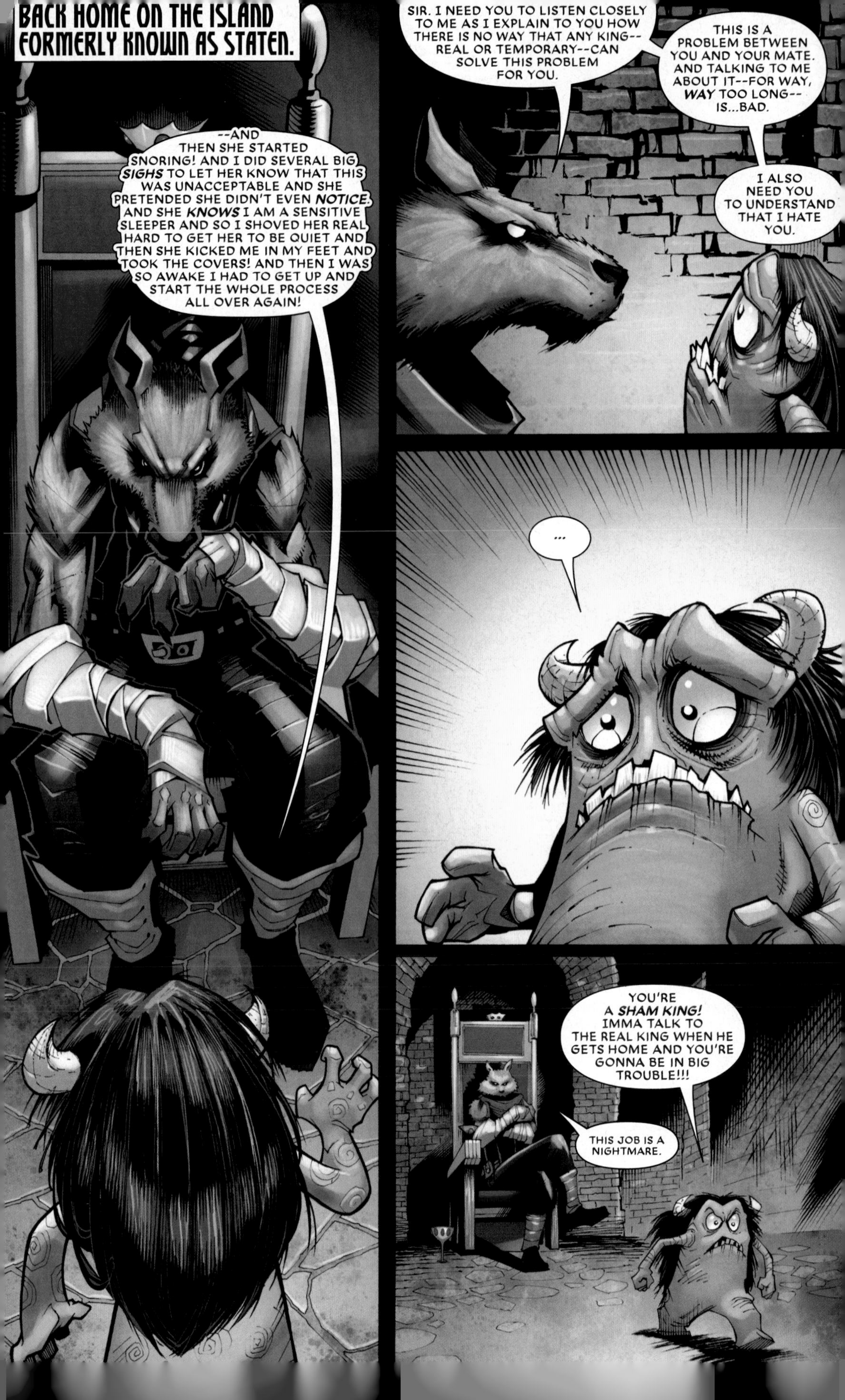
BACK HOME ON THE ISLAND FORMERLY KNOWN AS STATEN.
--AND THEN SHE STARTED SNORING! AND I DID SEVERAL BIG SIGHS TO LET HER KNOW THAT THIS WAS UNACCEPTABLE AND SHE PRETENDED SHE DIDN'T EVEN NOTICE. AND SHE KNOWS I AM A SENSITIVE SLEEPER AND SO I SHOVED HER REAL HARD TO GET HER TO BE QUIET AND THEN SHE KICKED ME IN MY FEET AND TOOK THE COVERS! AND THEN I WAS SO AWAKE I HAD TO GET UP AND START THE WHOLE PROCESS ALL OVER AGAIN!
SIR. I NEED YOU TO LISTEN CLOSELY TO ME AS I EXPLAIN TO YOU HOW THERE IS NO WAY THAT ANY KING--REAL OR TEMPORARY--CAN SOLVE THIS PROBLEM FOR YOU.
THIS IS A PROBLEM BETWEEN YOU AND YOUR MATE. AND TALKING TO ME ABOUT IT--FOR WAY, WAY TOO LONG--IS...BAD.
I ALSO NEED YOU TO UNDERSTAND THAT I HATE YOU.
...
YOU'RE A SHAM KING! IMMA TALK TO THE REAL KING WHEN HE GETS HOME AND YOU'RE GONNA BE IN BIG TROUBLE!!!
THIS JOB IS A NIGHTMARE.

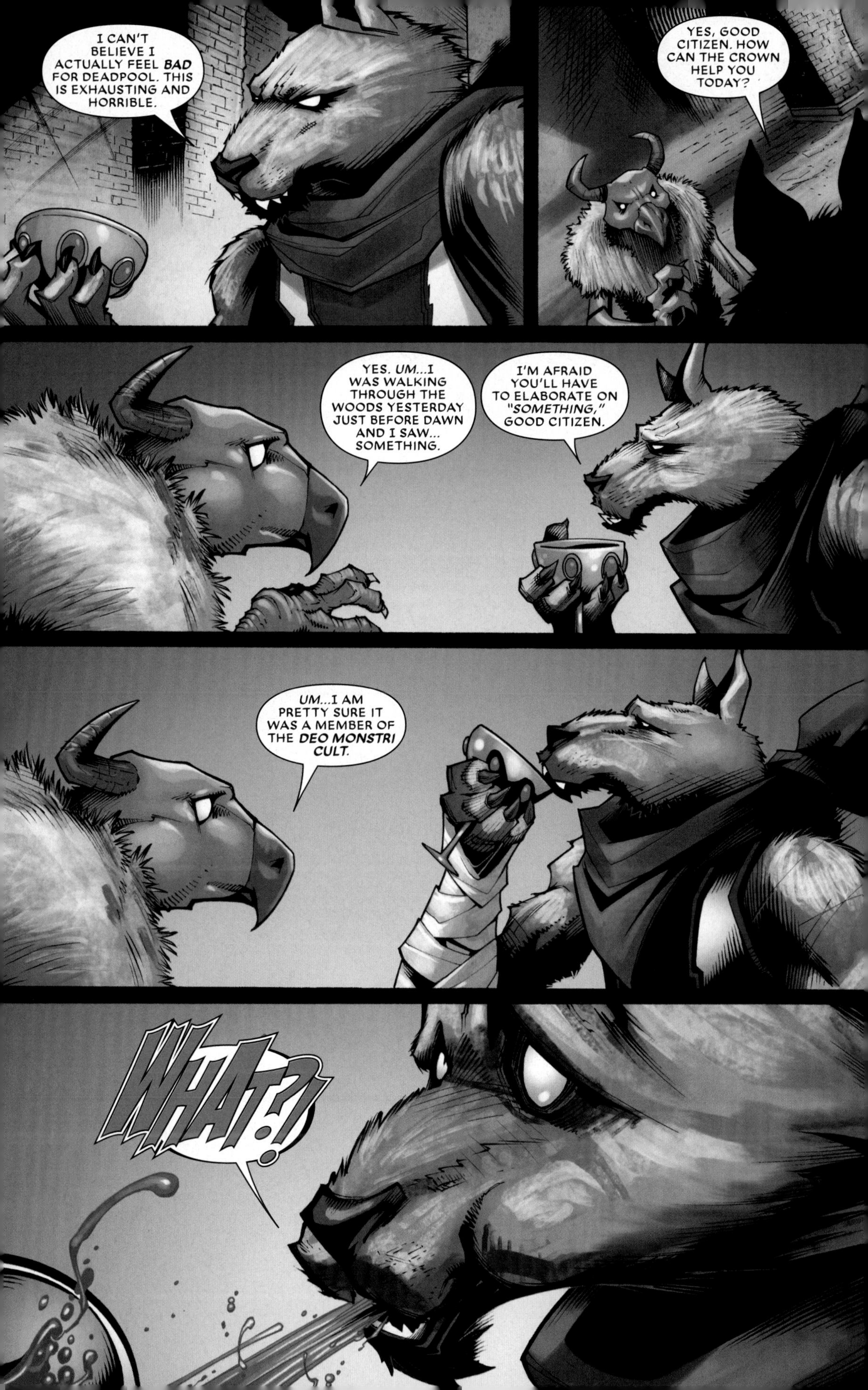
I CAN'T BELIEVE I ACTUALLY FEEL BAD FOR DEADPOOL. THIS IS EXHAUSTING AND HORRIBLE.
YES, GOOD CITIZEN. HOW CAN THE CROWN HELP YOU TODAY?
YES. UM...I WAS WALKING THROUGH THE WOODS YESTERDAY JUST BEFORE DAWN AND I SAW... SOMETHING.
I'M AFRAID YOU'LL HAVE TO ELABORATE ON "SOMETHING," GOOD CITIZEN.
UM...I AM PRETTY SURE IT WAS A MEMBER OF THE DEO MONSTRI CULT.
WHAT?!

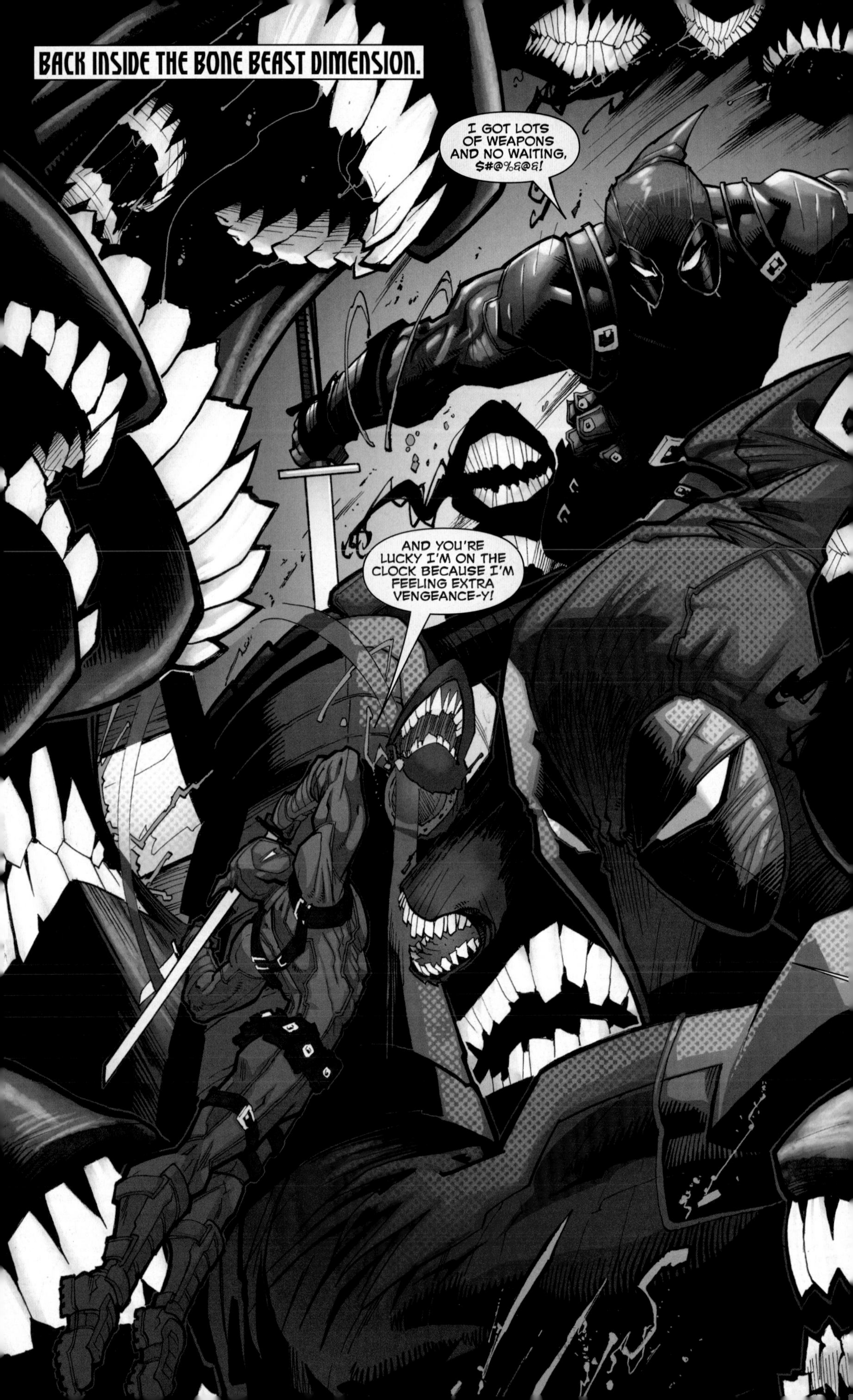
BACK INSIDE THE BONE BEAST DIMENSION.
I GOT LOTS OF WEAPONS AND NO WAITING, $#@%&@&!
AND YOU'RE LUCKY I'M ON THE CLOCK BECAUSE I'M FEELING EXTRA VENGEANCE-Y!

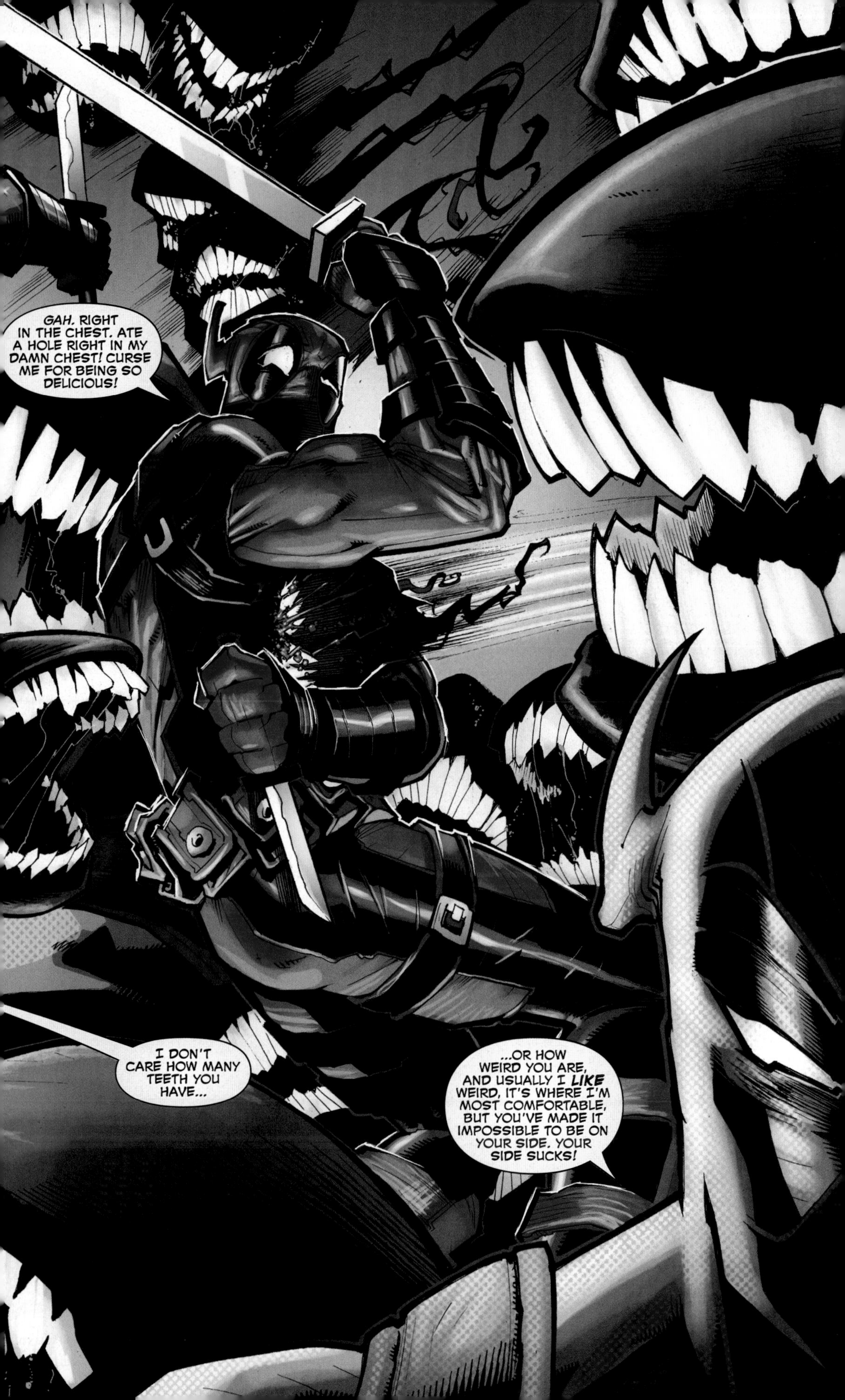
GAH. RIGHT IN THE CHEST. ATE A HOLE RIGHT IN MY DAMN CHEST! CURSE ME FOR BEING SO DELICIOUS!
I DON'T CARE HOW MANY TEETH YOU HAVE...
...OR HOW WEIRD YOU ARE, AND USUALLY I *LIKE* WEIRD, IT'S WHERE I'M MOST COMFORTABLE, BUT YOU'VE MADE IT IMPOSSIBLE TO BE ON YOUR SIDE. YOUR SIDE SUCKS!

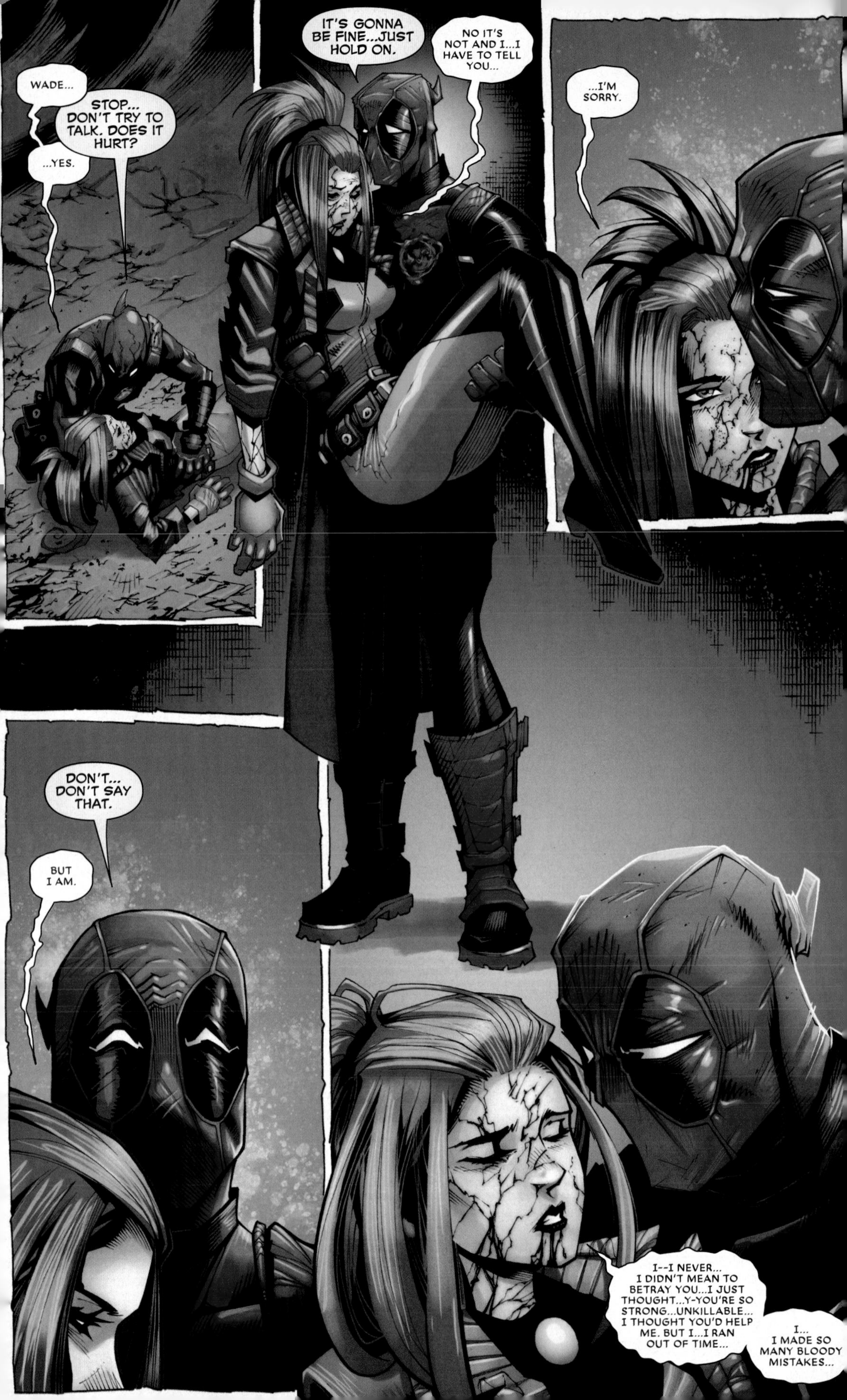
WADE...
STOP... DON'T TRY TO TALK. DOES IT HURT?
...YES.
IT'S GONNA BE FINE...JUST HOLD ON.
NO IT'S NOT AND I...I HAVE TO TELL YOU...
...I'M SORRY.
DON'T... DON'T SAY THAT.
BUT I AM.
I--I NEVER... I DIDN'T MEAN TO BETRAY YOU...I JUST THOUGHT...Y-YOU'RE SO STRONG...UNKILLABLE... I THOUGHT YOU'D HELP ME. BUT I...I RAN OUT OF TIME...
I... I MADE SO MANY BLOODY MISTAKES...

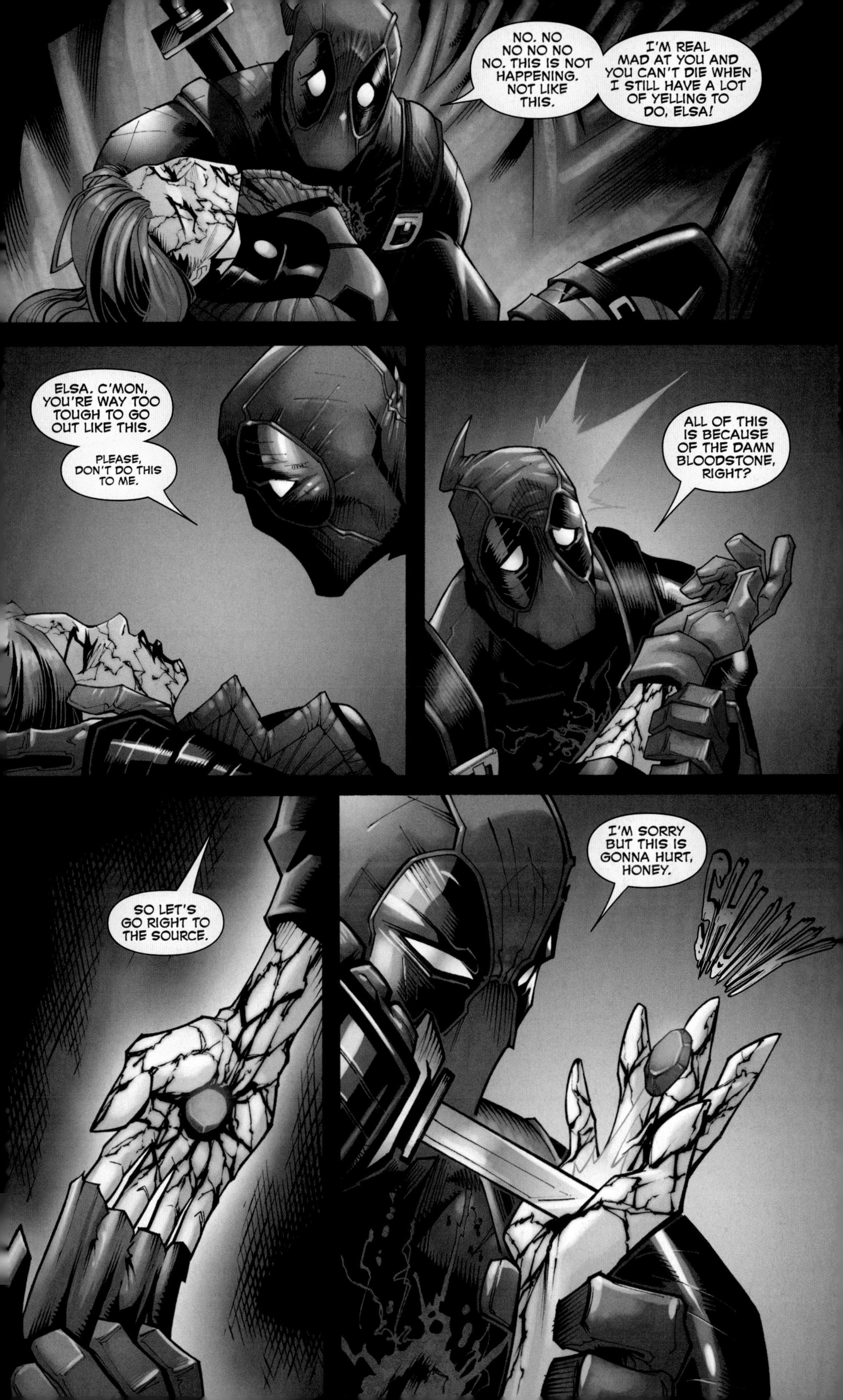

NO. NO NO NO NO NO. THIS IS NOT HAPPENING. NOT LIKE THIS.
I'M REAL MAD AT YOU AND YOU CAN'T DIE WHEN I STILL HAVE A LOT OF YELLING TO DO, ELSA!
ELSA. C'MON, YOU'RE WAY TOO TOUGH TO GO OUT LIKE THIS.
PLEASE, DON'T DO THIS TO ME.
ALL OF THIS IS BECAUSE OF THE DAMN BLOODSTONE, RIGHT?
SO LET'S GO RIGHT TO THE SOURCE.
I'M SORRY BUT THIS IS GONNA HURT, HONEY.

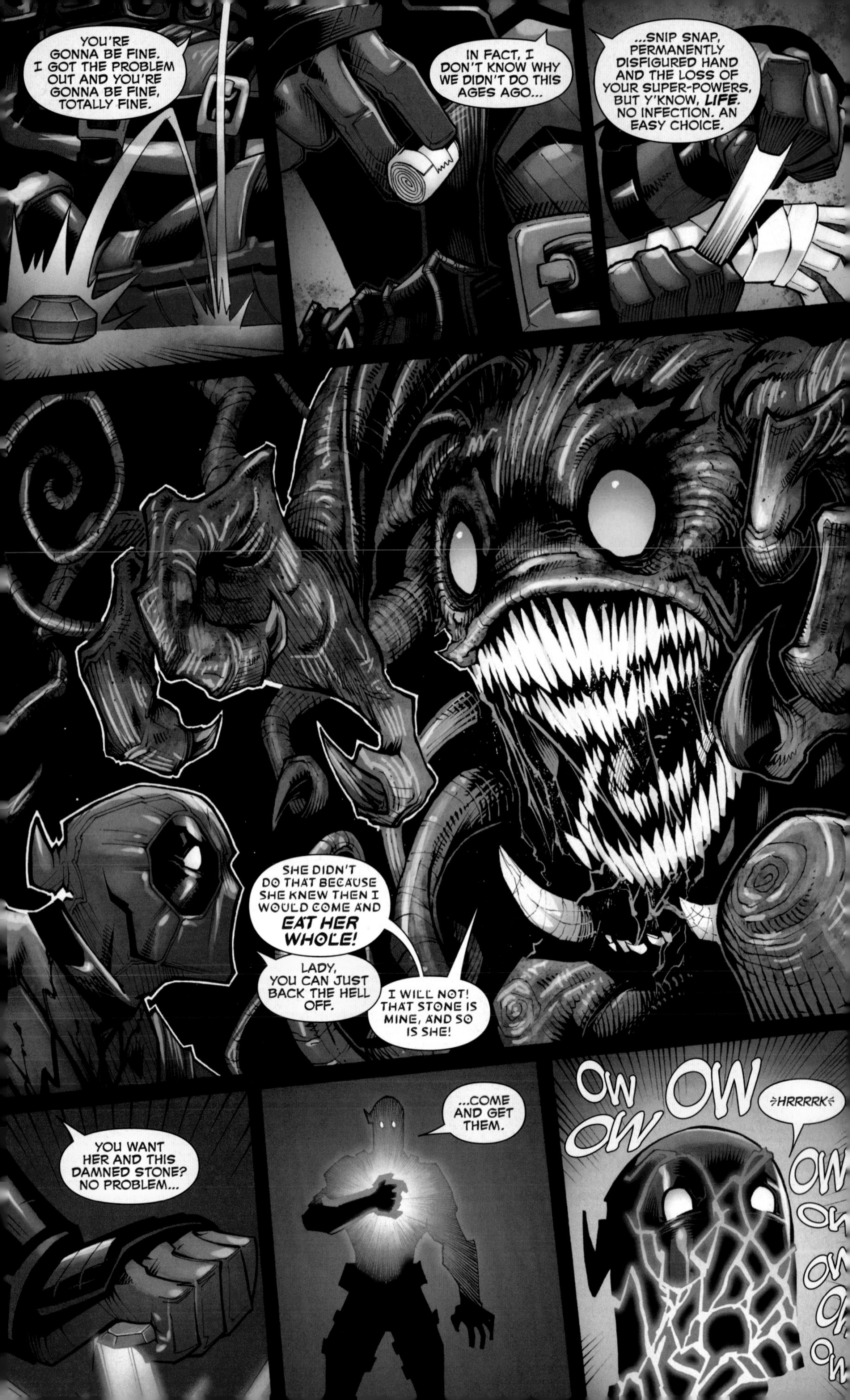
YOU'RE GONNA BE FINE. I GOT THE PROBLEM OUT AND YOU'RE GONNA BE FINE, TOTALLY FINE.
IN FACT, I DON'T KNOW WHY WE DIDN'T DO THIS AGES AGO...
...SNIP SNAP, PERMANENTLY DISFIGURED HAND AND THE LOSS OF YOUR SUPER-POWERS, BUT Y'KNOW, LIFE. NO INFECTION. AN EASY CHOICE.
SHE DIDN'T DO THAT BECAUSE SHE KNEW THEN I WOULD COME AND EAT HER WHOLE!
LADY, YOU CAN JUST BACK THE HELL OFF.
I WILL NOT! THAT STONE IS MINE, AND SO IS SHE!
YOU WANT HER AND THIS DAMNED STONE? NO PROBLEM...
...COME AND GET THEM.
OW OW OW OW
HRRRRK
OW OW OW OW OW OW

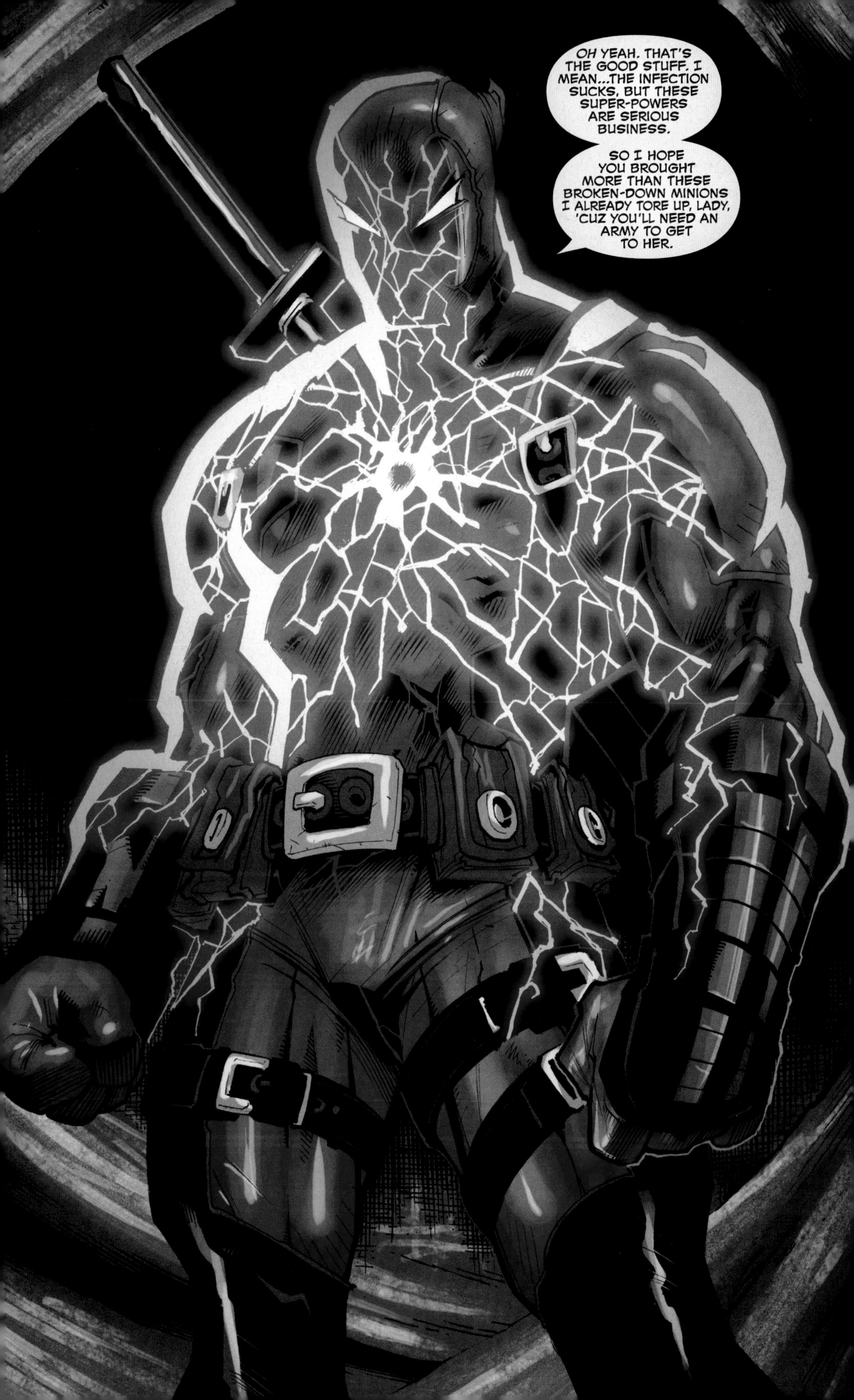
OH YEAH. THAT'S THE GOOD STUFF. I MEAN...THE INFECTION SUCKS, BUT THESE SUPER-POWERS ARE SERIOUS BUSINESS.
SO I HOPE YOU BROUGHT MORE THAN THESE BROKEN-DOWN MINIONS I ALREADY TORE UP, LADY, 'CUZ YOU'LL NEED AN ARMY TO GET TO HER.

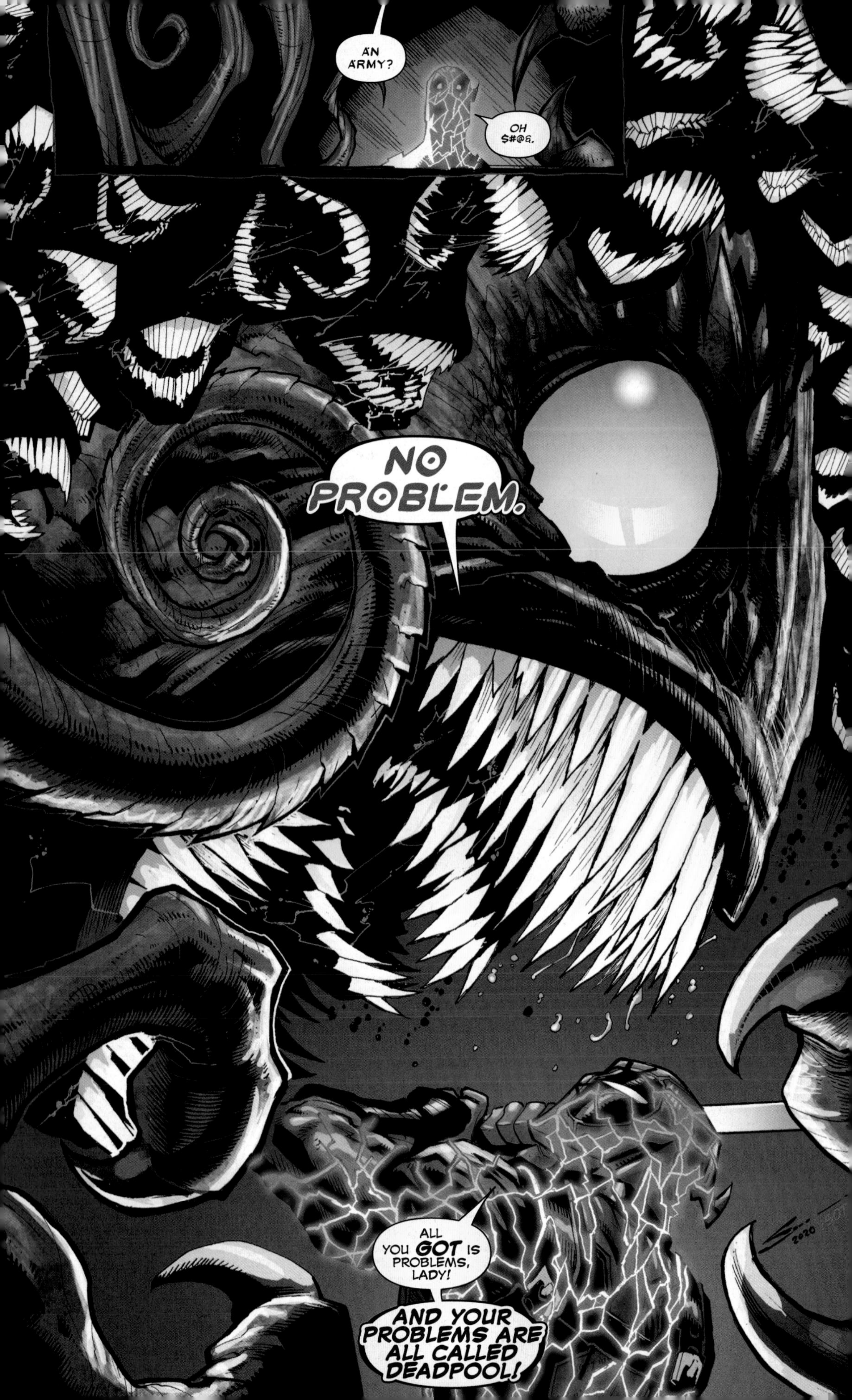
ÄN ÄRMY?
OH $#@&.
NO PROBLEM.
ALL YOU GOT IS PROBLEMS, LADY!
AND YOUR PROBLEMS ARE ALL CALLED DEADPOOL!

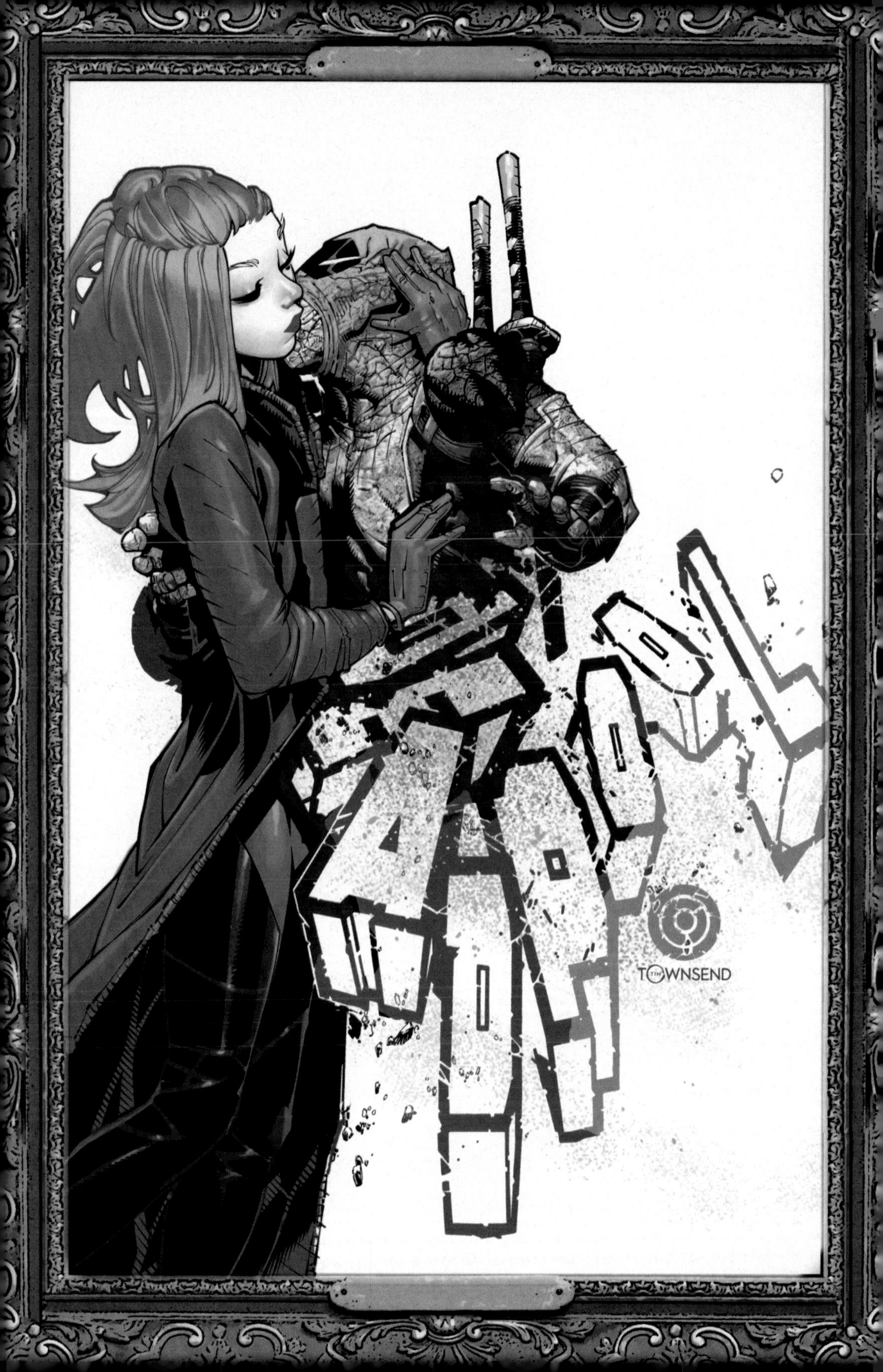
TOWNSEND

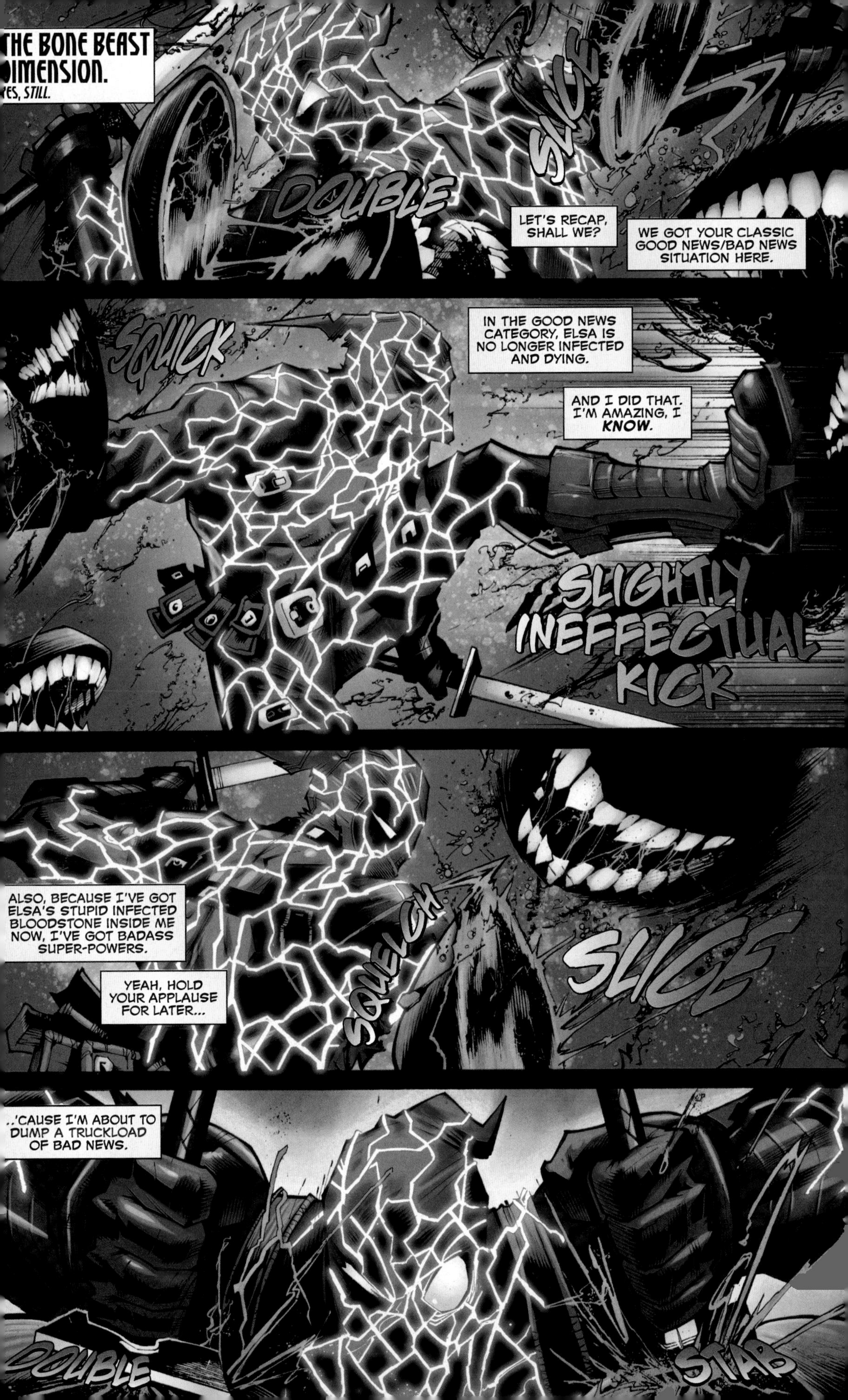
THE BONE BEAST DIMENSION.
YES, STILL.
SLICE
DOUBLE
LET'S RECAP, SHALL WE?
WE GOT YOUR CLASSIC GOOD NEWS/BAD NEWS SITUATION HERE.
SQUICK
IN THE GOOD NEWS CATEGORY, ELSA IS NO LONGER INFECTED AND DYING.
AND I DID THAT. I'M AMAZING, I KNOW.
SLIGHTLY INEFFECTUAL KICK
ALSO, BECAUSE I'VE GOT ELSA'S STUPID INFECTED BLOODSTONE INSIDE ME NOW, I'VE GOT BADASS SUPER-POWERS.
YEAH, HOLD YOUR APPLAUSE FOR LATER...
SQUELCH
SLICE
...'CAUSE I'M ABOUT TO DUMP A TRUCKLOAD OF BAD NEWS.
DOUBLE
STAB

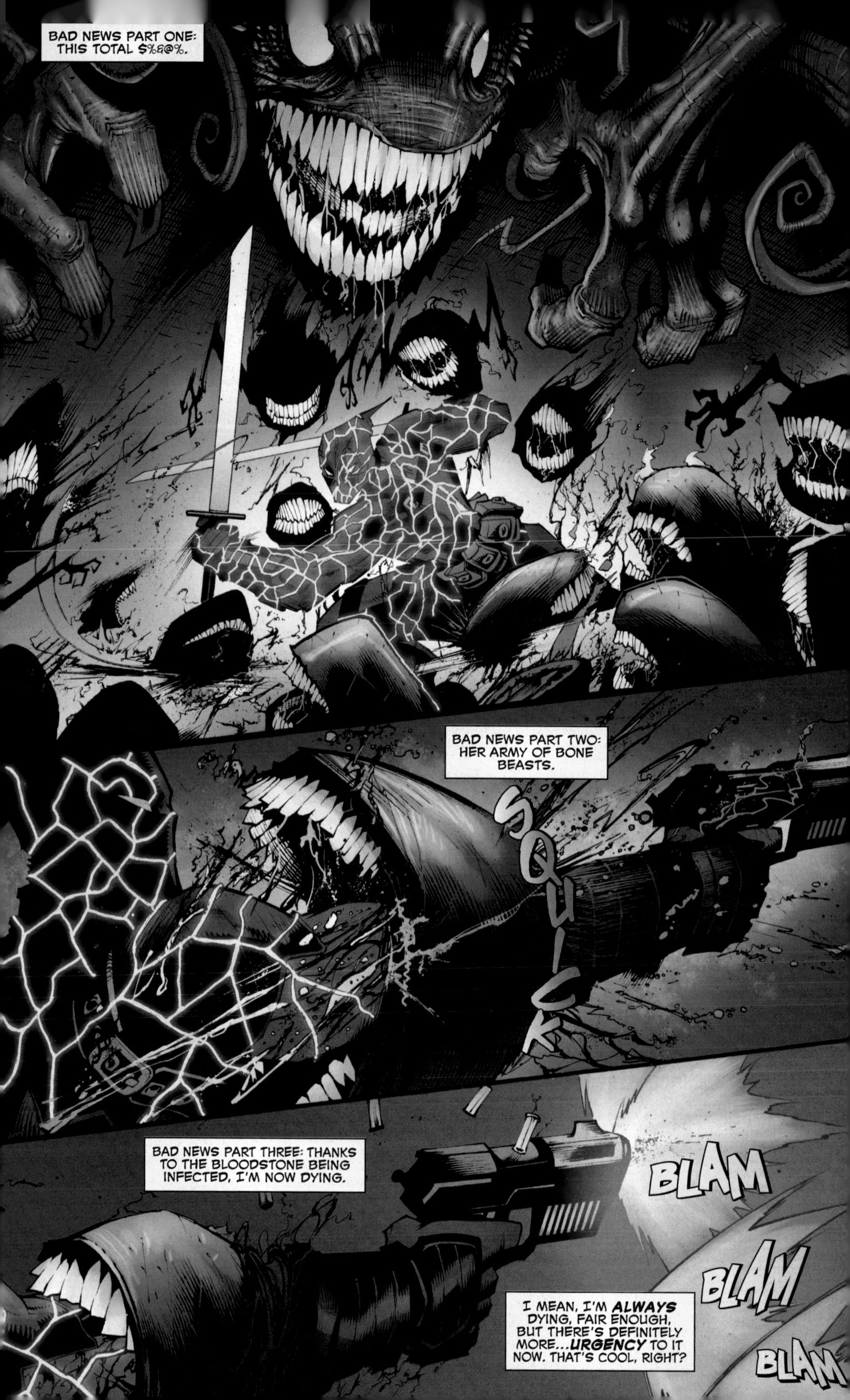
BAD NEWS PART ONE: THIS TOTAL $%&@%.
BAD NEWS PART TWO: HER ARMY OF BONE BEASTS.
SQUI-UK
BAD NEWS PART THREE: THANKS TO THE BLOODSTONE BEING INFECTED, I'M NOW DYING.
BLAM
BLAM
I MEAN, I'M **ALWAYS** DYING, FAIR ENOUGH, BUT THERE'S DEFINITELY MORE... **URGENCY** TO IT NOW. THAT'S COOL, RIGHT?
BLAM

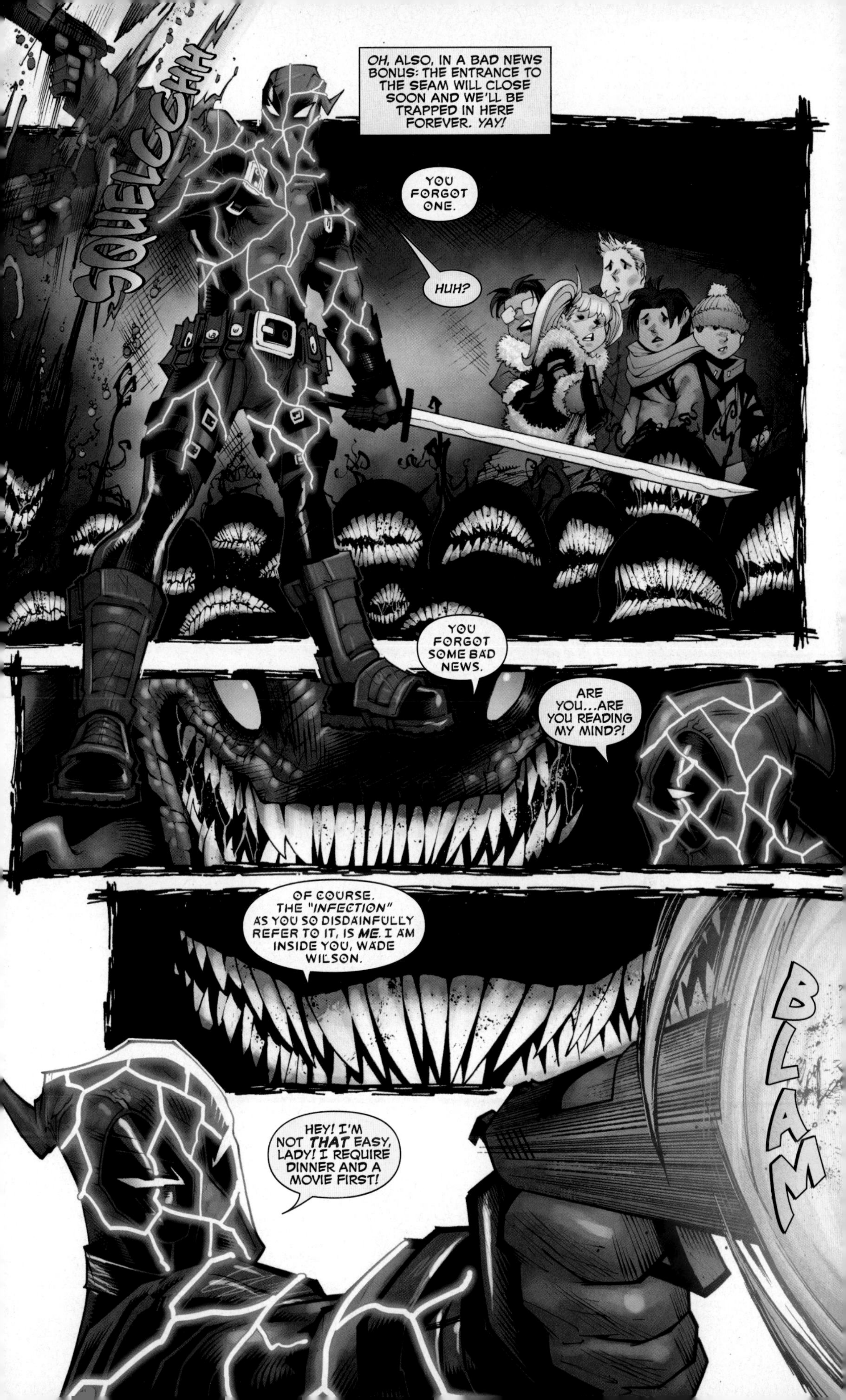
OH, ALSO, IN A BAD NEWS BONUS: THE ENTRANCE TO THE SEAM WILL CLOSE SOON AND WE'LL BE TRAPPED IN HERE FOREVER. YAY!
SQUELCCHH
YOU FORGOT ONE.
HUH?
YOU FORGOT SOME BAD NEWS.
ARE YOU...ARE YOU READING MY MIND?!
OF COURSE. THE "INFECTION" AS YOU SO DISDAINFULLY REFER TO IT, IS ME. I AM INSIDE YOU, WADE WILSON.
BLAM
HEY! I'M NOT THAT EASY, LADY! I REQUIRE DINNER AND A MOVIE FIRST!

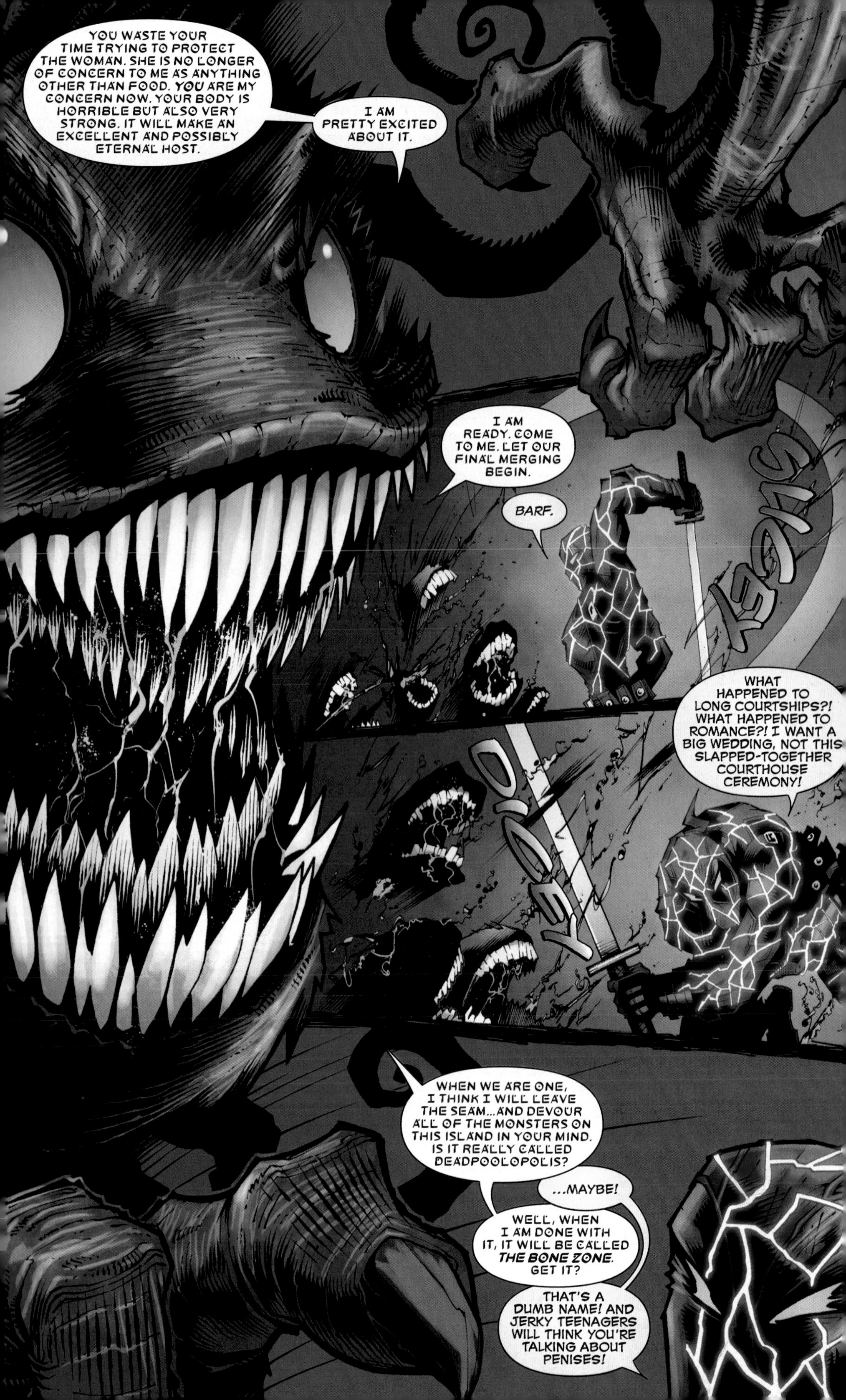
YOU WASTE YOUR TIME TRYING TO PROTECT THE WOMAN. SHE IS NO LONGER OF CONCERN TO ME AS ANYTHING OTHER THAN FOOD. *YOU* ARE MY CONCERN NOW. YOUR BODY IS HORRIBLE BUT ALSO VERY STRONG. IT WILL MAKE AN EXCELLENT AND POSSIBLY ETERNAL HOST.
I AM PRETTY EXCITED ABOUT IT.
I AM READY. COME TO ME. LET OUR FINAL MERGING BEGIN.
BARF.
WHAT HAPPENED TO LONG COURTSHIPS?! WHAT HAPPENED TO ROMANCE?! I WANT A BIG WEDDING, NOT THIS SLAPPED-TOGETHER COURTHOUSE CEREMONY!
WHEN WE ARE ONE, I THINK I WILL LEAVE THE SEAM... AND DEVOUR ALL OF THE MONSTERS ON THIS ISLAND IN YOUR MIND. IS IT REALLY CALLED DEADPOOLOPOLIS?
...MAYBE!
WELL, WHEN I AM DONE WITH IT, IT WILL BE CALLED *THE BONE ZONE*. GET IT?
THAT'S A DUMB NAME! AND JERKY TEENAGERS WILL THINK YOU'RE TALKING ABOUT PENISES!

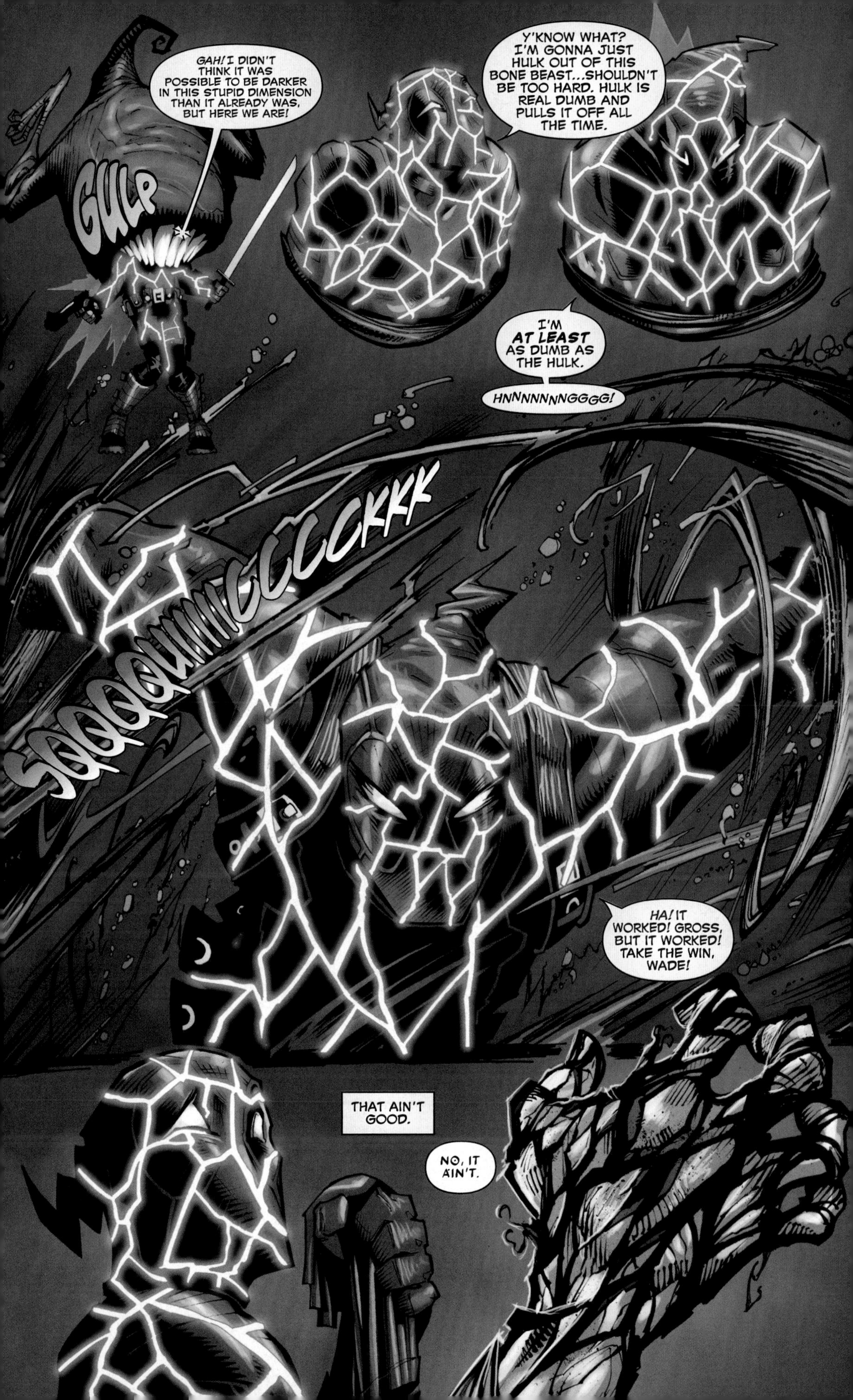
GAH! I DIDN'T THINK IT WAS POSSIBLE TO BE DARKER IN THIS STUPID DIMENSION THAN IT ALREADY WAS, BUT HERE WE ARE!
GULP
Y'KNOW WHAT? I'M GONNA JUST HULK OUT OF THIS BONE BEAST...SHOULDN'T BE TOO HARD. HULK IS REAL DUMB AND PULLS IT OFF ALL THE TIME.
I'M AT LEAST AS DUMB AS THE HULK.
HNNNNNNNGGGG!
SQQQUIIIICCCCCKKK
HA! IT WORKED! GROSS, BUT IT WORKED! TAKE THE WIN, WADE!
THAT AIN'T GOOD.
NO, IT AIN'T.

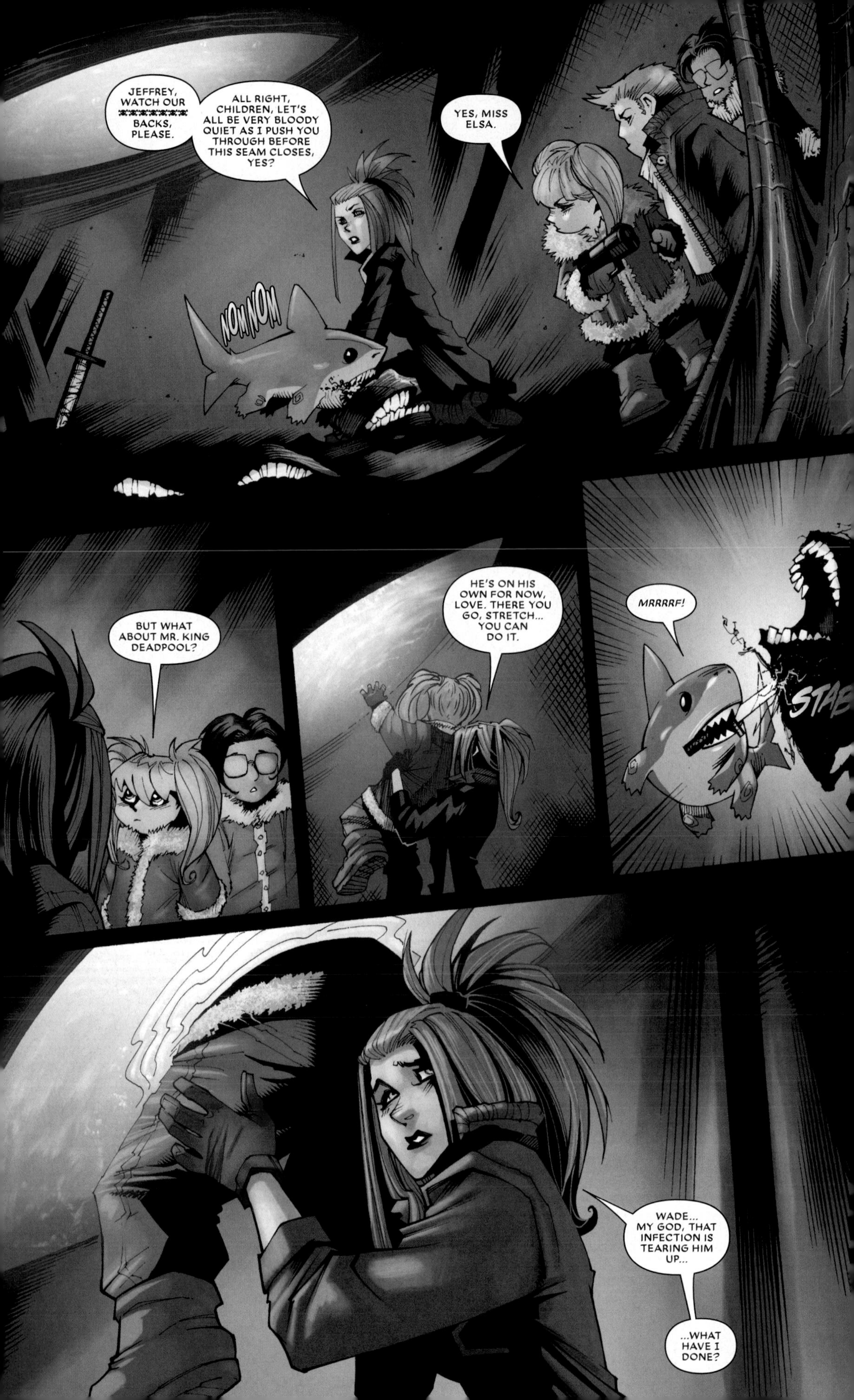
JEFFREY, WATCH OUR ☠☠☠☠☠☠☠ BACKS, PLEASE.
ALL RIGHT, CHILDREN, LET'S ALL BE VERY BLOODY QUIET AS I PUSH YOU THROUGH BEFORE THIS SEAM CLOSES, YES?
YES, MISS ELSA.
NOM NOM
BUT WHAT ABOUT MR. KING DEADPOOL?
HE'S ON HIS OWN FOR NOW, LOVE. THERE YOU GO, STRETCH... YOU CAN DO IT.
MRRRRF!
STAB
WADE... MY GOD, THAT INFECTION IS TEARING HIM UP...
...WHAT HAVE I DONE?

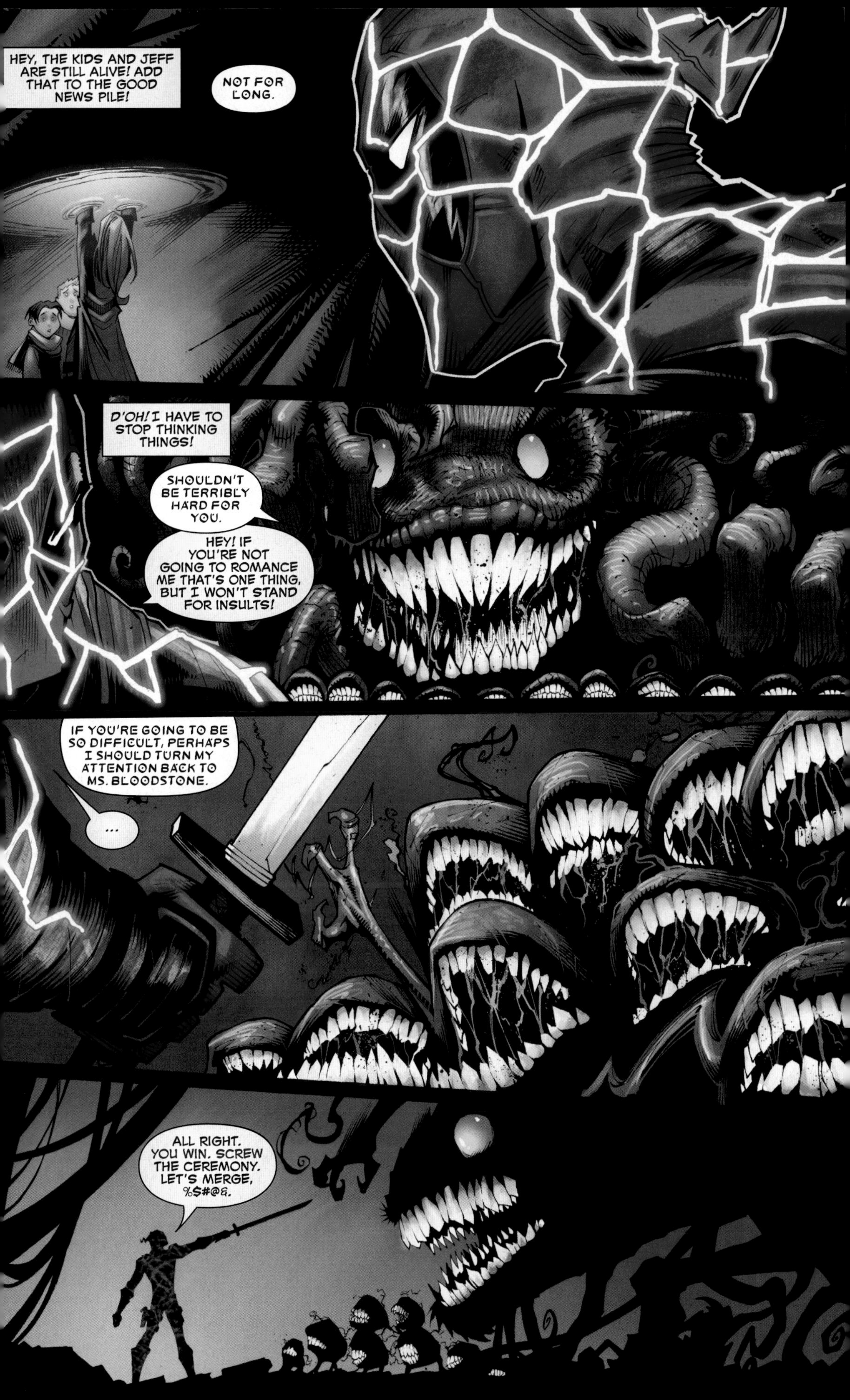
HEY, THE KIDS AND JEFF ARE STILL ALIVE! ADD THAT TO THE GOOD NEWS PILE!
NOT FOR LONG.
D'OH! I HAVE TO STOP THINKING THINGS!
SHOULDN'T BE TERRIBLY HARD FOR YOU.
HEY! IF YOU'RE NOT GOING TO ROMANCE ME THAT'S ONE THING, BUT I WON'T STAND FOR INSULTS!
IF YOU'RE GOING TO BE SO DIFFICULT, PERHAPS I SHOULD TURN MY ATTENTION BACK TO MS. BLOODSTONE.
...
ALL RIGHT. YOU WIN. SCREW THE CEREMONY. LET'S MERGE, %$#@&.

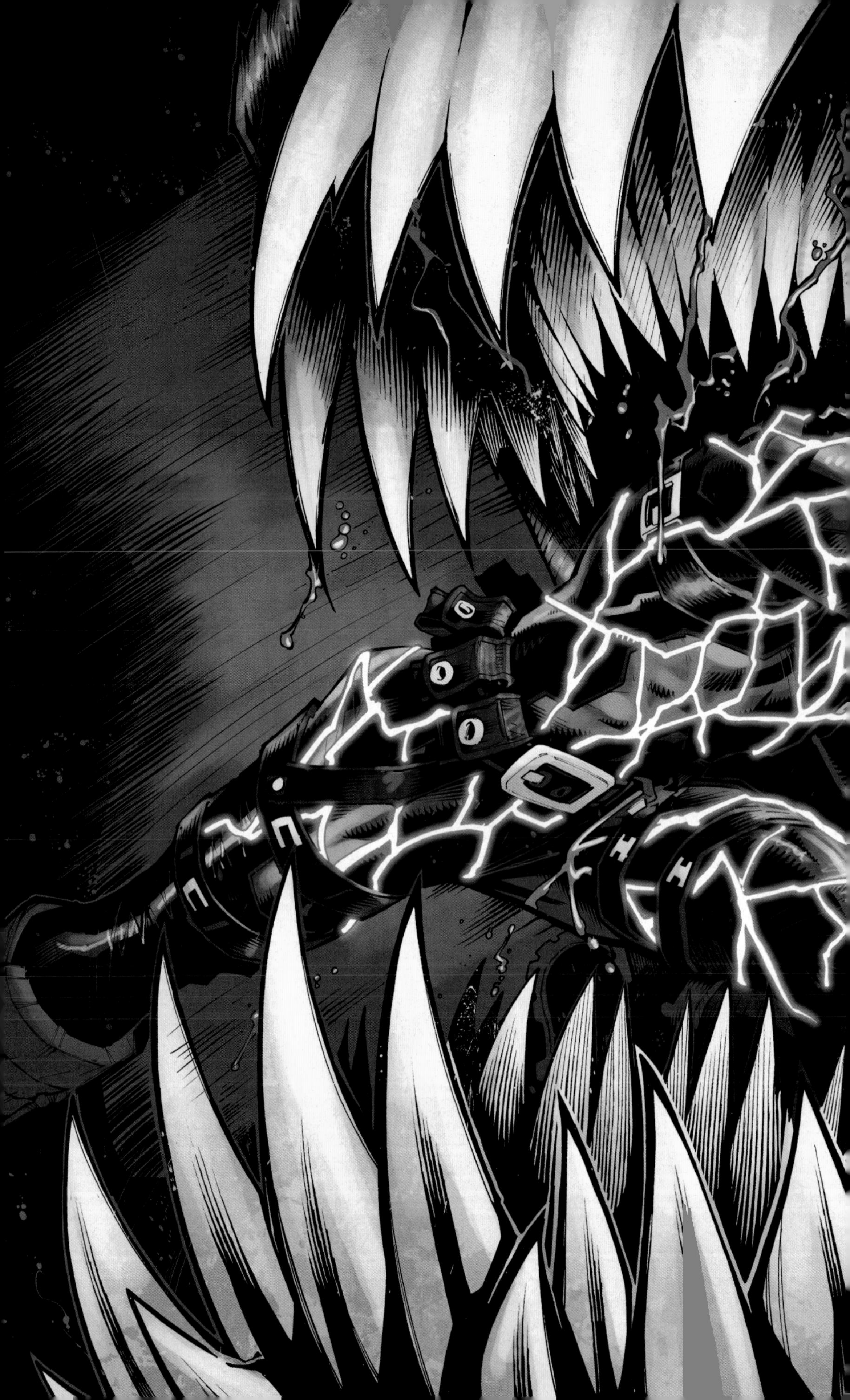

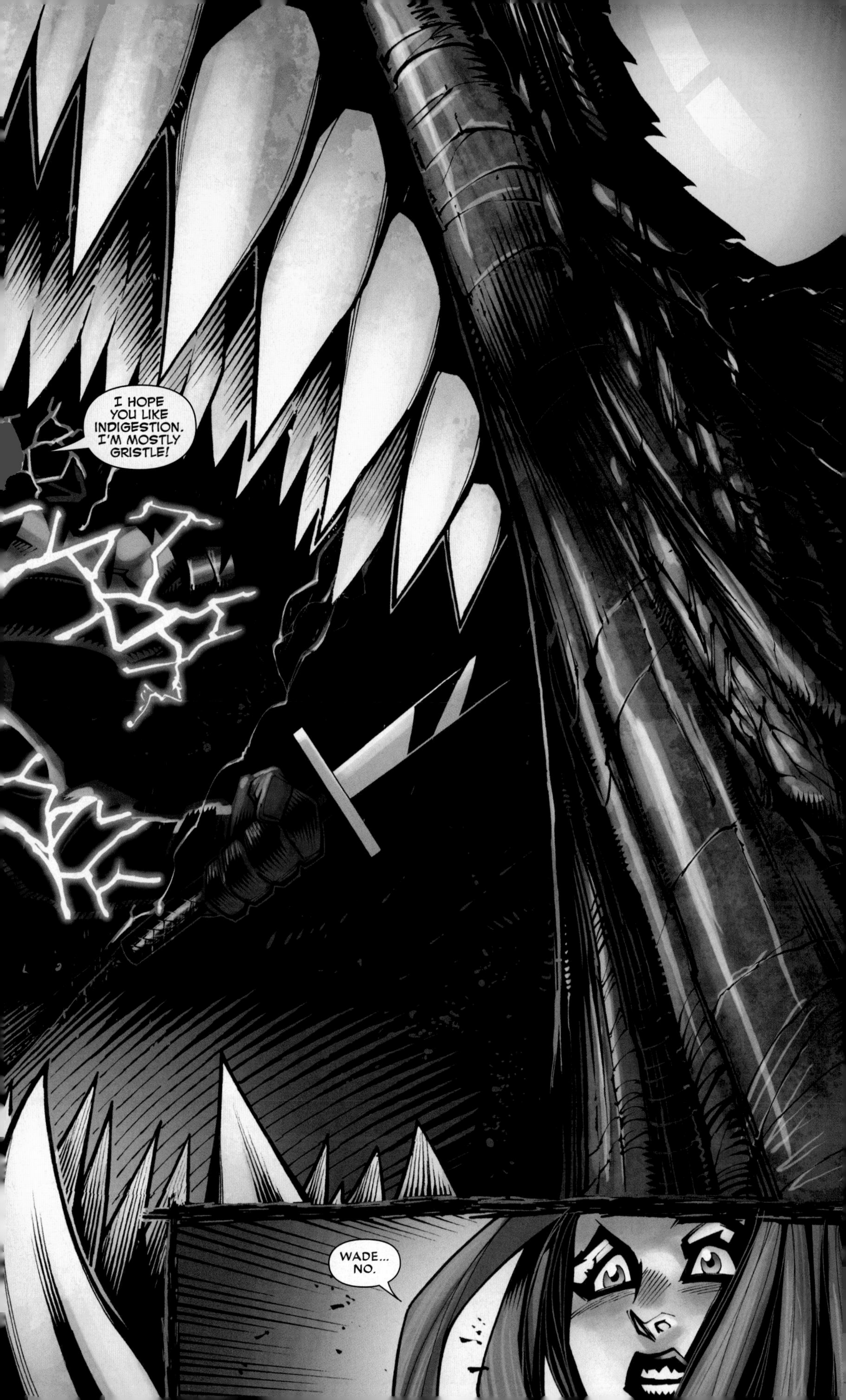
I HOPE YOU LIKE INDIGESTION. I'M MOSTLY GRISTLE!
WADE... NO.

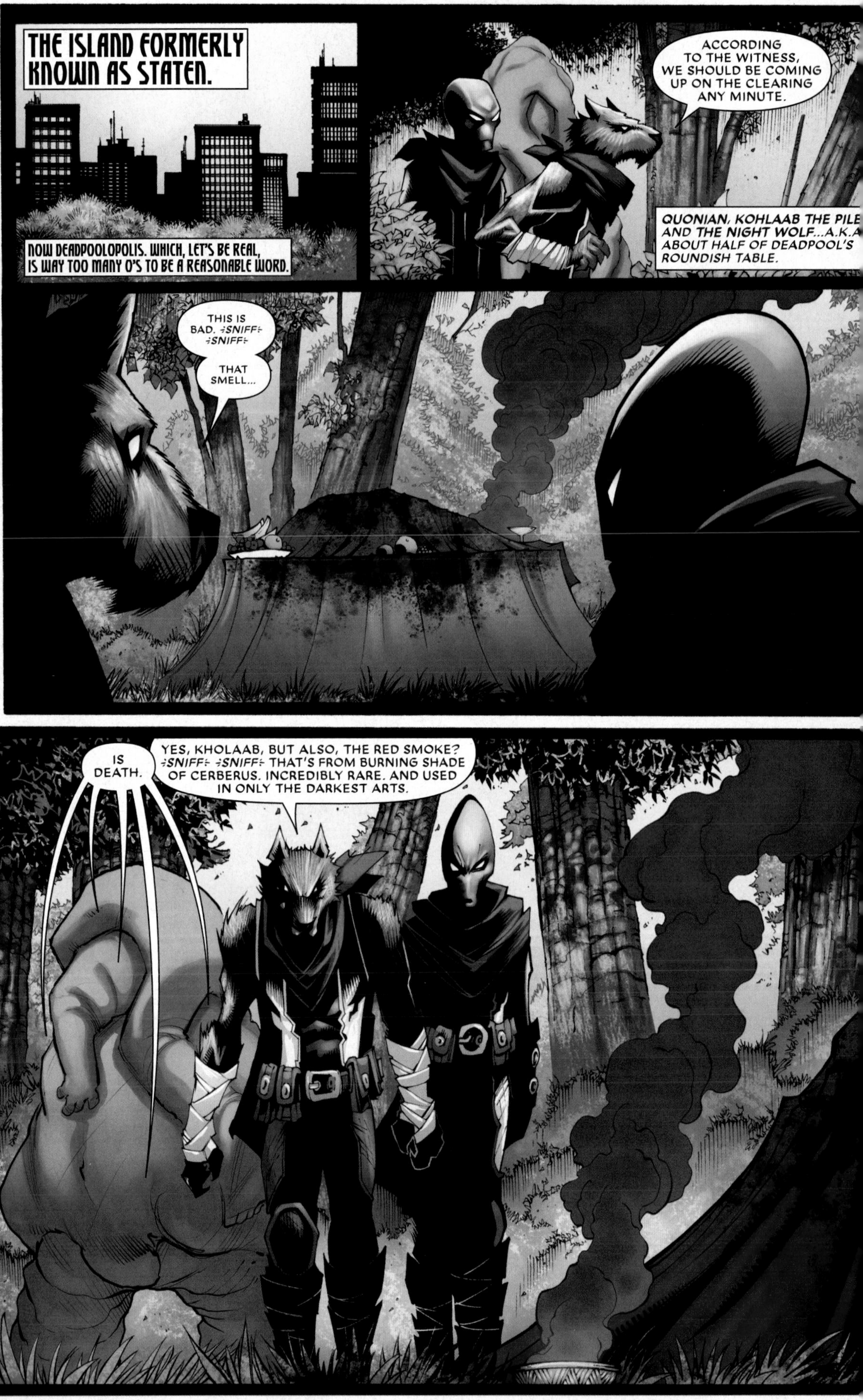
THE ISLAND FORMERLY KNOWN AS STATEN.
NOW DEADPOOLOPOLIS. WHICH, LET'S BE REAL, IS WAY TOO MANY O'S TO BE A REASONABLE WORD.
ACCORDING TO THE WITNESS, WE SHOULD BE COMING UP ON THE CLEARING ANY MINUTE.
QUONIAN, KOHLAAB THE PILE AND THE NIGHT WOLF...A.K.A. ABOUT HALF OF DEADPOOL'S ROUNDISH TABLE.
THIS IS BAD. ÷SNIFF÷ ÷SNIFF÷
THAT SMELL...
IS DEATH.
YES, KHOLAAB, BUT ALSO, THE RED SMOKE? ÷SNIFF÷ ÷SNIFF÷ THAT'S FROM BURNING SHADE OF CERBERUS. INCREDIBLY RARE. AND USED IN ONLY THE DARKEST ARTS.

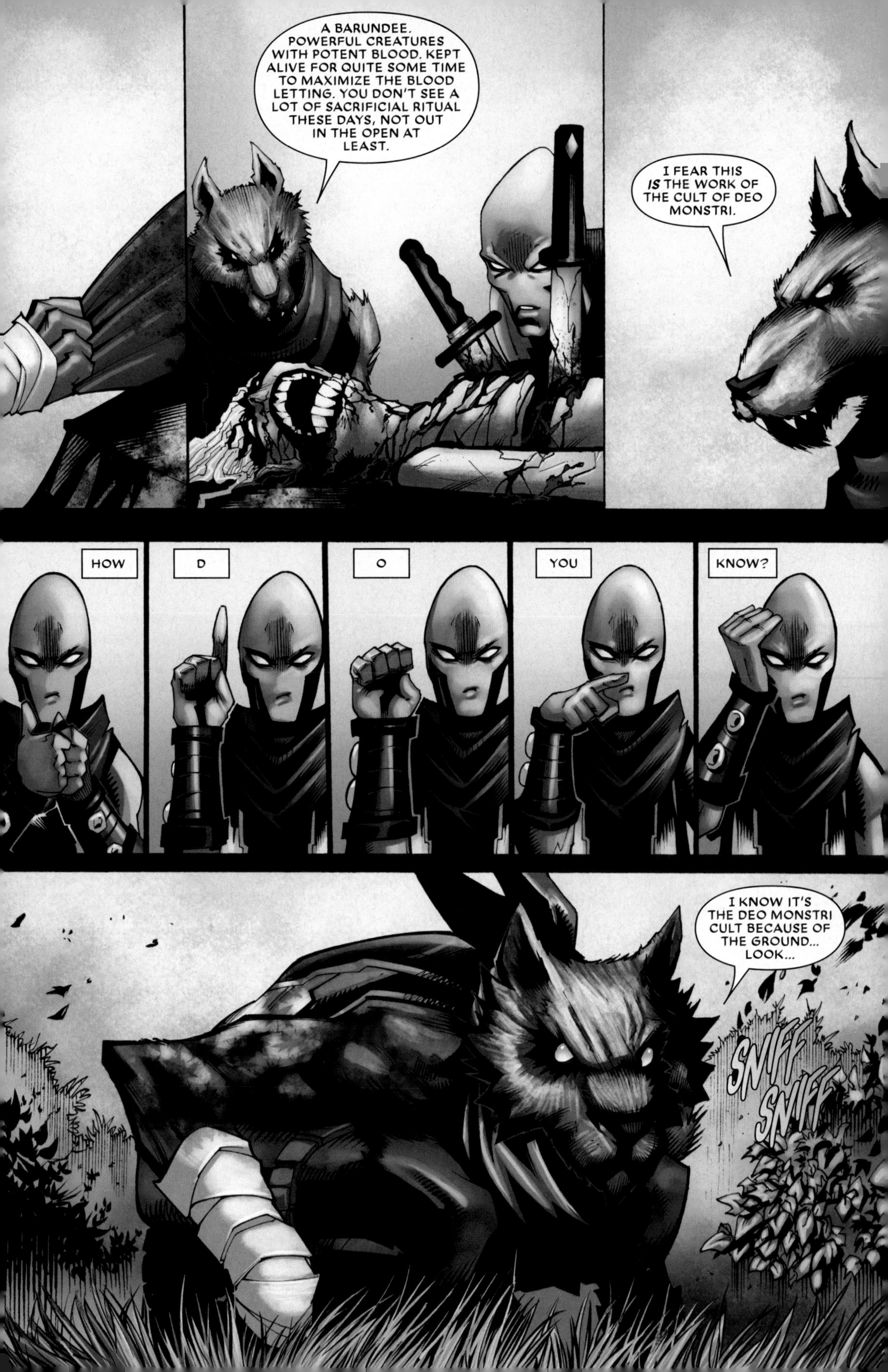
A BARUNDEE. POWERFUL CREATURES WITH POTENT BLOOD. KEPT ALIVE FOR QUITE SOME TIME TO MAXIMIZE THE BLOOD LETTING. YOU DON'T SEE A LOT OF SACRIFICIAL RITUAL THESE DAYS, NOT OUT IN THE OPEN AT LEAST.
I FEAR THIS *IS* THE WORK OF THE CULT OF DEO MONSTRI.
HOW
D
O
YOU
KNOW?
I KNOW IT'S THE DEO MONSTRI CULT BECAUSE OF THE GROUND... LOOK...
SNIFF SNIFF

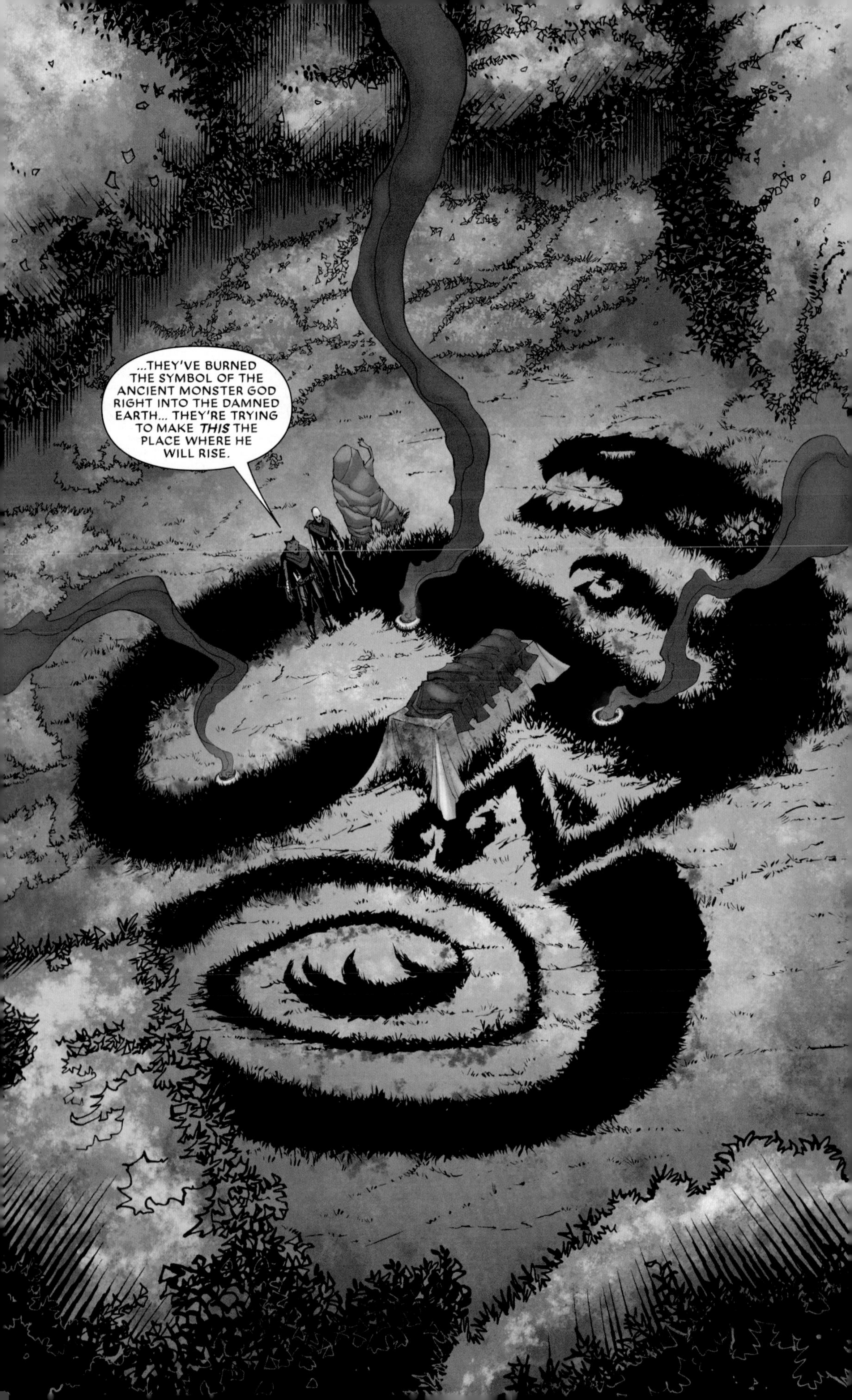
...THEY'VE BURNED THE SYMBOL OF THE ANCIENT MONSTER GOD RIGHT INTO THE DAMNED EARTH... THEY'RE TRYING TO MAKE *THIS* THE PLACE WHERE HE WILL RISE.

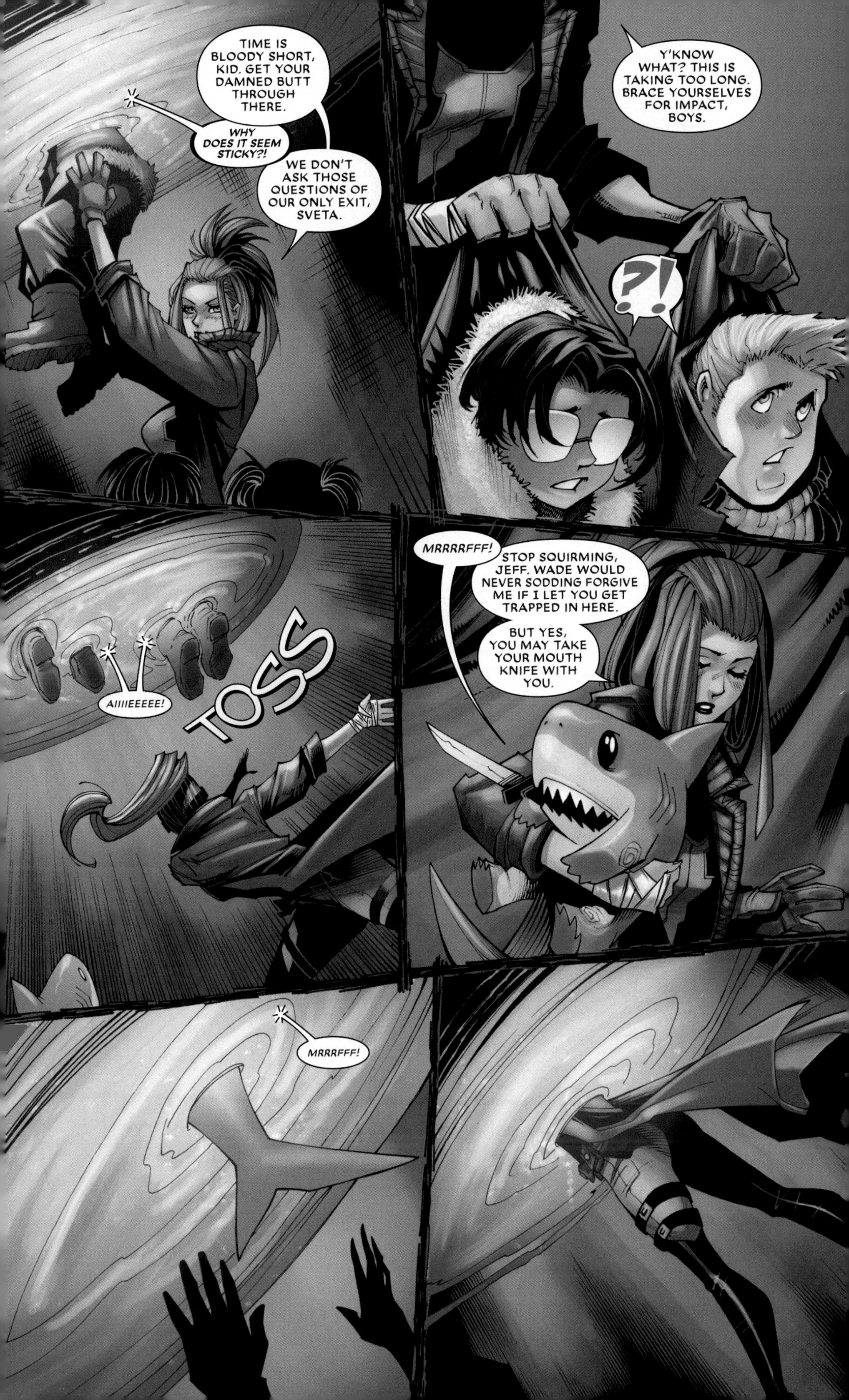
TIME IS BLOODY SHORT, KID. GET YOUR DAMNED BUTT THROUGH THERE.
WHY DOES IT SEEM STICKY?!
WE DON'T ASK THOSE QUESTIONS OF OUR ONLY EXIT, SVETA.
Y'KNOW WHAT? THIS IS TAKING TOO LONG. BRACE YOURSELVES FOR IMPACT, BOYS.
?!
AIIIIEEEEE!
TOSS
MRRRRFFF!
STOP SQUIRMING, JEFF. WADE WOULD NEVER SODDING FORGIVE ME IF I LET YOU GET TRAPPED IN HERE.
BUT YES, YOU MAY TAKE YOUR MOUTH KNIFE WITH YOU.
MRRRFFF!

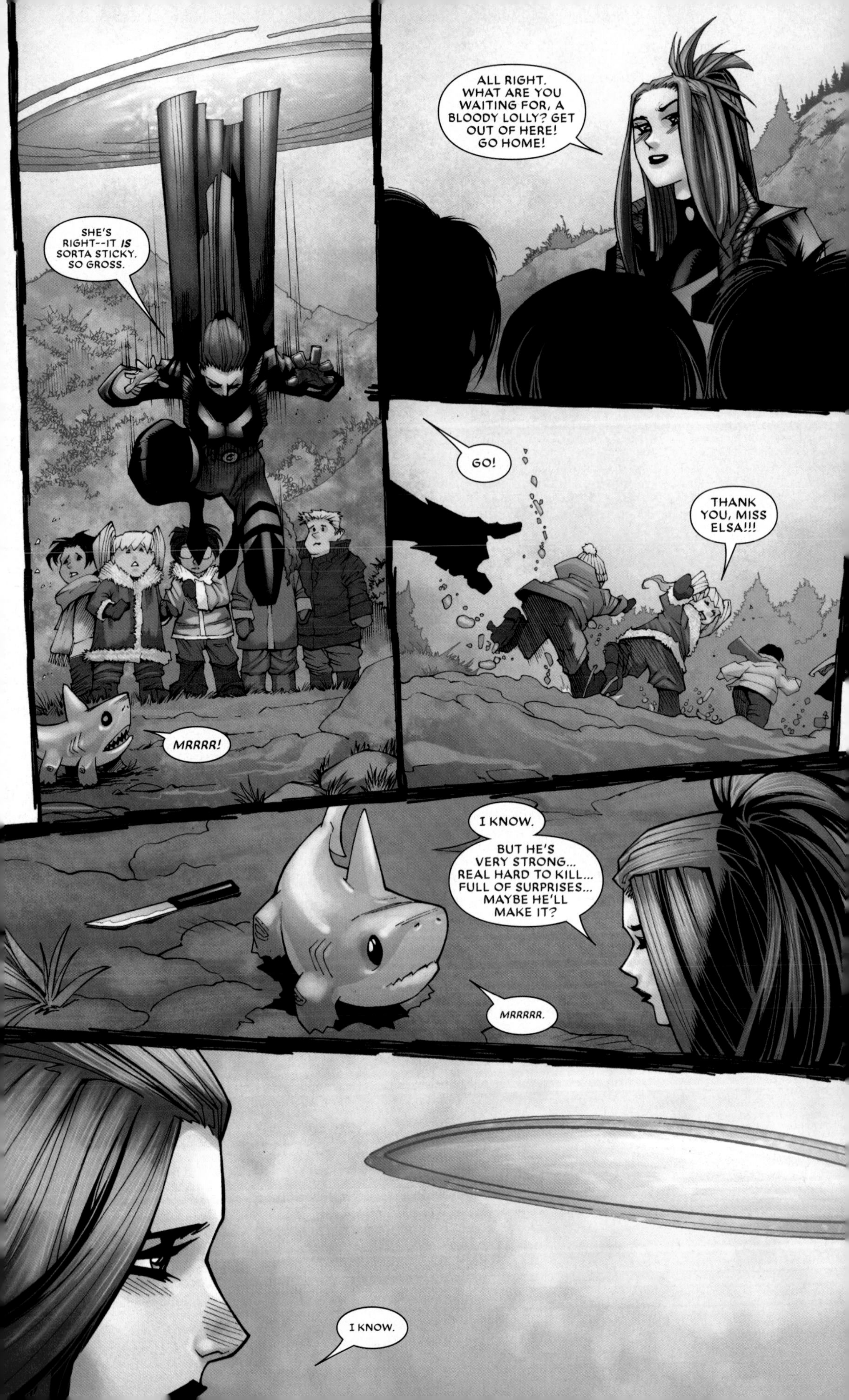
SHE'S RIGHT--IT IS SORTA STICKY. SO GROSS.
MRRRR!
ALL RIGHT. WHAT ARE YOU WAITING FOR, A BLOODY LOLLY? GET OUT OF HERE! GO HOME!
GO!
THANK YOU, MISS ELSA!!!
I KNOW.
BUT HE'S VERY STRONG... REAL HARD TO KILL... FULL OF SURPRISES... MAYBE HE'LL MAKE IT?
MRRRRR.
I KNOW.

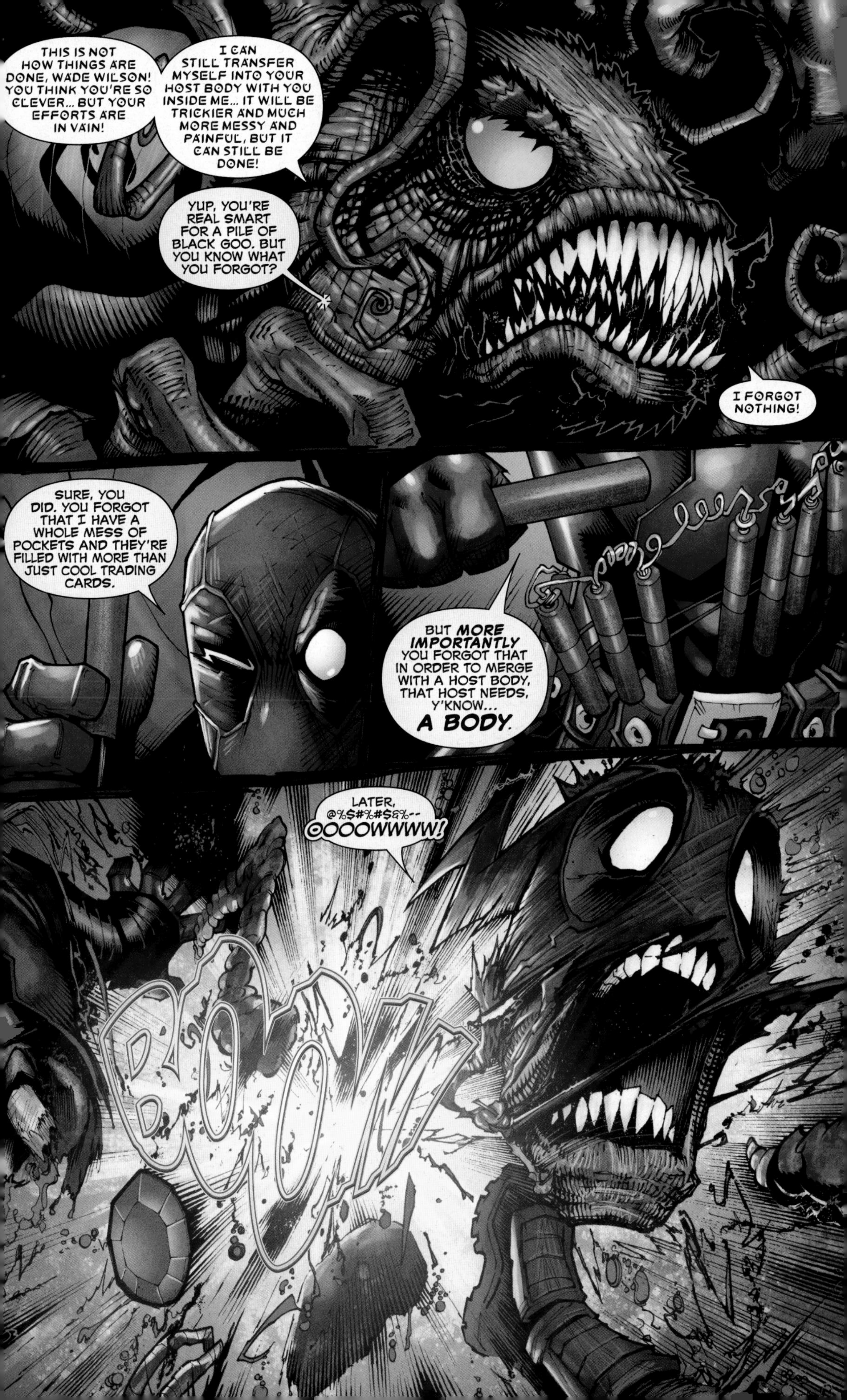
THIS IS NOT HOW THINGS ARE DONE, WADE WILSON! YOU THINK YOU'RE SO CLEVER... BUT YOUR EFFORTS ARE IN VAIN!
I CAN STILL TRANSFER MYSELF INTO YOUR HOST BODY WITH YOU INSIDE ME... IT WILL BE TRICKIER AND MUCH MORE MESSY AND PAINFUL, BUT IT CAN STILL BE DONE!
YUP, YOU'RE REAL SMART FOR A PILE OF BLACK GOO. BUT YOU KNOW WHAT YOU FORGOT?
I FORGOT NOTHING!
SURE, YOU DID. YOU FORGOT THAT I HAVE A WHOLE MESS OF POCKETS AND THEY'RE FILLED WITH MORE THAN JUST COOL TRADING CARDS.
BUT MORE IMPORTANTLY YOU FORGOT THAT IN ORDER TO MERGE WITH A HOST BODY, THAT HOST NEEDS, Y'KNOW... A BODY.
LATER, @%$#%#$&%-- OOOOWWWW!
BOOM

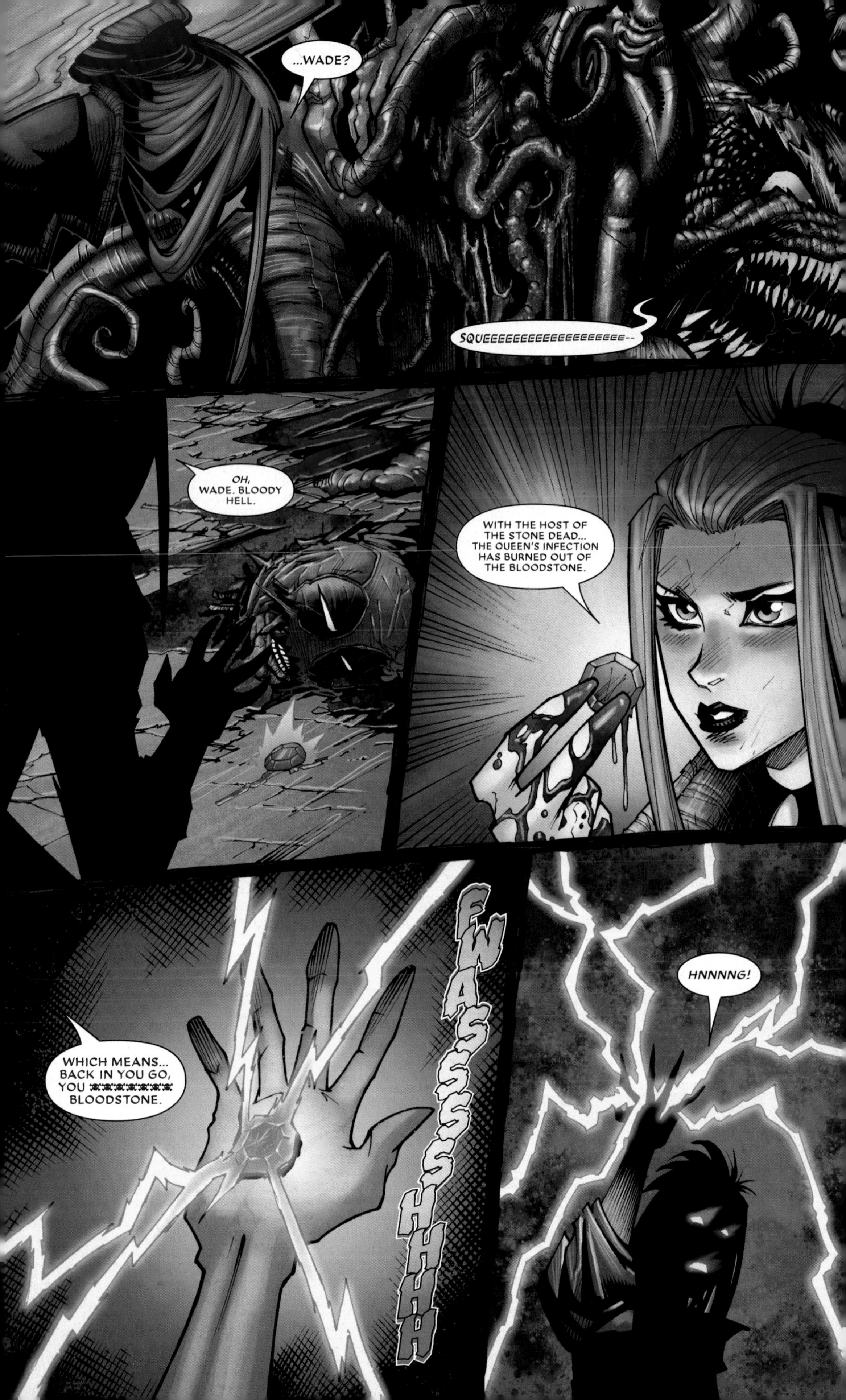
...WADE?
SQUEEEEEEEEEEEEEEEEEEE--
OH, WADE. BLOODY HELL.
WITH THE HOST OF THE STONE DEAD... THE QUEEN'S INFECTION HAS BURNED OUT OF THE BLOODSTONE.
WHICH MEANS... BACK IN YOU GO, YOU BLOODSTONE.
FWASSSSSHHHHH
HNNNNG!

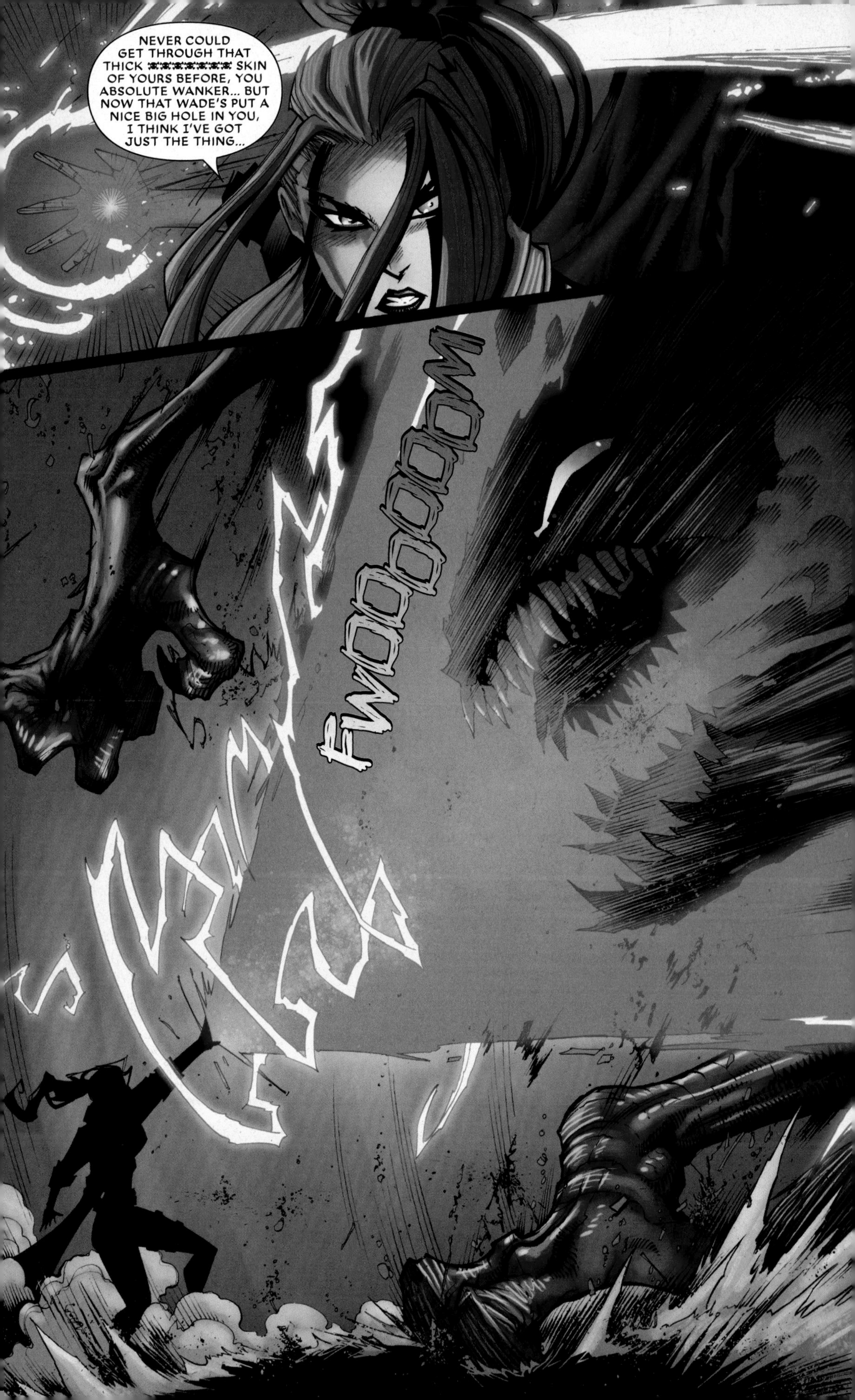
NEVER COULD GET THROUGH THAT THICK ☠☠☠☠☠☠☠ SKIN OF YOURS BEFORE, YOU ABSOLUTE WANKER... BUT NOW THAT WADE'S PUT A NICE BIG HOLE IN YOU, I THINK I'VE GOT JUST THE THING...
FWOOOOOOM

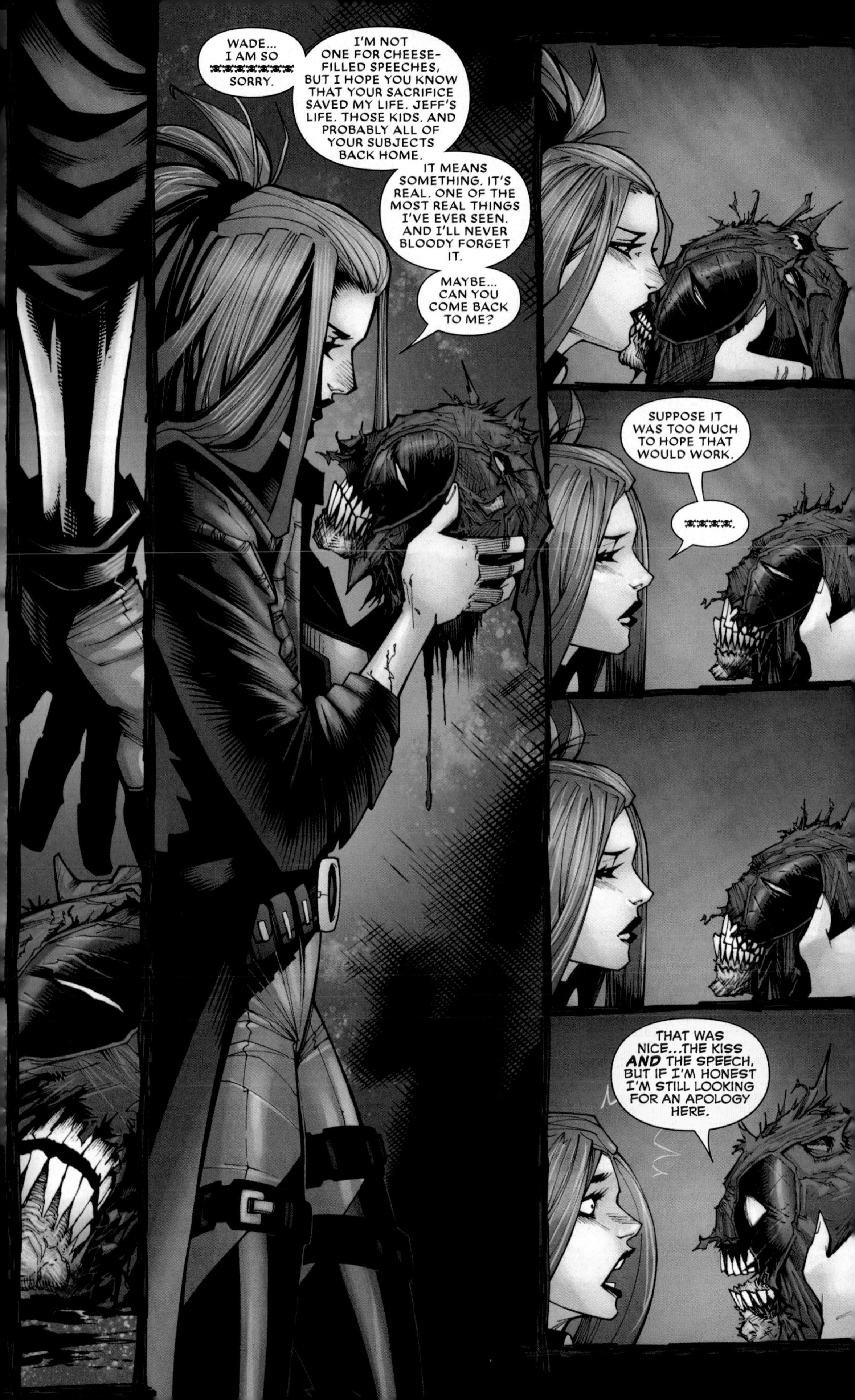
WADE... I AM SO SORRY.
I'M NOT ONE FOR CHEESE-FILLED SPEECHES, BUT I HOPE YOU KNOW THAT YOUR SACRIFICE SAVED MY LIFE. JEFF'S LIFE. THOSE KIDS. AND PROBABLY ALL OF YOUR SUBJECTS BACK HOME.
IT MEANS SOMETHING. IT'S REAL. ONE OF THE MOST REAL THINGS I'VE EVER SEEN. AND I'LL NEVER BLOODY FORGET IT.
MAYBE... CAN YOU COME BACK TO ME?
SUPPOSE IT WAS TOO MUCH TO HOPE THAT WOULD WORK.
THAT WAS NICE...THE KISS **AND** THE SPEECH, BUT IF I'M HONEST I'M STILL LOOKING FOR AN APOLOGY HERE.

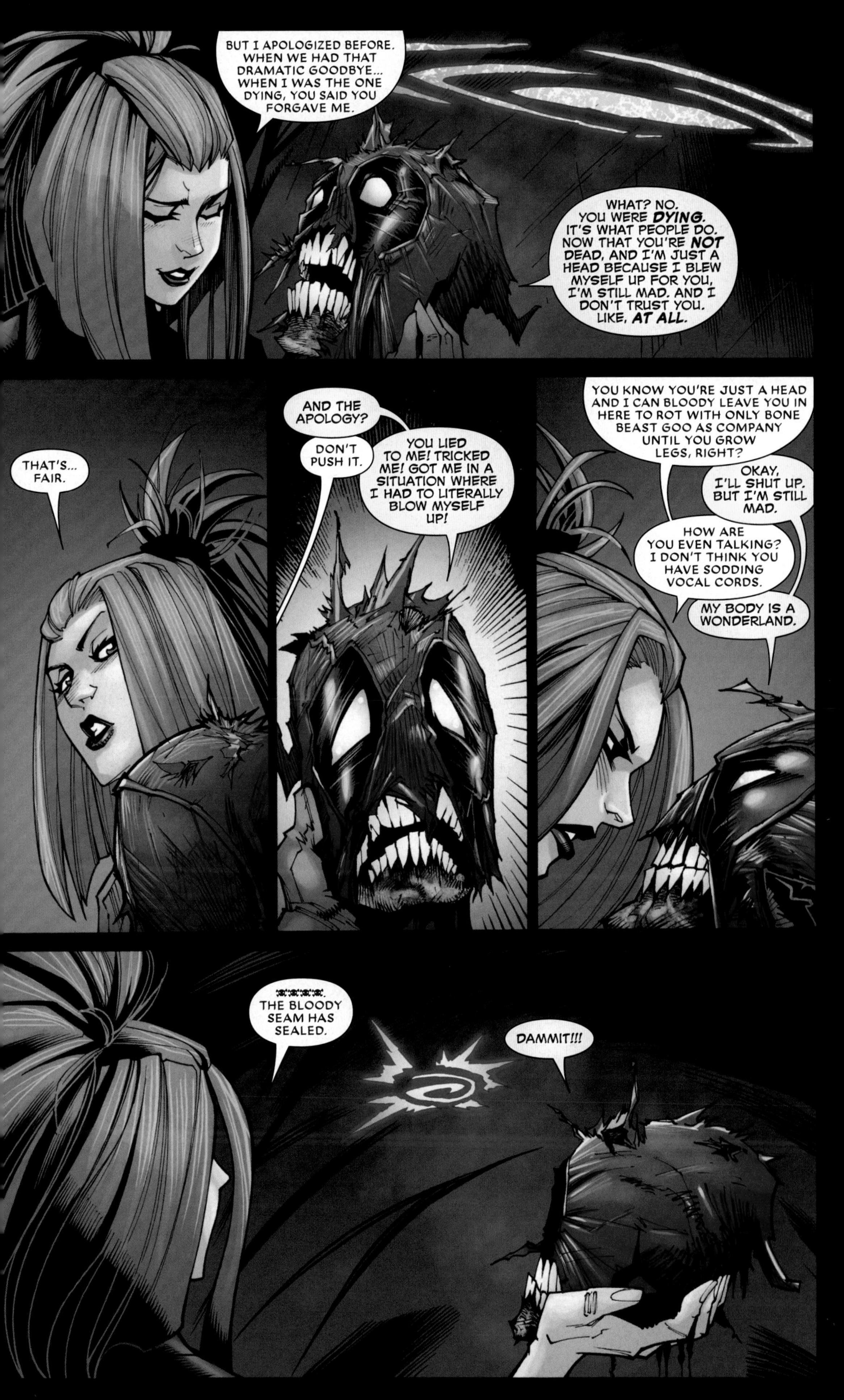
BUT I APOLOGIZED BEFORE. WHEN WE HAD THAT DRAMATIC GOODBYE... WHEN I WAS THE ONE DYING, YOU SAID YOU FORGAVE ME.
WHAT? NO. YOU WERE DYING. IT'S WHAT PEOPLE DO. NOW THAT YOU'RE NOT DEAD, AND I'M JUST A HEAD BECAUSE I BLEW MYSELF UP FOR YOU, I'M STILL MAD. AND I DON'T TRUST YOU. LIKE, AT ALL.
THAT'S... FAIR.
AND THE APOLOGY?
DON'T PUSH IT.
YOU LIED TO ME! TRICKED ME! GOT ME IN A SITUATION WHERE I HAD TO LITERALLY BLOW MYSELF UP!
YOU KNOW YOU'RE JUST A HEAD AND I CAN BLOODY LEAVE YOU IN HERE TO ROT WITH ONLY BONE BEAST GOO AS COMPANY UNTIL YOU GROW LEGS, RIGHT?
OKAY, I'LL SHUT UP. BUT I'M STILL MAD.
HOW ARE YOU EVEN TALKING? I DON'T THINK YOU HAVE SODDING VOCAL CORDS.
MY BODY IS A WONDERLAND.
THE BLOODY SEAM HAS SEALED.
DAMMIT!!!

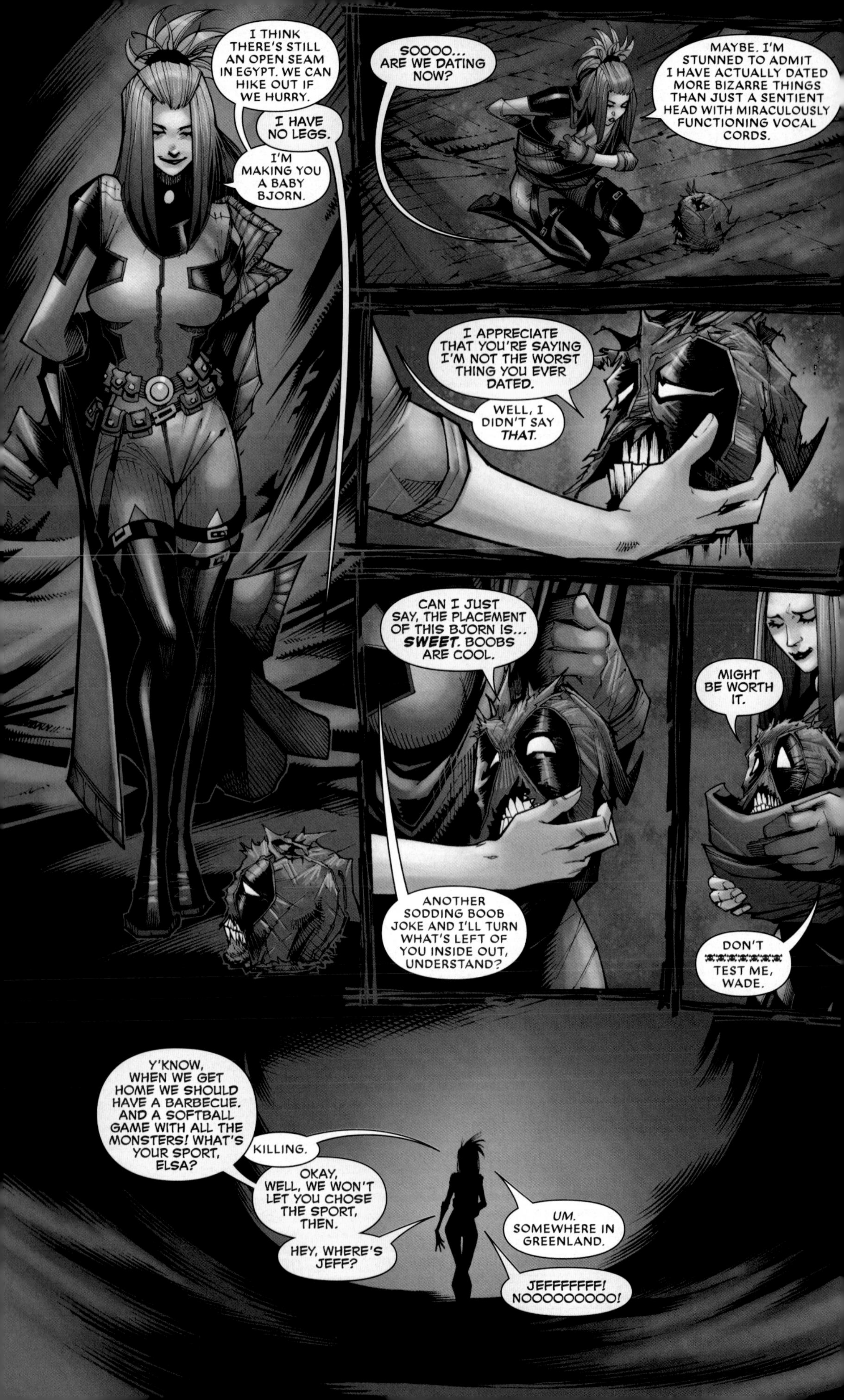

I THINK THERE'S STILL AN OPEN SEAM IN EGYPT. WE CAN HIKE OUT IF WE HURRY.
I HAVE NO LEGS.
I'M MAKING YOU A BABY BJORN.
SOOOO... ARE WE DATING NOW?
MAYBE. I'M STUNNED TO ADMIT I HAVE ACTUALLY DATED MORE BIZARRE THINGS THAN JUST A SENTIENT HEAD WITH MIRACULOUSLY FUNCTIONING VOCAL CORDS.
I APPRECIATE THAT YOU'RE SAYING I'M NOT THE WORST THING YOU EVER DATED.
WELL, I DIDN'T SAY THAT.
CAN I JUST SAY, THE PLACEMENT OF THIS BJORN IS... SWEET. BOOBS ARE COOL.
ANOTHER SODDING BOOB JOKE AND I'LL TURN WHAT'S LEFT OF YOU INSIDE OUT, UNDERSTAND?
MIGHT BE WORTH IT.
DON'T TEST ME, WADE.
Y'KNOW, WHEN WE GET HOME WE SHOULD HAVE A BARBECUE. AND A SOFTBALL GAME WITH ALL THE MONSTERS! WHAT'S YOUR SPORT, ELSA?
KILLING.
OKAY, WELL, WE WON'T LET YOU CHOSE THE SPORT, THEN.
HEY, WHERE'S JEFF?
UM. SOMEWHERE IN GREENLAND.
JEFFFFFFFF! NOOOOOOOOO!

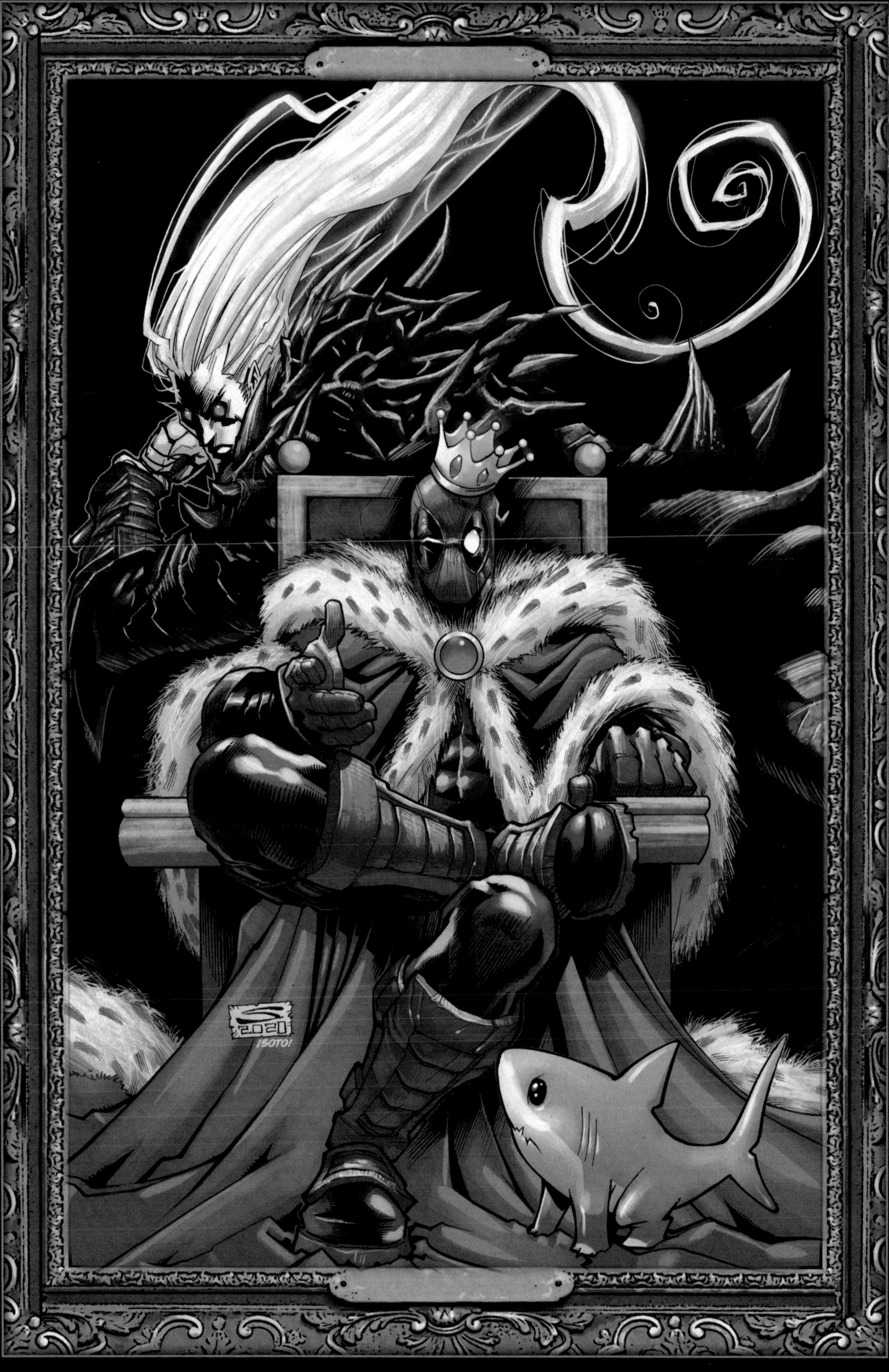
2020
¡SOTO!

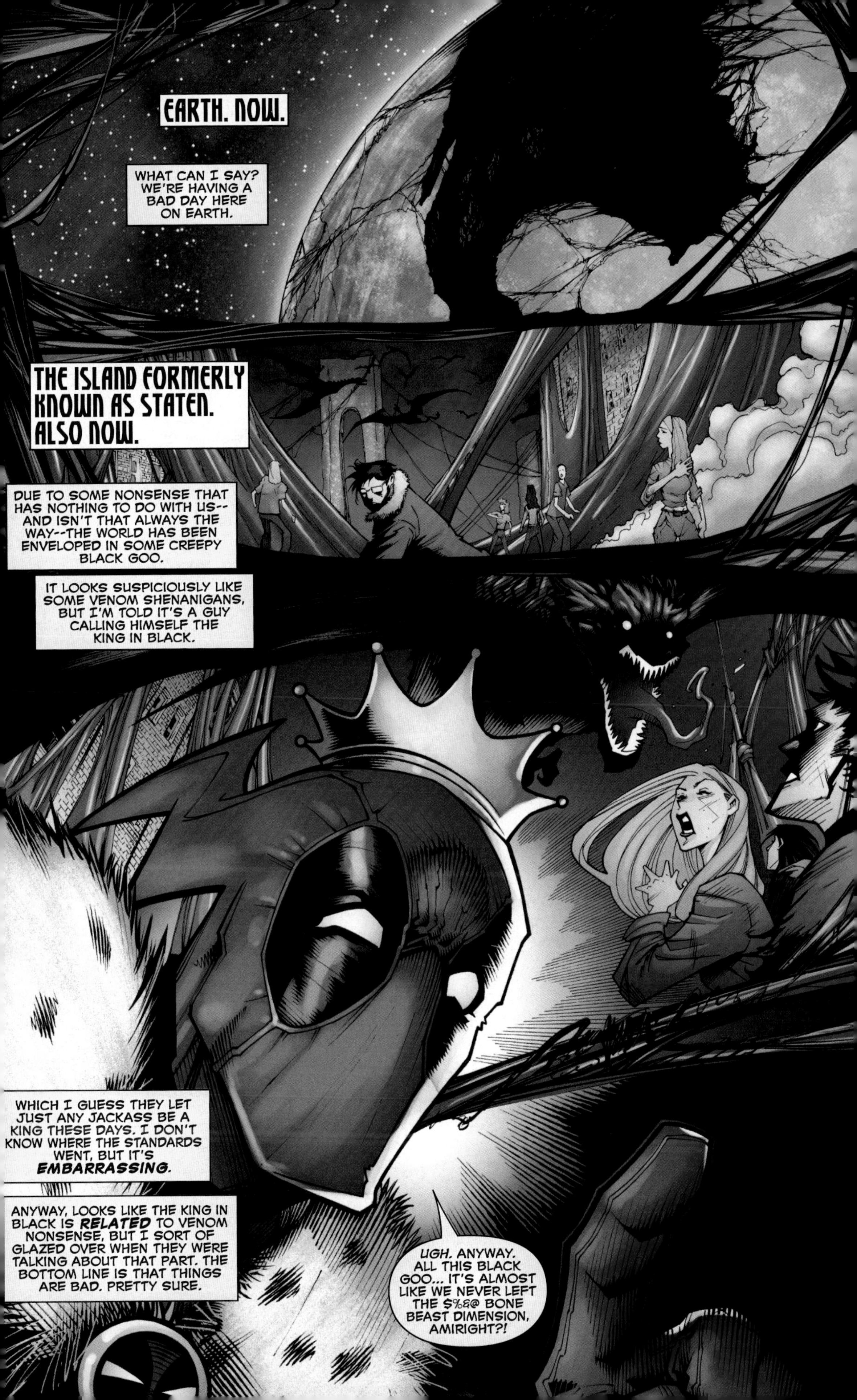
EARTH. NOW.
WHAT CAN I SAY? WE'RE HAVING A BAD DAY HERE ON EARTH.
THE ISLAND FORMERLY KNOWN AS STATEN. ALSO NOW.
DUE TO SOME NONSENSE THAT HAS NOTHING TO DO WITH US-- AND ISN'T THAT ALWAYS THE WAY--THE WORLD HAS BEEN ENVELOPED IN SOME CREEPY BLACK GOO.
IT LOOKS SUSPICIOUSLY LIKE SOME VENOM SHENANIGANS, BUT I'M TOLD IT'S A GUY CALLING HIMSELF THE KING IN BLACK.
WHICH I GUESS THEY LET JUST ANY JACKASS BE A KING THESE DAYS. I DON'T KNOW WHERE THE STANDARDS WENT, BUT IT'S EMBARRASSING.
ANYWAY, LOOKS LIKE THE KING IN BLACK IS RELATED TO VENOM NONSENSE, BUT I SORT OF GLAZED OVER WHEN THEY WERE TALKING ABOUT THAT PART. THE BOTTOM LINE IS THAT THINGS ARE BAD. PRETTY SURE.
UGH. ANYWAY. ALL THIS BLACK GOO... IT'S ALMOST LIKE WE NEVER LEFT THE $%&@ BONE BEAST DIMENSION, AMIRIGHT?!

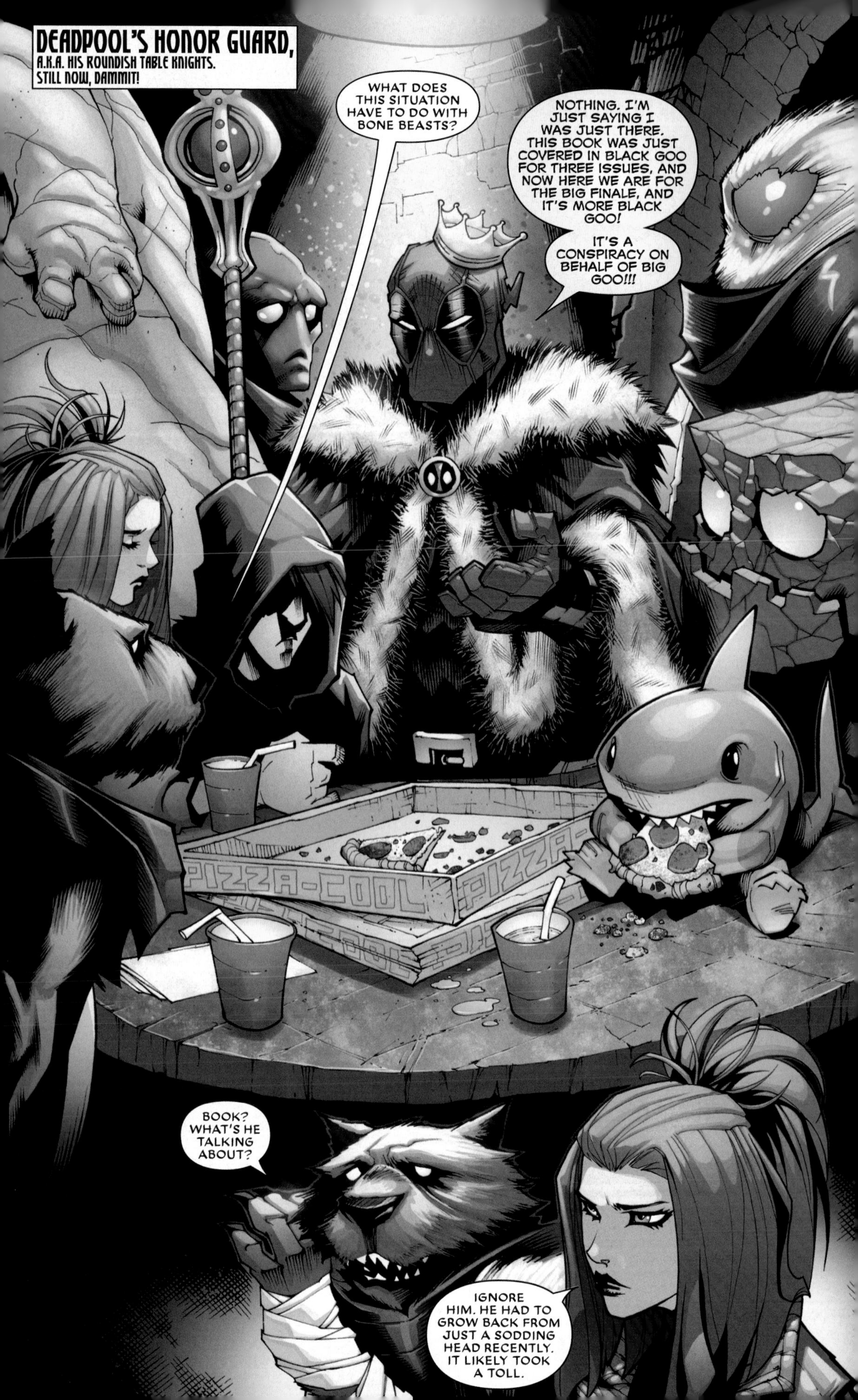
DEADPOOL'S HONOR GUARD,
A.K.A. HIS ROUNDISH TABLE KNIGHTS. STILL NOW, DAMMIT!
WHAT DOES THIS SITUATION HAVE TO DO WITH BONE BEASTS?
NOTHING. I'M JUST SAYING I WAS JUST THERE. THIS BOOK WAS JUST COVERED IN BLACK GOO FOR THREE ISSUES, AND NOW HERE WE ARE FOR THE BIG FINALE, AND IT'S MORE BLACK GOO!
IT'S A CONSPIRACY ON BEHALF OF BIG GOO!!!
PIZZA-COOL
BOOK? WHAT'S HE TALKING ABOUT?
IGNORE HIM. HE HAD TO GROW BACK FROM JUST A SODDING HEAD RECENTLY. IT LIKELY TOOK A TOLL.

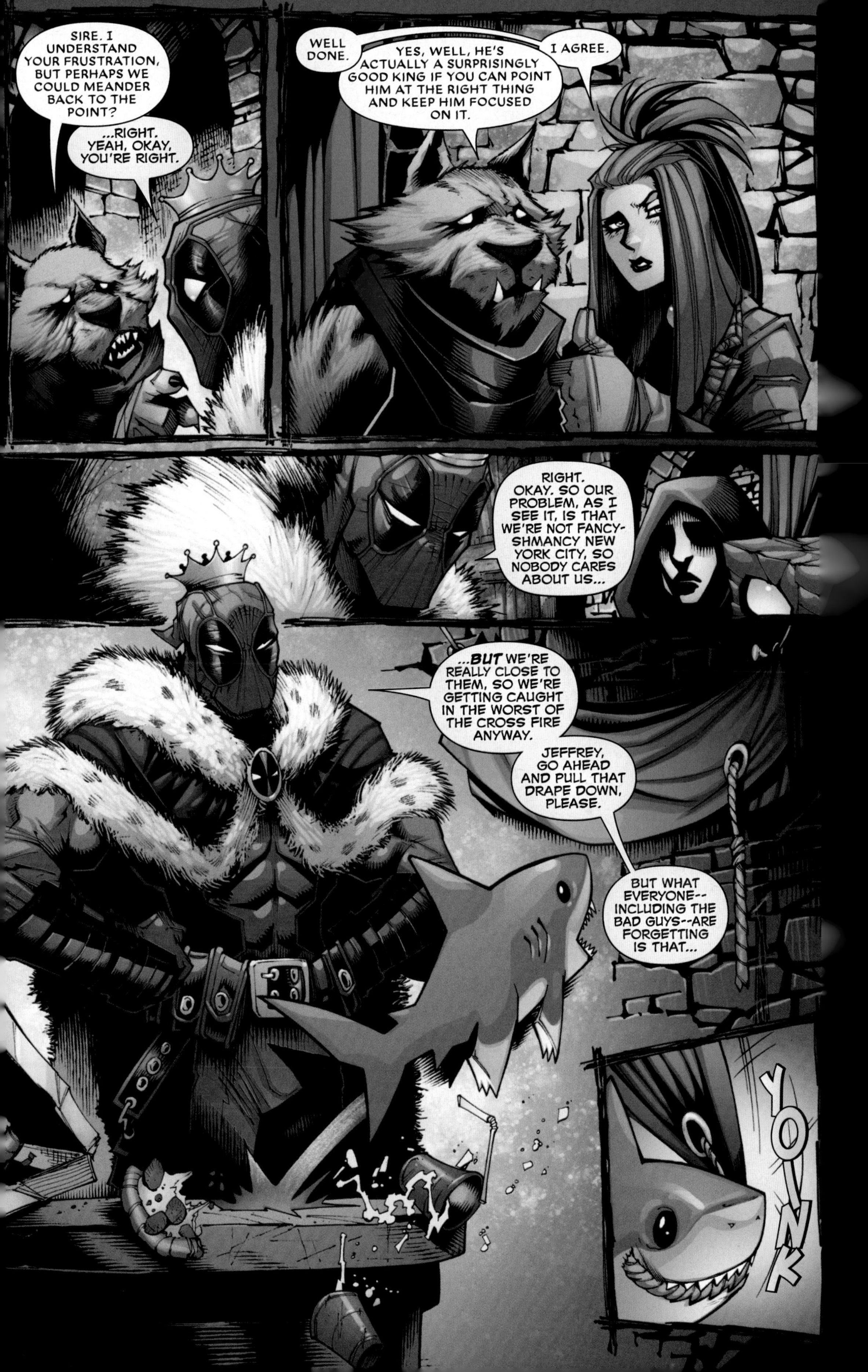
SIRE. I UNDERSTAND YOUR FRUSTRATION, BUT PERHAPS WE COULD MEANDER BACK TO THE POINT?
...RIGHT. YEAH, OKAY, YOU'RE RIGHT.
WELL DONE.
YES, WELL, HE'S ACTUALLY A SURPRISINGLY GOOD KING IF YOU CAN POINT HIM AT THE RIGHT THING AND KEEP HIM FOCUSED ON IT.
I AGREE.
RIGHT. OKAY. SO OUR PROBLEM, AS I SEE IT, IS THAT WE'RE NOT FANCY-SHMANCY NEW YORK CITY, SO NOBODY CARES ABOUT US...
...**BUT** WE'RE REALLY CLOSE TO THEM, SO WE'RE GETTING CAUGHT IN THE WORST OF THE CROSS FIRE ANYWAY.
JEFFREY, GO AHEAD AND PULL THAT DRAPE DOWN, PLEASE.
BUT WHAT EVERYONE--INCLUDING THE BAD GUYS--ARE FORGETTING IS THAT...
YOINK

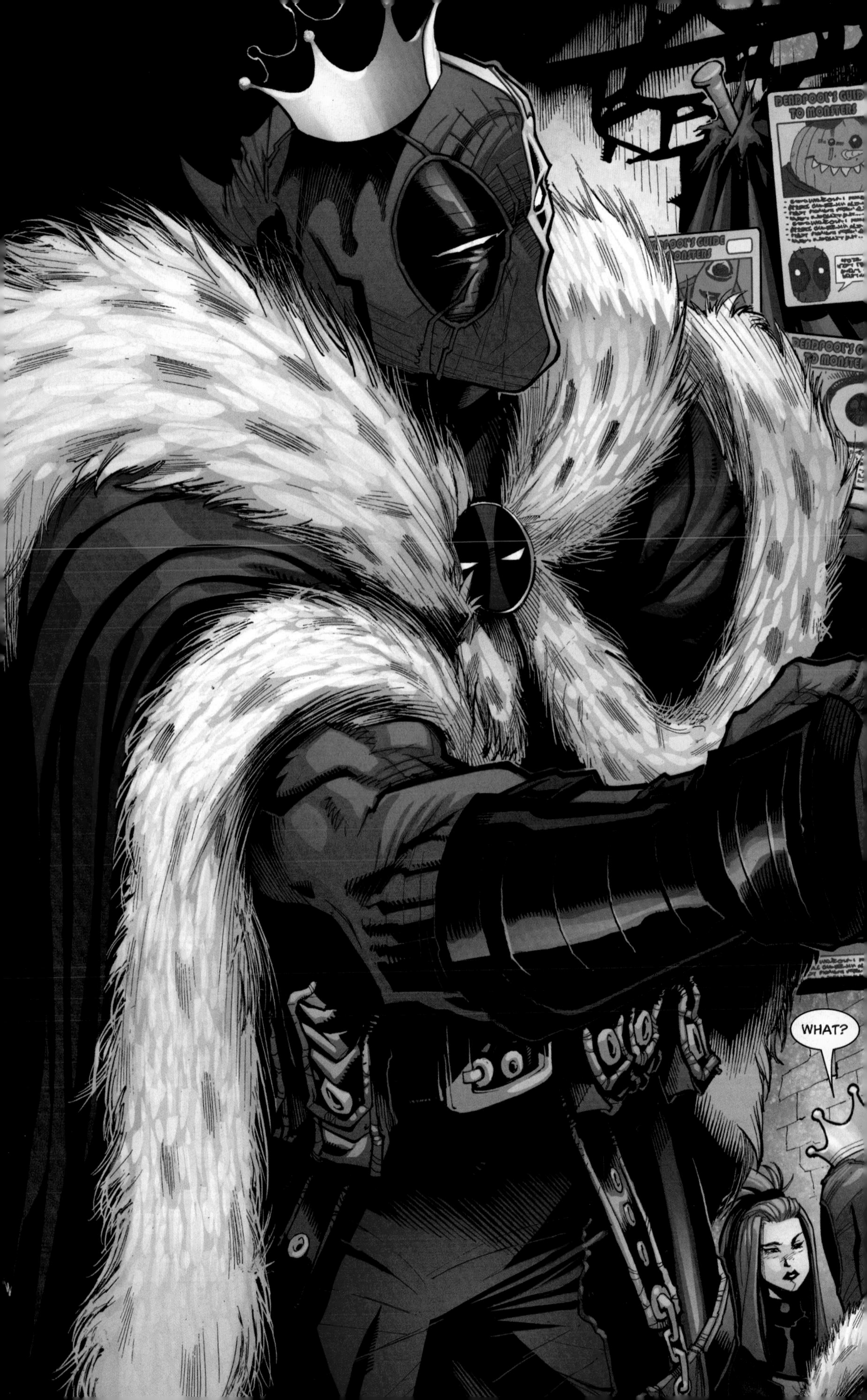
DEADPOOL'S GUIDE TO MONSTERS
WHAT?

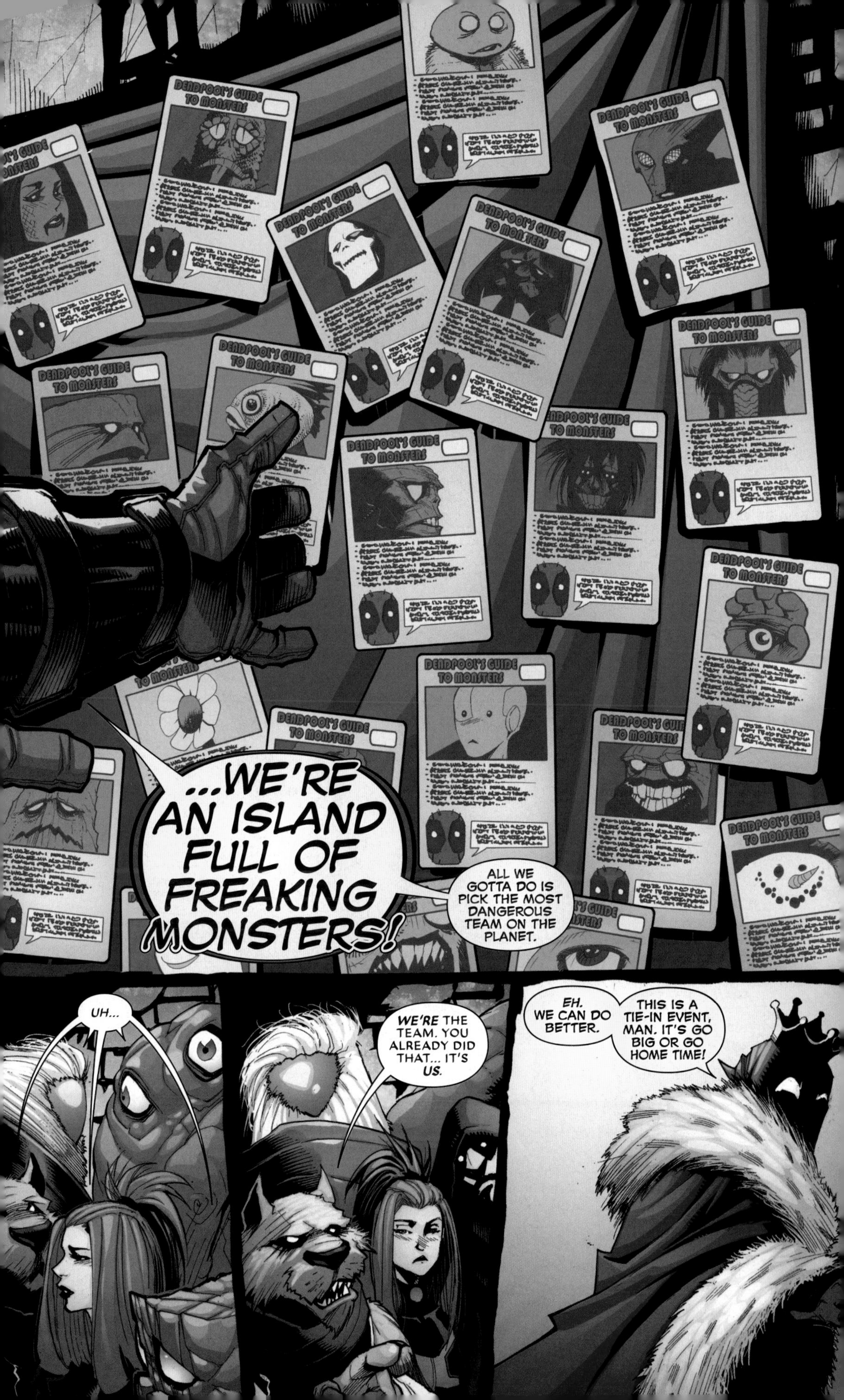
DEADPOOL'S GUIDE TO MONSTERS
...WE'RE AN ISLAND FULL OF FREAKING MONSTERS!
ALL WE GOTTA DO IS PICK THE MOST DANGEROUS TEAM ON THE PLANET.
UH...
WE'RE THE TEAM. YOU ALREADY DID THAT... IT'S US.
EH. WE CAN DO BETTER.
THIS IS A TIE-IN EVENT, MAN. IT'S GO BIG OR GO HOME TIME!

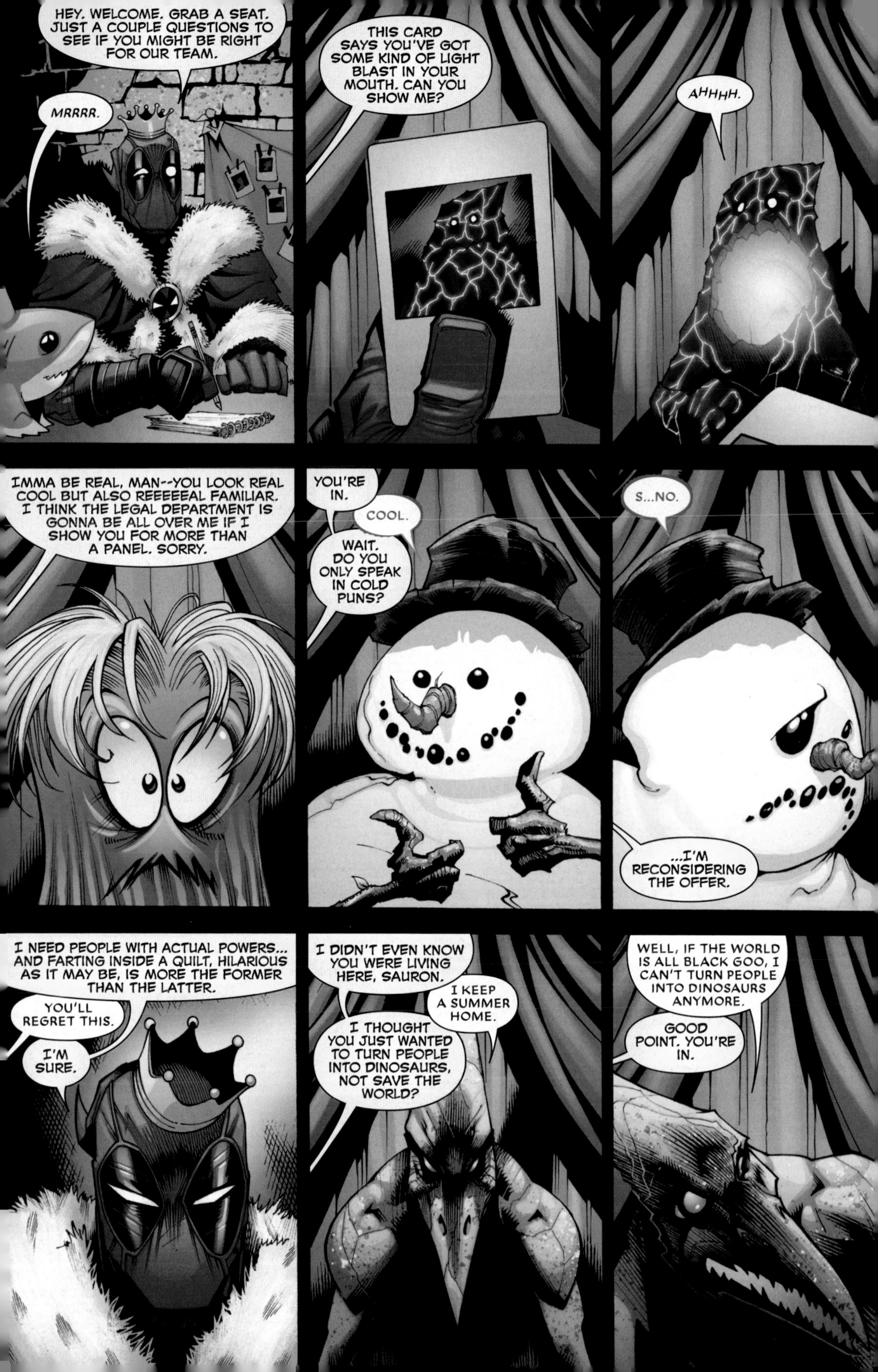
HEY. WELCOME. GRAB A SEAT. JUST A COUPLE QUESTIONS TO SEE IF YOU MIGHT BE RIGHT FOR OUR TEAM.
MRRRR.
THIS CARD SAYS YOU'VE GOT SOME KIND OF LIGHT BLAST IN YOUR MOUTH. CAN YOU SHOW ME?
AHHHH.
IMMA BE REAL, MAN--YOU LOOK REAL COOL BUT ALSO REEEEEAL FAMILIAR. I THINK THE LEGAL DEPARTMENT IS GONNA BE ALL OVER ME IF I SHOW YOU FOR MORE THAN A PANEL. SORRY.
YOU'RE IN.
COOL.
WAIT. DO YOU ONLY SPEAK IN COLD PUNS?
S...NO.
...I'M RECONSIDERING THE OFFER.
I NEED PEOPLE WITH ACTUAL POWERS... AND FARTING INSIDE A QUILT, HILARIOUS AS IT MAY BE, IS MORE THE FORMER THAN THE LATTER.
YOU'LL REGRET THIS.
I'M SURE.
I DIDN'T EVEN KNOW YOU WERE LIVING HERE, SAURON.
I KEEP A SUMMER HOME.
I THOUGHT YOU JUST WANTED TO TURN PEOPLE INTO DINOSAURS, NOT SAVE THE WORLD?
WELL, IF THE WORLD IS ALL BLACK GOO, I CAN'T TURN PEOPLE INTO DINOSAURS ANYMORE.
GOOD POINT. YOU'RE IN.

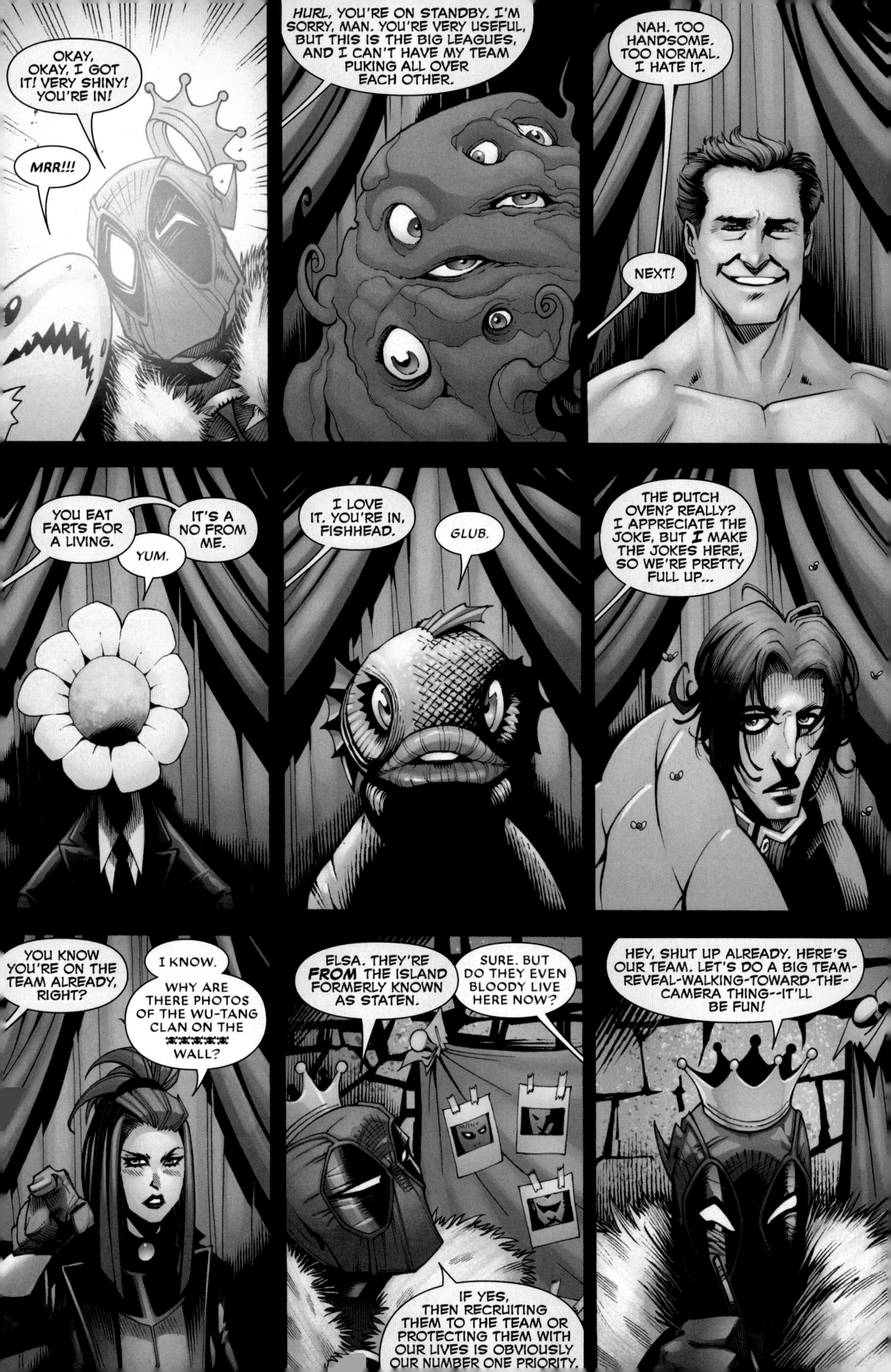

OKAY, OKAY, I GOT IT! VERY SHINY! YOU'RE IN!
MRR!!!
HURL, YOU'RE ON STANDBY. I'M SORRY, MAN. YOU'RE VERY USEFUL, BUT THIS IS THE BIG LEAGUES, AND I CAN'T HAVE MY TEAM PUKING ALL OVER EACH OTHER.
NAH. TOO HANDSOME. TOO NORMAL. I HATE IT.
NEXT!
YOU EAT FARTS FOR A LIVING.
IT'S A NO FROM ME.
YUM.
I LOVE IT. YOU'RE IN, FISHHEAD.
GLUB.
THE DUTCH OVEN? REALLY? I APPRECIATE THE JOKE, BUT I MAKE THE JOKES HERE, SO WE'RE PRETTY FULL UP...
YOU KNOW YOU'RE ON THE TEAM ALREADY, RIGHT?
I KNOW.
WHY ARE THERE PHOTOS OF THE WU-TANG CLAN ON THE WALL?
ELSA. THEY'RE FROM THE ISLAND FORMERLY KNOWN AS STATEN.
SURE. BUT DO THEY EVEN BLOODY LIVE HERE NOW?
IF YES, THEN RECRUITING THEM TO THE TEAM OR PROTECTING THEM WITH OUR LIVES IS OBVIOUSLY OUR NUMBER ONE PRIORITY.
HEY, SHUT UP ALREADY. HERE'S OUR TEAM. LET'S DO A BIG TEAM-REVEAL-WALKING-TOWARD-THE-CAMERA THING--IT'LL BE FUN!

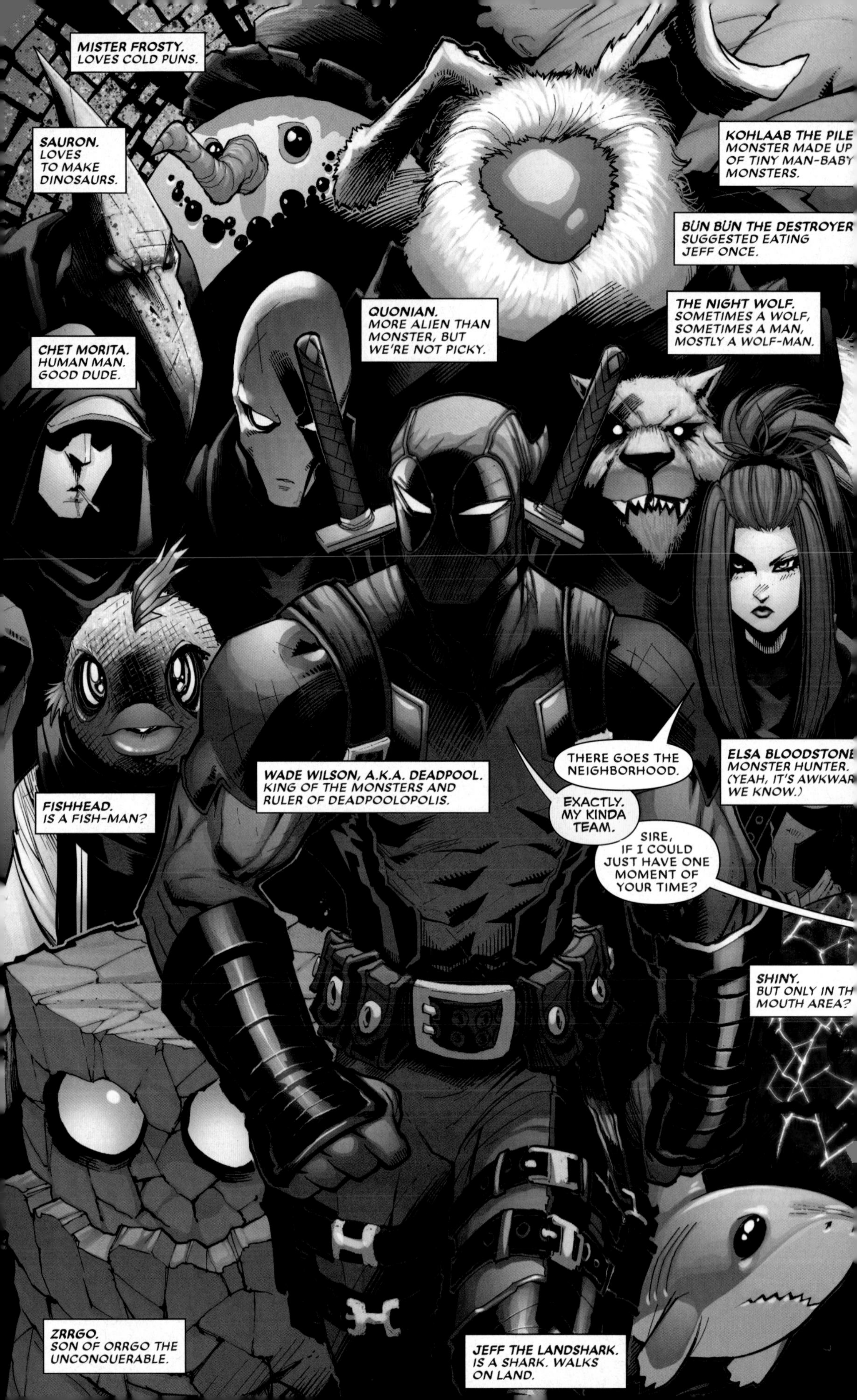
MISTER FROSTY. LOVES COLD PUNS.
SAURON. LOVES TO MAKE DINOSAURS.
KOHLAAB THE PILE MONSTER MADE UP OF TINY MAN-BABY MONSTERS.
BÜN BÜN THE DESTROYER SUGGESTED EATING JEFF ONCE.
QUONIAN. MORE ALIEN THAN MONSTER, BUT WE'RE NOT PICKY.
THE NIGHT WOLF. SOMETIMES A WOLF, SOMETIMES A MAN, MOSTLY A WOLF-MAN.
CHET MORITA. HUMAN MAN. GOOD DUDE.
THERE GOES THE NEIGHBORHOOD.
ELSA BLOODSTONE MONSTER HUNTER. (YEAH, IT'S AWKWAR WE KNOW.)
WADE WILSON, A.K.A. DEADPOOL. KING OF THE MONSTERS AND RULER OF DEADPOOLOPOLIS.
EXACTLY. MY KINDA TEAM.
FISHHEAD. IS A FISH-MAN?
SIRE, IF I COULD JUST HAVE ONE MOMENT OF YOUR TIME?
SHINY. BUT ONLY IN TH MOUTH AREA?
ZRRGO. SON OF ORRGO THE UNCONQUERABLE.
JEFF THE LANDSHARK. IS A SHARK. WALKS ON LAND.

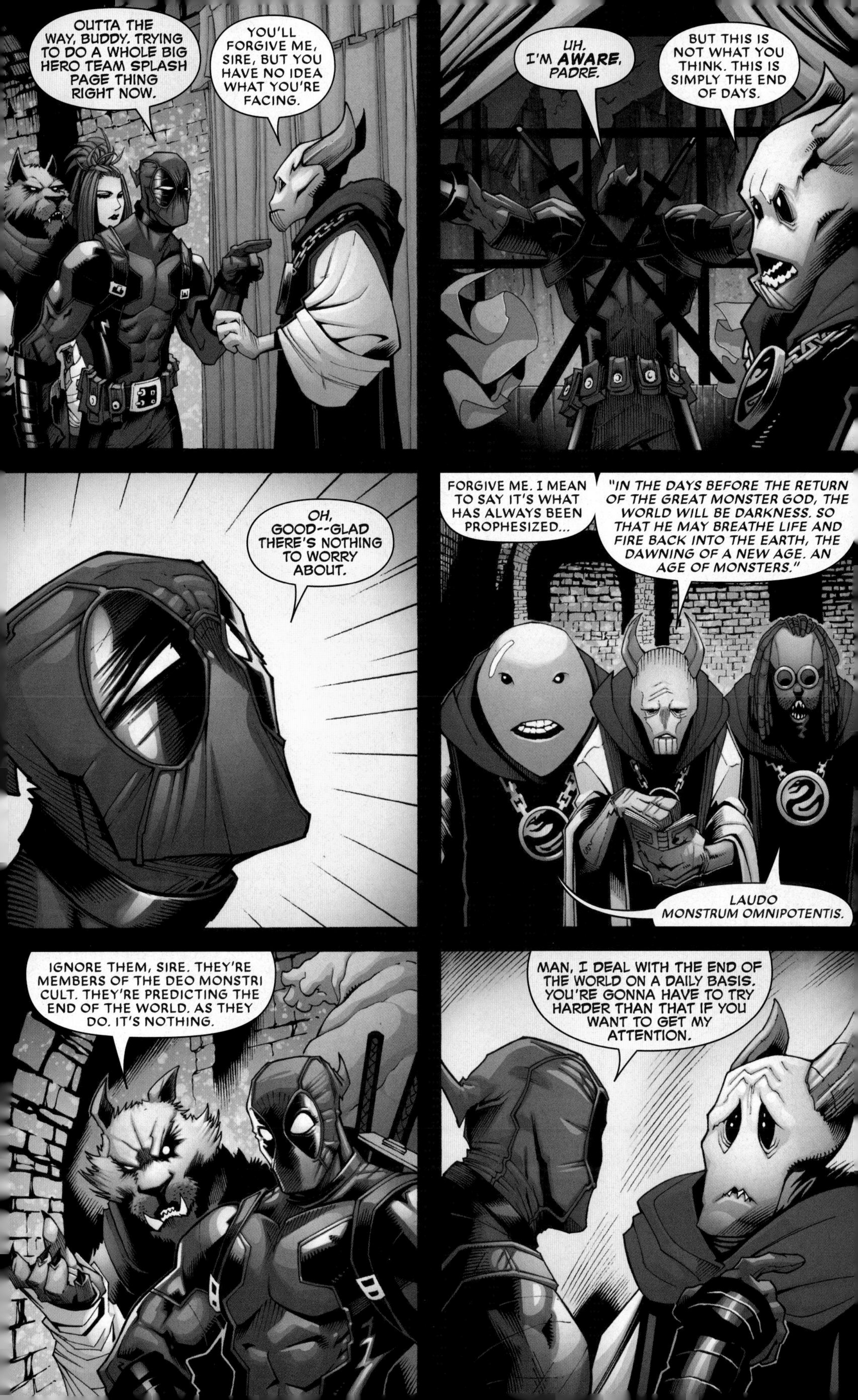
OUTTA THE WAY, BUDDY. TRYING TO DO A WHOLE BIG HERO TEAM SPLASH PAGE THING RIGHT NOW.
YOU'LL FORGIVE ME, SIRE, BUT YOU HAVE NO IDEA WHAT YOU'RE FACING.
UH. I'M **AWARE**, PADRE.
BUT THIS IS NOT WHAT YOU THINK. THIS IS SIMPLY THE END OF DAYS.
OH, GOOD--GLAD THERE'S NOTHING TO WORRY ABOUT.
FORGIVE ME. I MEAN TO SAY IT'S WHAT HAS ALWAYS BEEN PROPHESIZED...
"IN THE DAYS BEFORE THE RETURN OF THE GREAT MONSTER GOD, THE WORLD WILL BE DARKNESS. SO THAT HE MAY BREATHE LIFE AND FIRE BACK INTO THE EARTH, THE DAWNING OF A NEW AGE. AN AGE OF MONSTERS."
LAUDO MONSTRUM OMNIPOTENTIS.
IGNORE THEM, SIRE. THEY'RE MEMBERS OF THE DEO MONSTRI CULT. THEY'RE PREDICTING THE END OF THE WORLD. AS THEY DO. IT'S NOTHING.
MAN, I DEAL WITH THE END OF THE WORLD ON A DAILY BASIS. YOU'RE GONNA HAVE TO TRY HARDER THAN THAT IF YOU WANT TO GET MY ATTENTION.

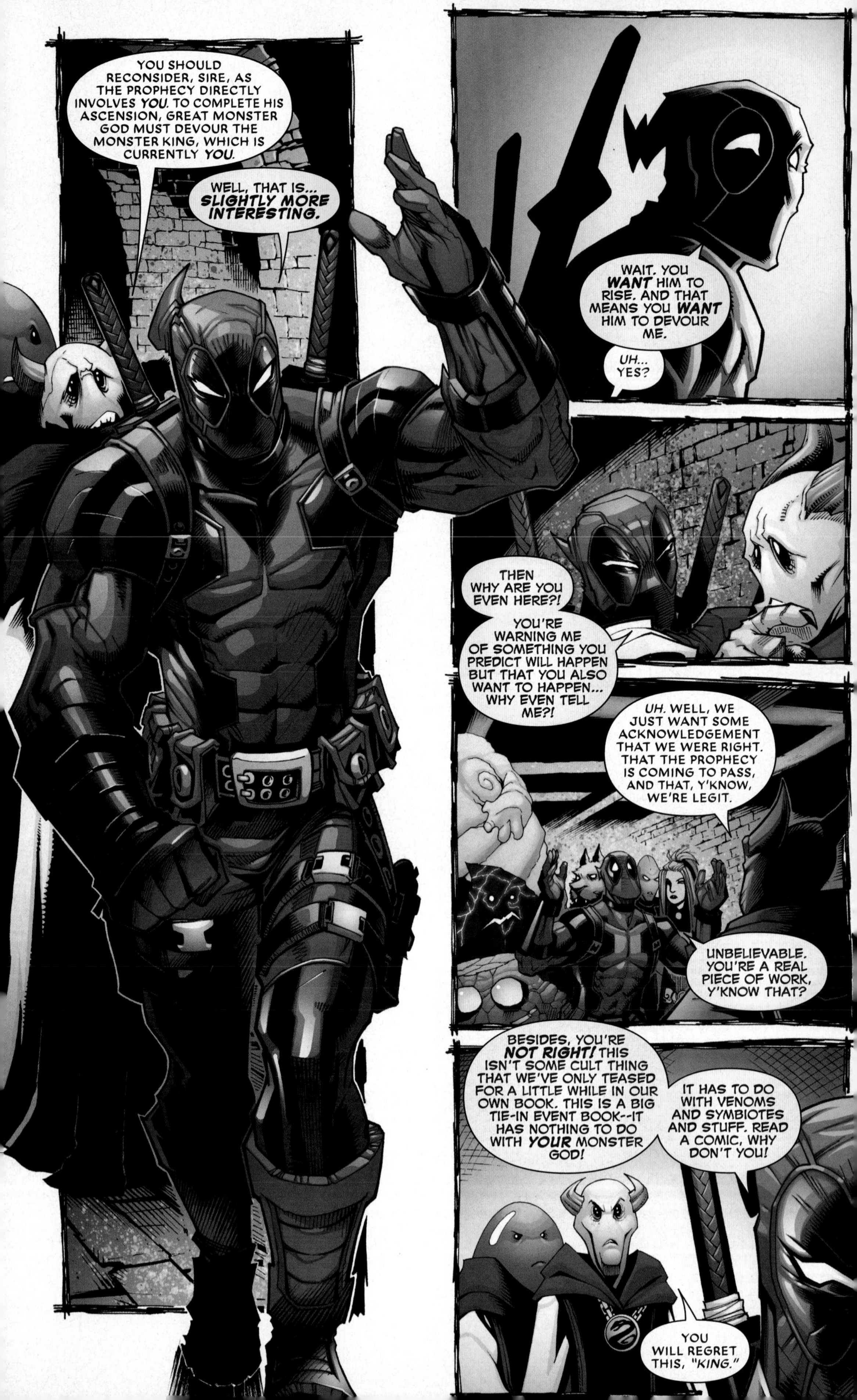
YOU SHOULD RECONSIDER, SIRE, AS THE PROPHECY DIRECTLY INVOLVES *YOU.* TO COMPLETE HIS ASCENSION, GREAT MONSTER GOD MUST DEVOUR THE MONSTER KING, WHICH IS CURRENTLY *YOU.*
WELL, THAT IS... ***SLIGHTLY MORE INTERESTING.***
WAIT. YOU ***WANT*** HIM TO RISE. AND THAT MEANS YOU ***WANT*** HIM TO DEVOUR ME.
UH... YES?
THEN WHY ARE YOU EVEN HERE?!
YOU'RE WARNING ME OF SOMETHING YOU PREDICT WILL HAPPEN BUT THAT YOU ALSO WANT TO HAPPEN... WHY EVEN TELL ME?!
UH. WELL, WE JUST WANT SOME ACKNOWLEDGEMENT THAT WE WERE RIGHT. THAT THE PROPHECY IS COMING TO PASS, AND THAT, Y'KNOW, WE'RE LEGIT.
UNBELIEVABLE. YOU'RE A REAL PIECE OF WORK, Y'KNOW THAT?
BESIDES, YOU'RE ***NOT RIGHT!*** THIS ISN'T SOME CULT THING THAT WE'VE ONLY TEASED FOR A LITTLE WHILE IN OUR OWN BOOK. THIS IS A BIG TIE-IN EVENT BOOK--IT HAS NOTHING TO DO WITH ***YOUR*** MONSTER GOD!
IT HAS TO DO WITH VENOMS AND SYMBIOTES AND STUFF. READ A COMIC, WHY DON'T YOU!
YOU WILL REGRET THIS, *"KING."*

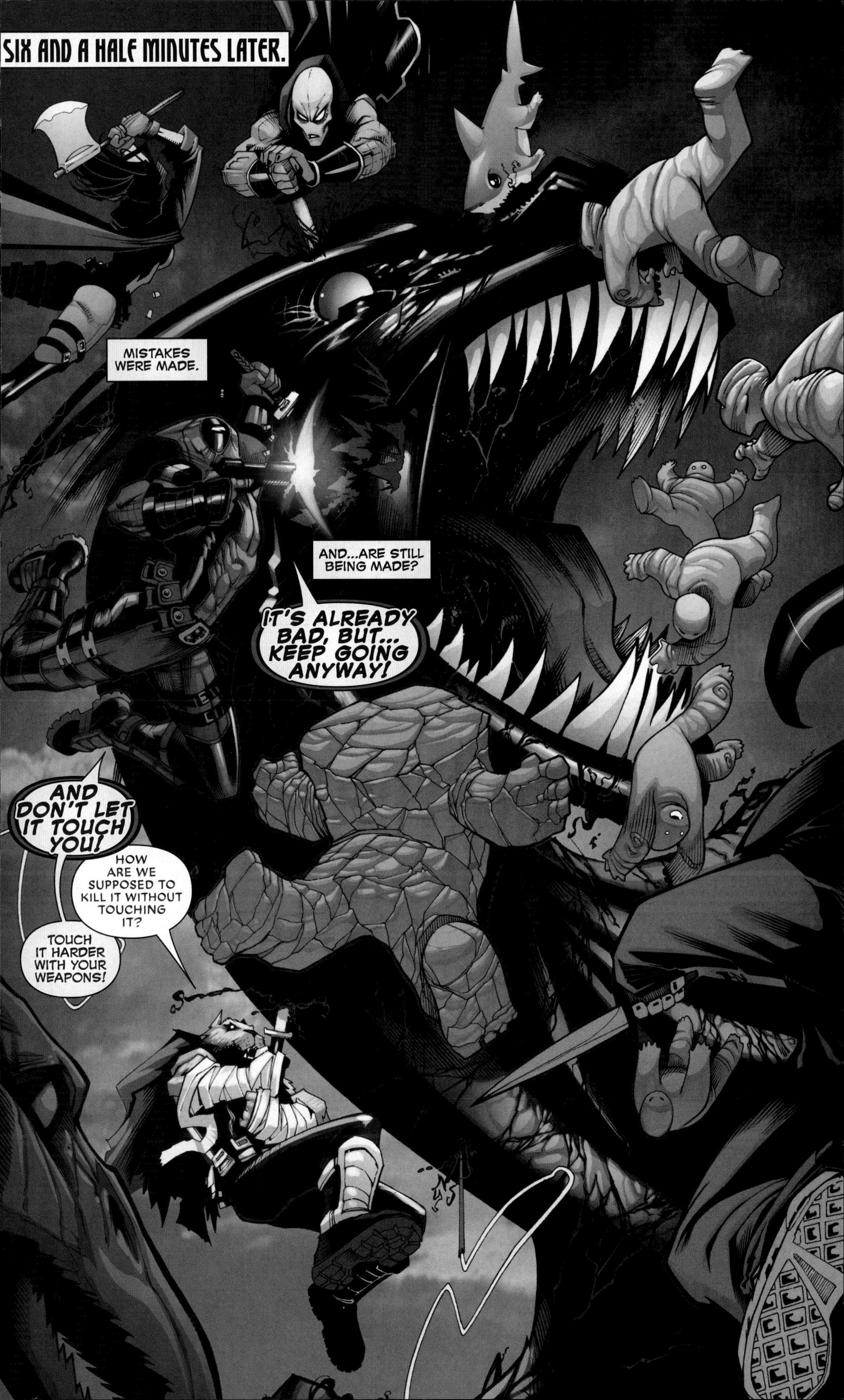
SIX AND A HALF MINUTES LATER.
MISTAKES WERE MADE.
AND...ARE STILL BEING MADE?
IT'S ALREADY BAD, BUT... KEEP GOING ANYWAY!
AND DON'T LET IT TOUCH YOU!
HOW ARE WE SUPPOSED TO KILL IT WITHOUT TOUCHING IT?
TOUCH IT HARDER WITH YOUR WEAPONS!

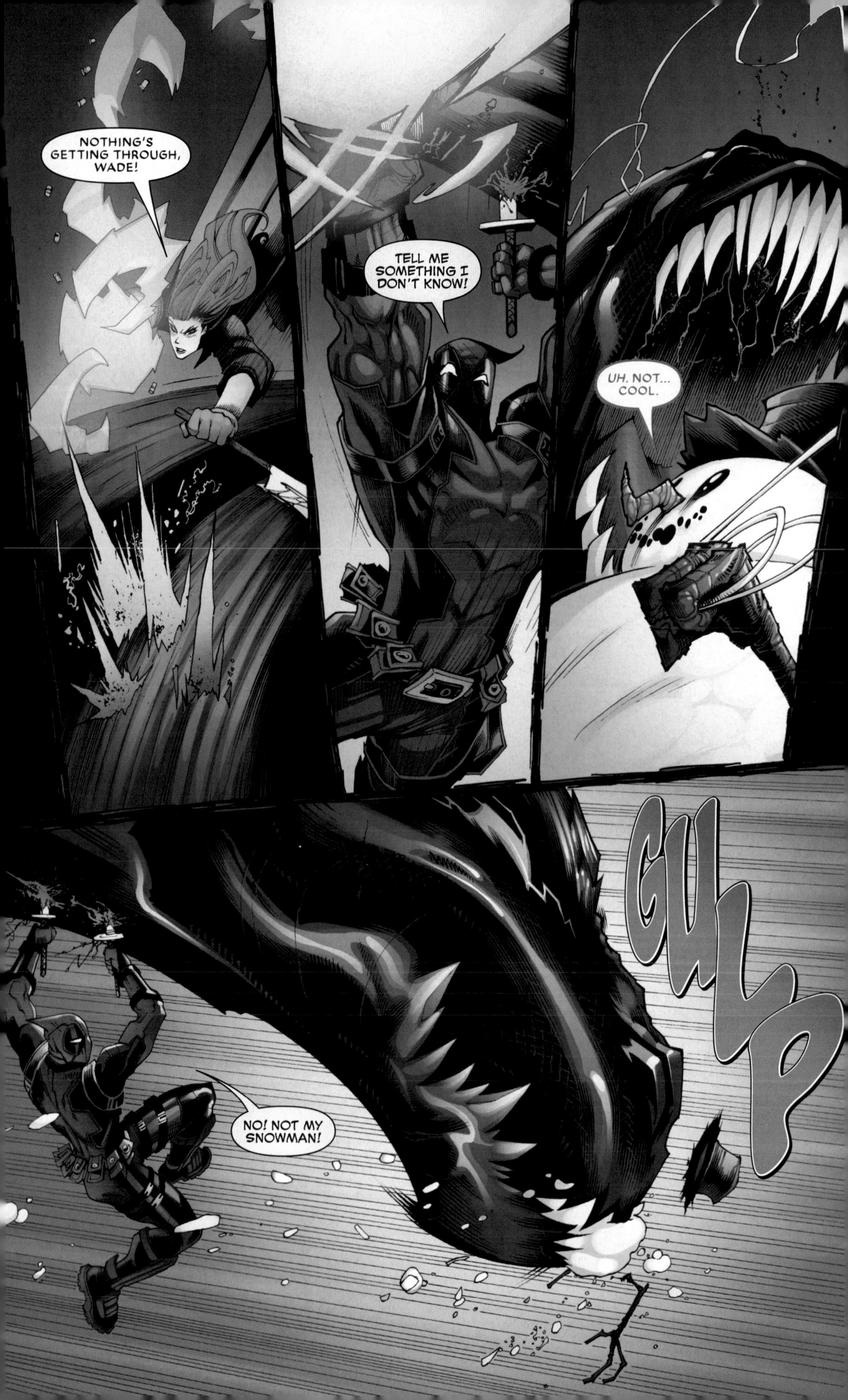
NOTHING'S GETTING THROUGH, WADE!
TELL ME SOMETHING I DON'T KNOW!
UH. NOT... COOL.
GULP
NO! NOT MY SNOWMAN!

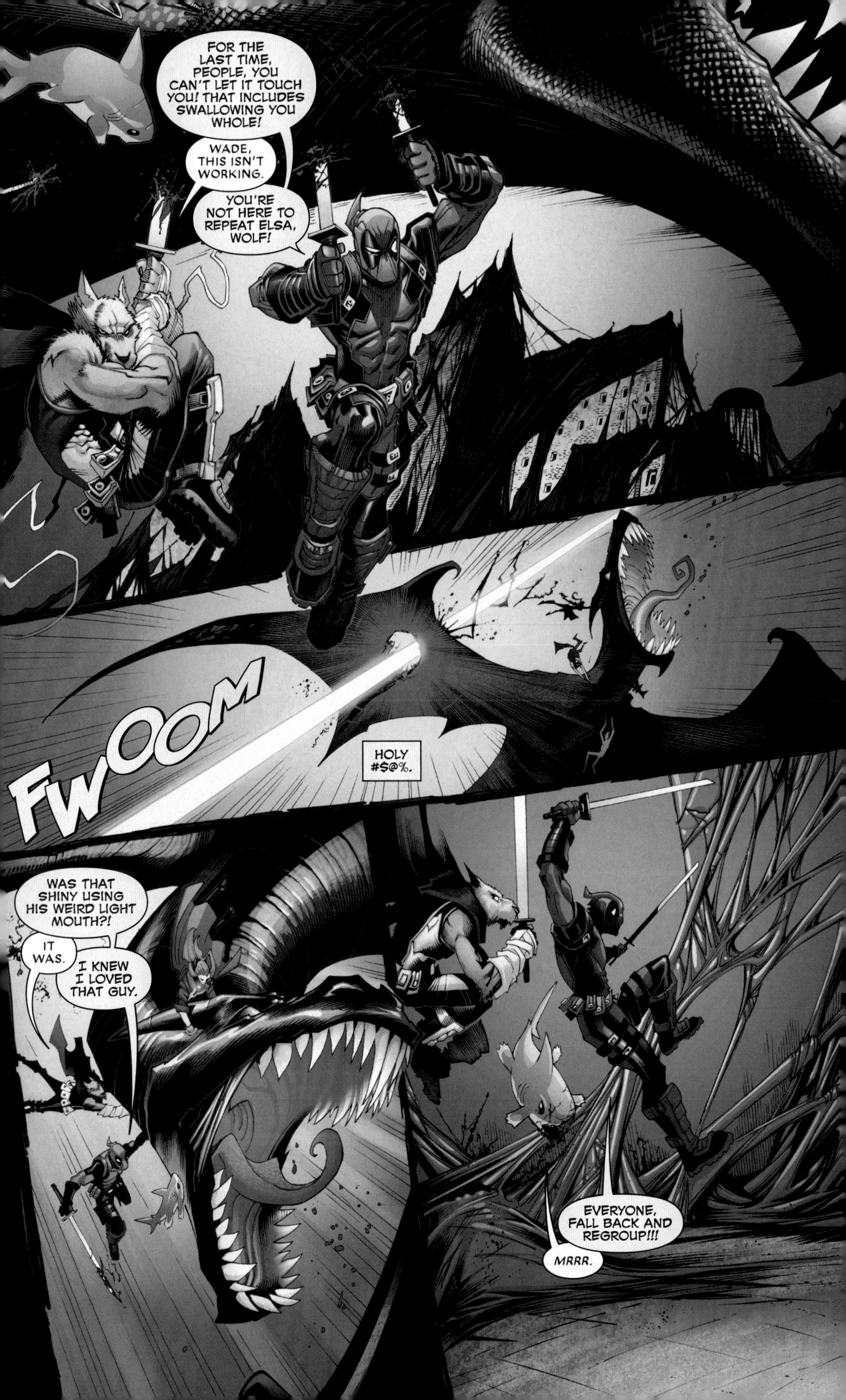
FOR THE LAST TIME, PEOPLE, YOU CAN'T LET IT TOUCH YOU! THAT INCLUDES SWALLOWING YOU WHOLE!
WADE, THIS ISN'T WORKING.
YOU'RE NOT HERE TO REPEAT ELSA, WOLF!
FWOOOM
HOLY #$@%.
WAS THAT SHINY USING HIS WEIRD LIGHT MOUTH?!
IT WAS.
I KNEW I LOVED THAT GUY.
EVERYONE, FALL BACK AND REGROUP!!!
MRRR.

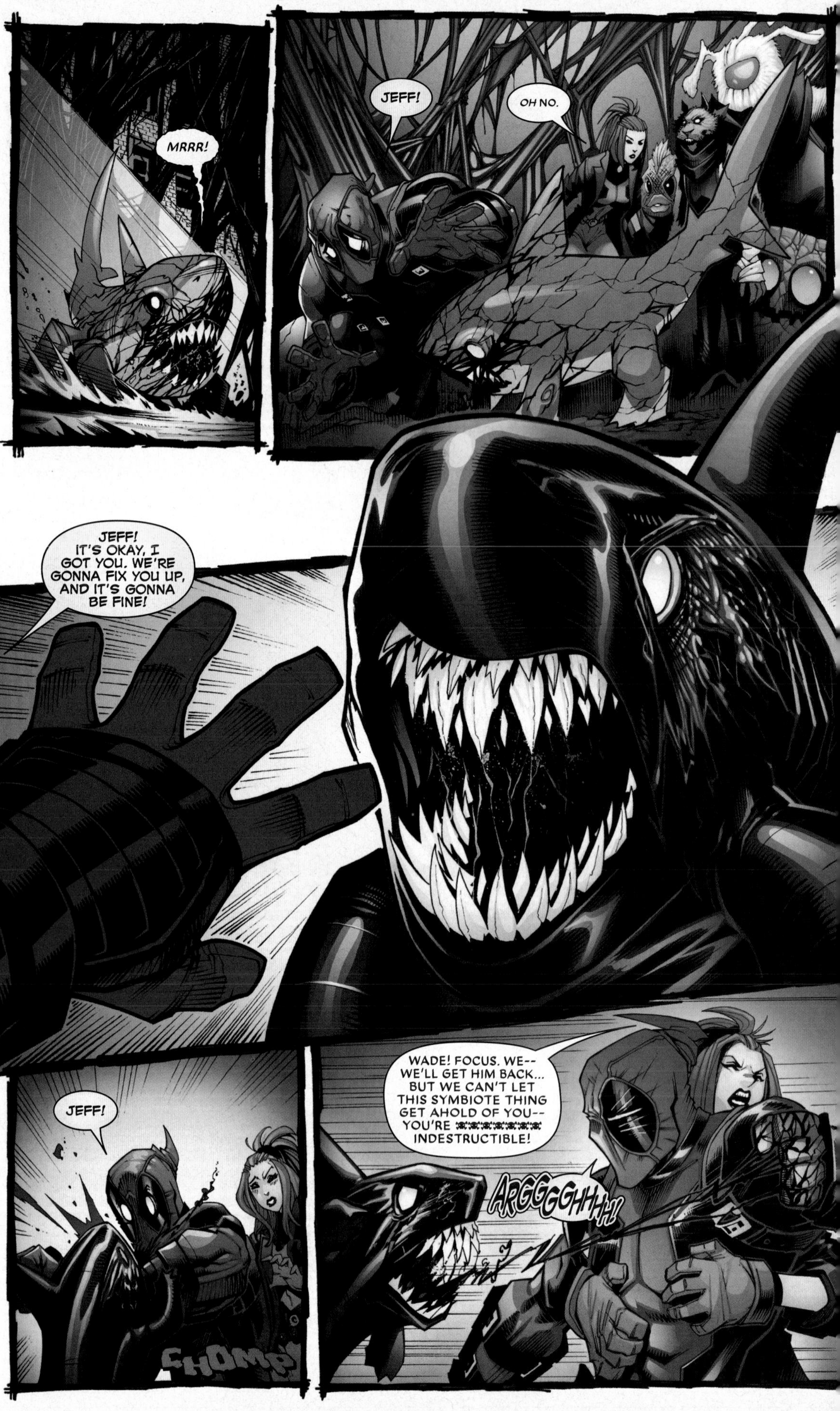
MRRR!
JEFF!
OH NO.
JEFF! IT'S OKAY, I GOT YOU. WE'RE GONNA FIX YOU UP, AND IT'S GONNA BE FINE!
JEFF!
CHOMP!
WADE! FOCUS. WE-- WE'LL GET HIM BACK... BUT WE CAN'T LET THIS SYMBIOTE THING GET AHOLD OF YOU-- YOU'RE INDESTRUCTIBLE!
ARGGGGHHHH!

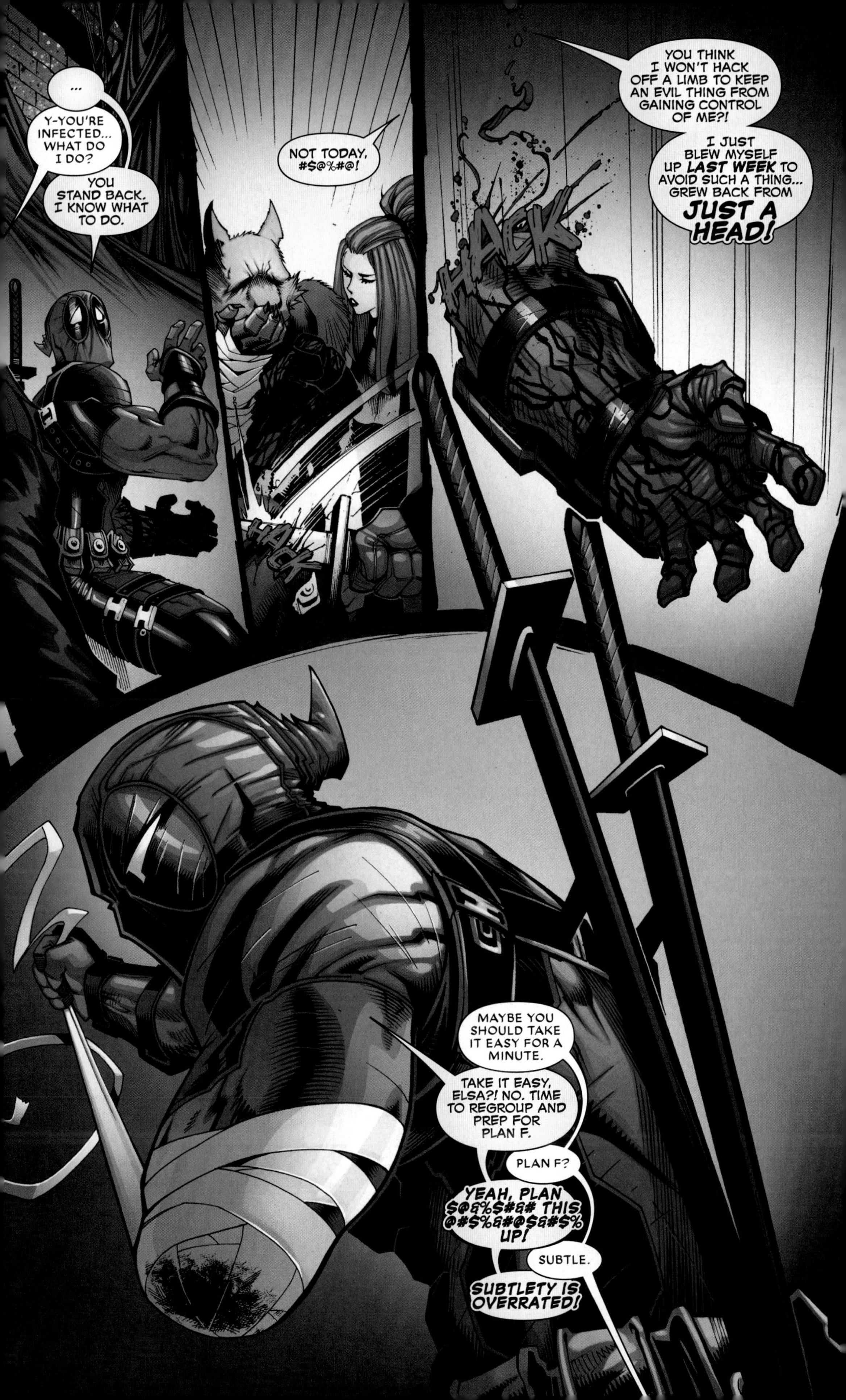
...
Y-YOU'RE INFECTED... WHAT DO I DO?
YOU STAND BACK. I KNOW WHAT TO DO.
NOT TODAY, #$@%#@!
HACK
YOU THINK I WON'T HACK OFF A LIMB TO KEEP AN EVIL THING FROM GAINING CONTROL OF ME?!
I JUST BLEW MYSELF UP LAST WEEK TO AVOID SUCH A THING... GREW BACK FROM JUST A HEAD!
HACK
MAYBE YOU SHOULD TAKE IT EASY FOR A MINUTE.
TAKE IT EASY, ELSA?! NO. TIME TO REGROUP AND PREP FOR PLAN F.
PLAN F?
YEAH, PLAN $@&%$#&# THIS @#$%&#@$&#$% UP!
SUBTLE.
SUBTLETY IS OVERRATED!

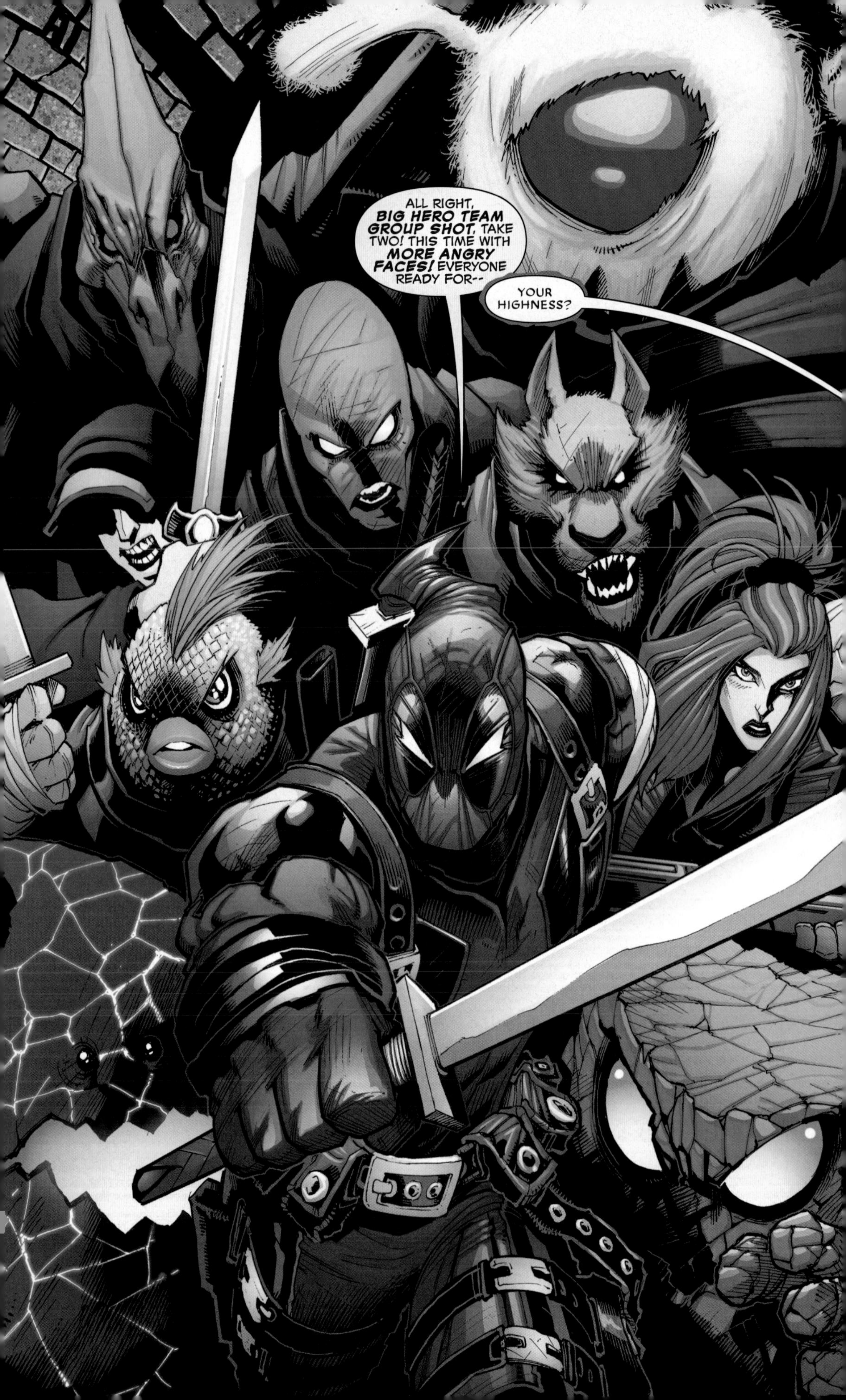
ALL RIGHT, **BIG HERO TEAM GROUP SHOT,** TAKE TWO! THIS TIME WITH **MORE ANGRY FACES!** EVERYONE READY FOR--
YOUR HIGHNESS?

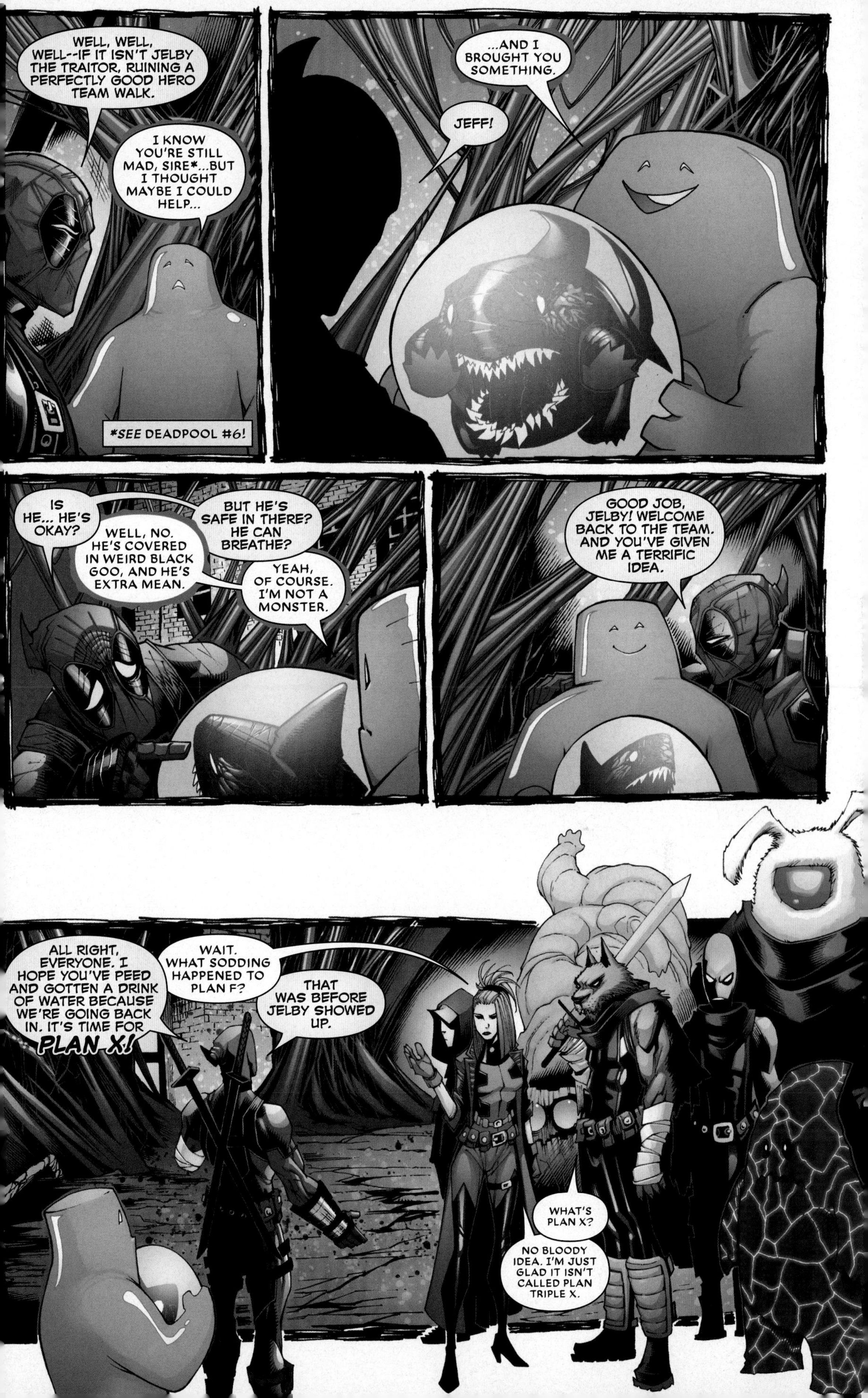
WELL, WELL, WELL--IF IT ISN'T JELBY THE TRAITOR, RUINING A PERFECTLY GOOD HERO TEAM WALK.
I KNOW YOU'RE STILL MAD, SIRE*...BUT I THOUGHT MAYBE I COULD HELP...
*SEE DEADPOOL #6!
...AND I BROUGHT YOU SOMETHING.
JEFF!
IS HE... HE'S OKAY?
WELL, NO. HE'S COVERED IN WEIRD BLACK GOO, AND HE'S EXTRA MEAN.
BUT HE'S SAFE IN THERE? HE CAN BREATHE?
YEAH, OF COURSE. I'M NOT A MONSTER.
GOOD JOB, JELBY! WELCOME BACK TO THE TEAM. AND YOU'VE GIVEN ME A TERRIFIC IDEA.
ALL RIGHT, EVERYONE. I HOPE YOU'VE PEED AND GOTTEN A DRINK OF WATER BECAUSE WE'RE GOING BACK IN. IT'S TIME FOR PLAN X!
WAIT. WHAT SODDING HAPPENED TO PLAN F?
THAT WAS BEFORE JELBY SHOWED UP.
WHAT'S PLAN X?
NO BLOODY IDEA. I'M JUST GLAD IT ISN'T CALLED PLAN TRIPLE X.

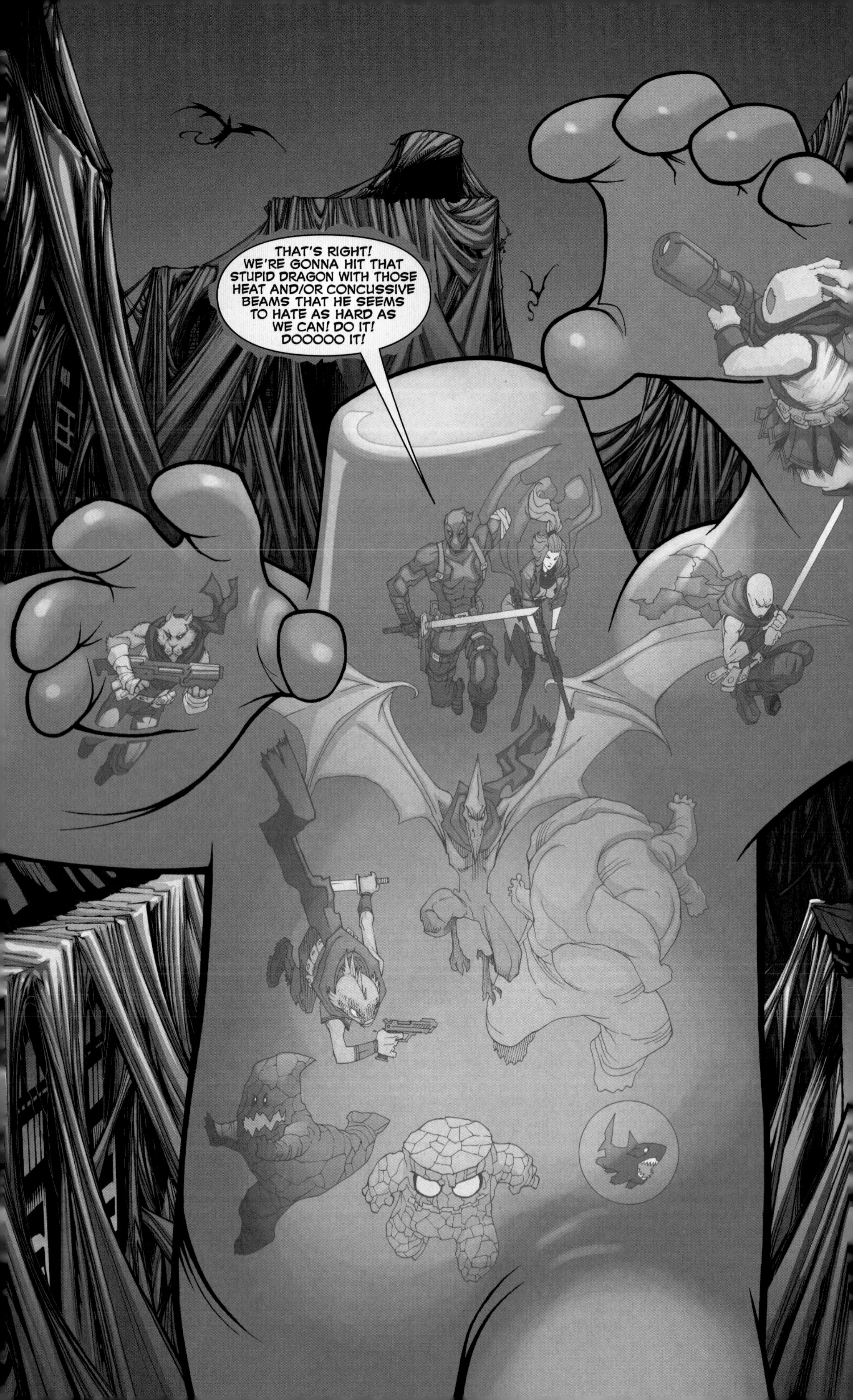
THAT'S RIGHT! WE'RE GONNA HIT THAT STUPID DRAGON WITH THOSE HEAT AND/OR CONCUSSIVE BEAMS THAT HE SEEMS TO HATE AS HARD AS WE CAN! DO IT! DOOOOO IT!

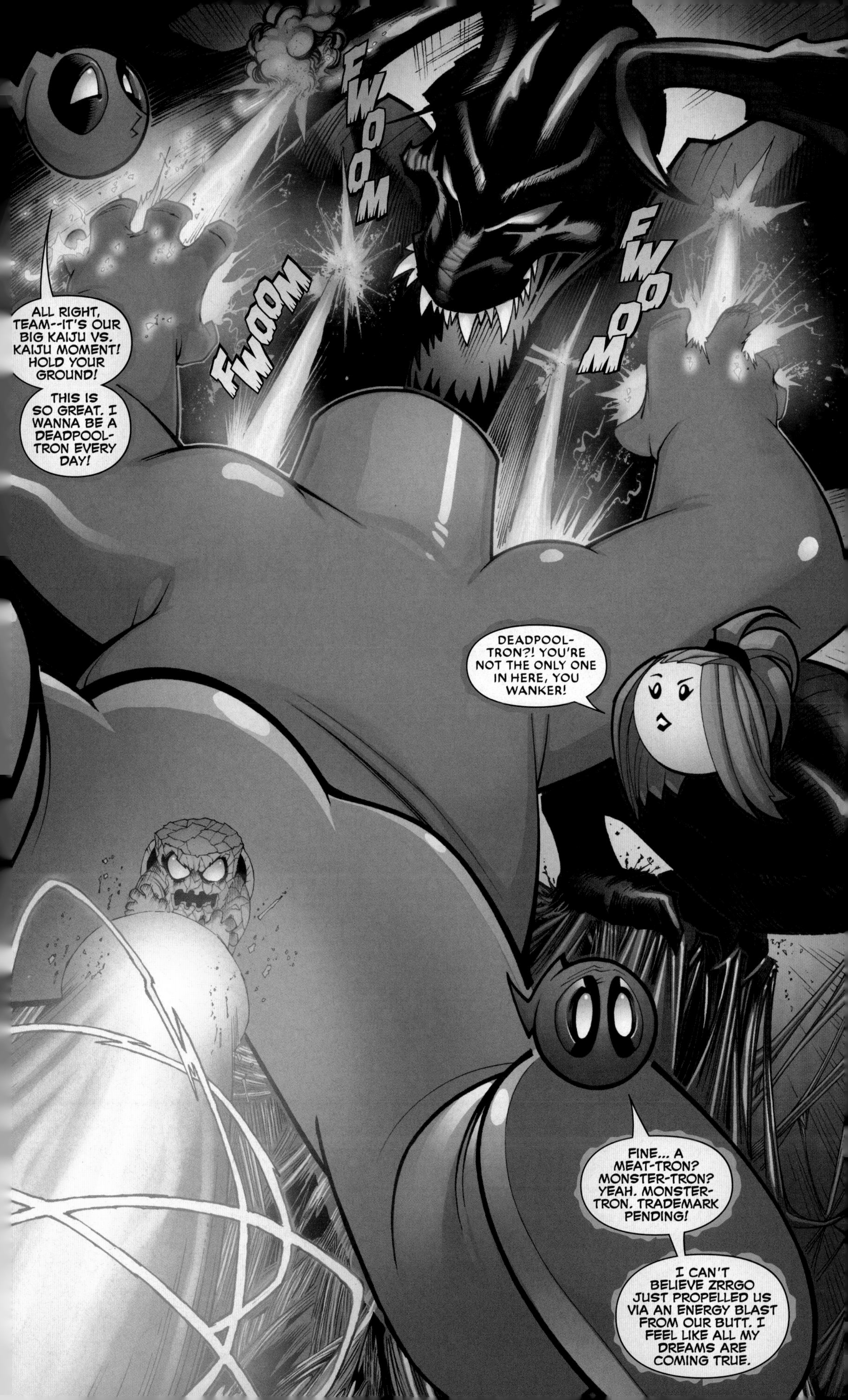
FWOOM
ALL RIGHT, TEAM--IT'S OUR BIG KAIJU VS. KAIJU MOMENT! HOLD YOUR GROUND!
THIS IS SO GREAT. I WANNA BE A DEADPOOL-TRON EVERY DAY!
FWOOM
FWOOM
DEADPOOL-TRON?! YOU'RE NOT THE ONLY ONE IN HERE, YOU WANKER!
FINE... A MEAT-TRON? MONSTER-TRON? YEAH. MONSTER-TRON. TRADEMARK PENDING!
I CAN'T BELIEVE ZRRGO JUST PROPELLED US VIA AN ENERGY BLAST FROM OUR BUTT. I FEEL LIKE ALL MY DREAMS ARE COMING TRUE.

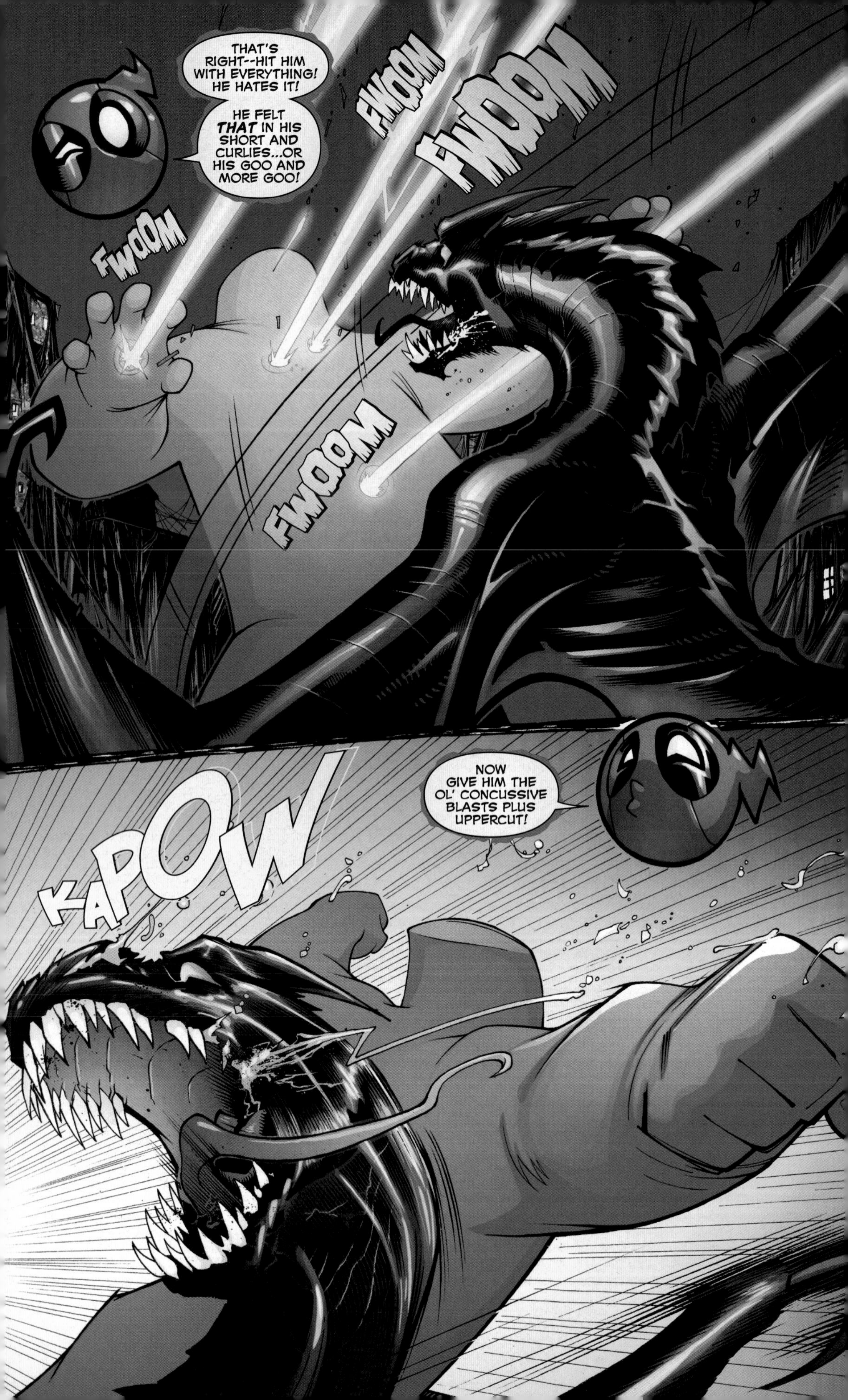
THAT'S RIGHT--HIT HIM WITH EVERYTHING! HE HATES IT!
HE FELT *THAT* IN HIS SHORT AND CURLIES...OR HIS GOO AND MORE GOO!
FWOOM
FWOOM
FWOOM
FWOOM
FWOOM
NOW GIVE HIM THE OL' CONCUSSIVE BLASTS PLUS UPPERCUT!
KAPOW

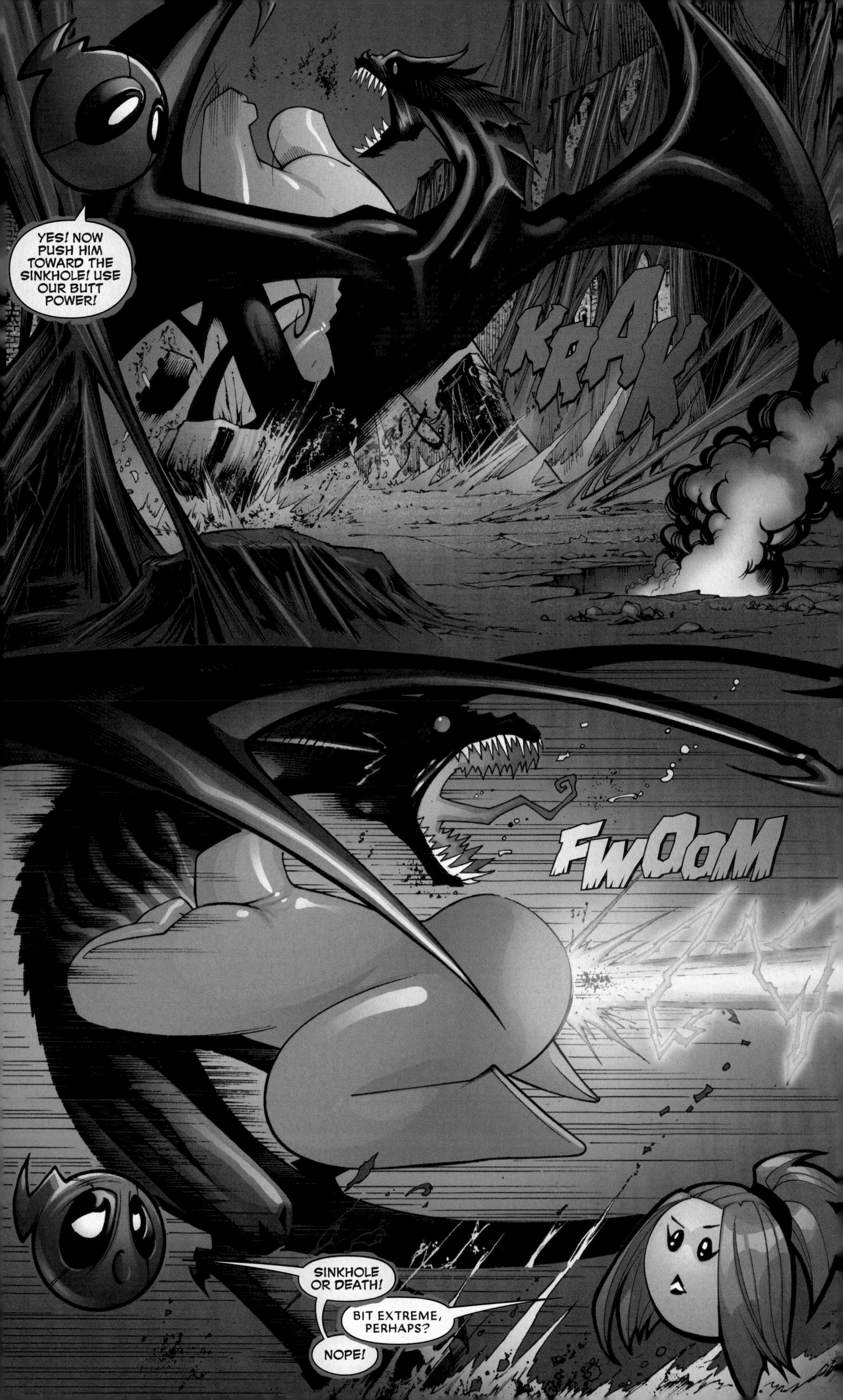
YES! NOW PUSH HIM TOWARD THE SINKHOLE! USE OUR BUTT POWER!
KRAK
FWOOM
SINKHOLE OR DEATH!
BIT EXTREME, PERHAPS?
NOPE!

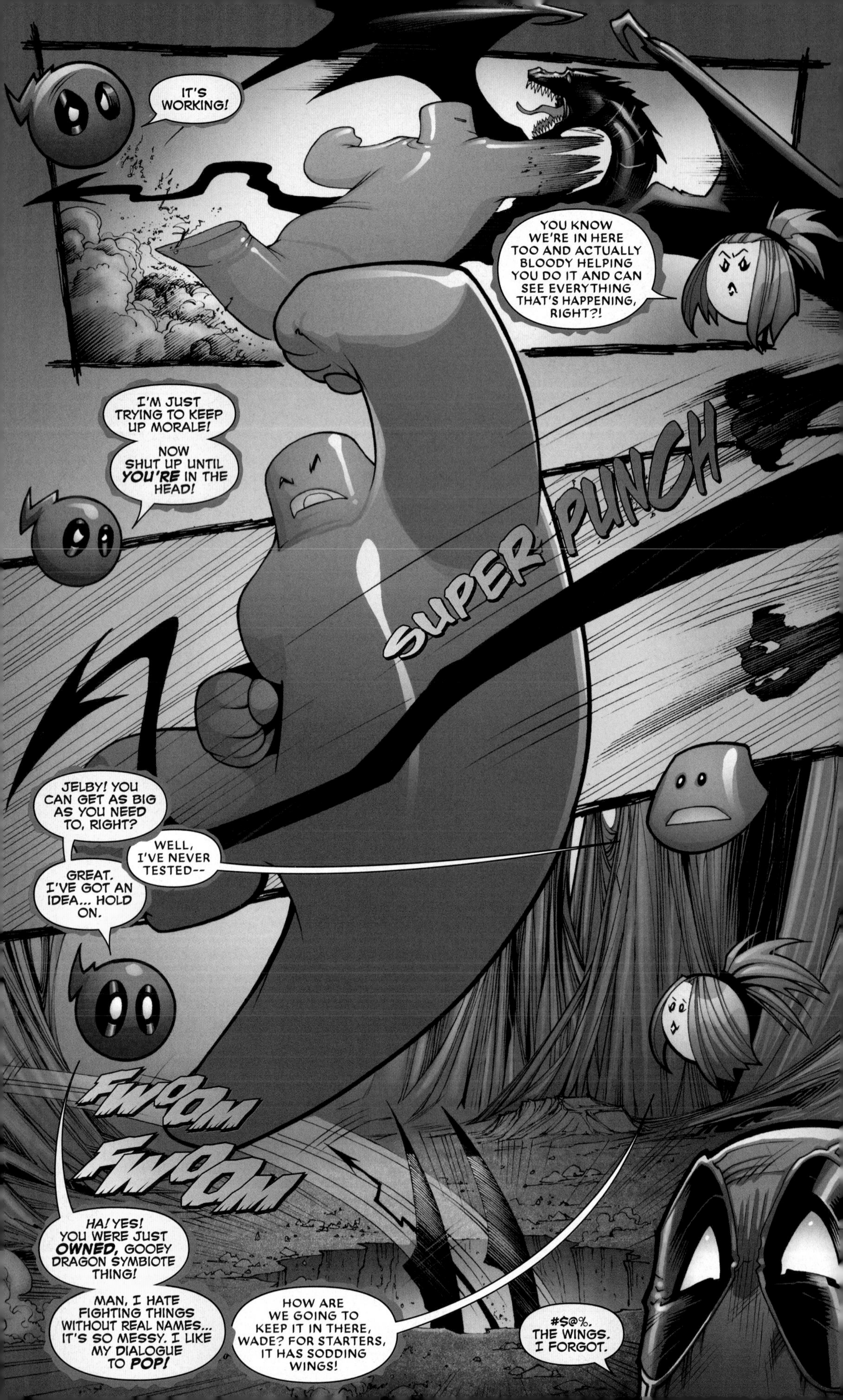
IT'S WORKING!
YOU KNOW WE'RE IN HERE TOO AND ACTUALLY BLOODY HELPING YOU DO IT AND CAN SEE EVERYTHING THAT'S HAPPENING, RIGHT?!
I'M JUST TRYING TO KEEP UP MORALE!
NOW SHUT UP UNTIL YOU'RE IN THE HEAD!
SUPER PUNCH
JELBY! YOU CAN GET AS BIG AS YOU NEED TO, RIGHT?
WELL, I'VE NEVER TESTED--
GREAT. I'VE GOT AN IDEA... HOLD ON.
FWOOM
FWOOM
HA! YES! YOU WERE JUST OWNED, GOOEY DRAGON SYMBIOTE THING!
MAN, I HATE FIGHTING THINGS WITHOUT REAL NAMES... IT'S SO MESSY. I LIKE MY DIALOGUE TO POP!
HOW ARE WE GOING TO KEEP IT IN THERE, WADE? FOR STARTERS, IT HAS SODDING WINGS!
#$@%. THE WINGS. I FORGOT.

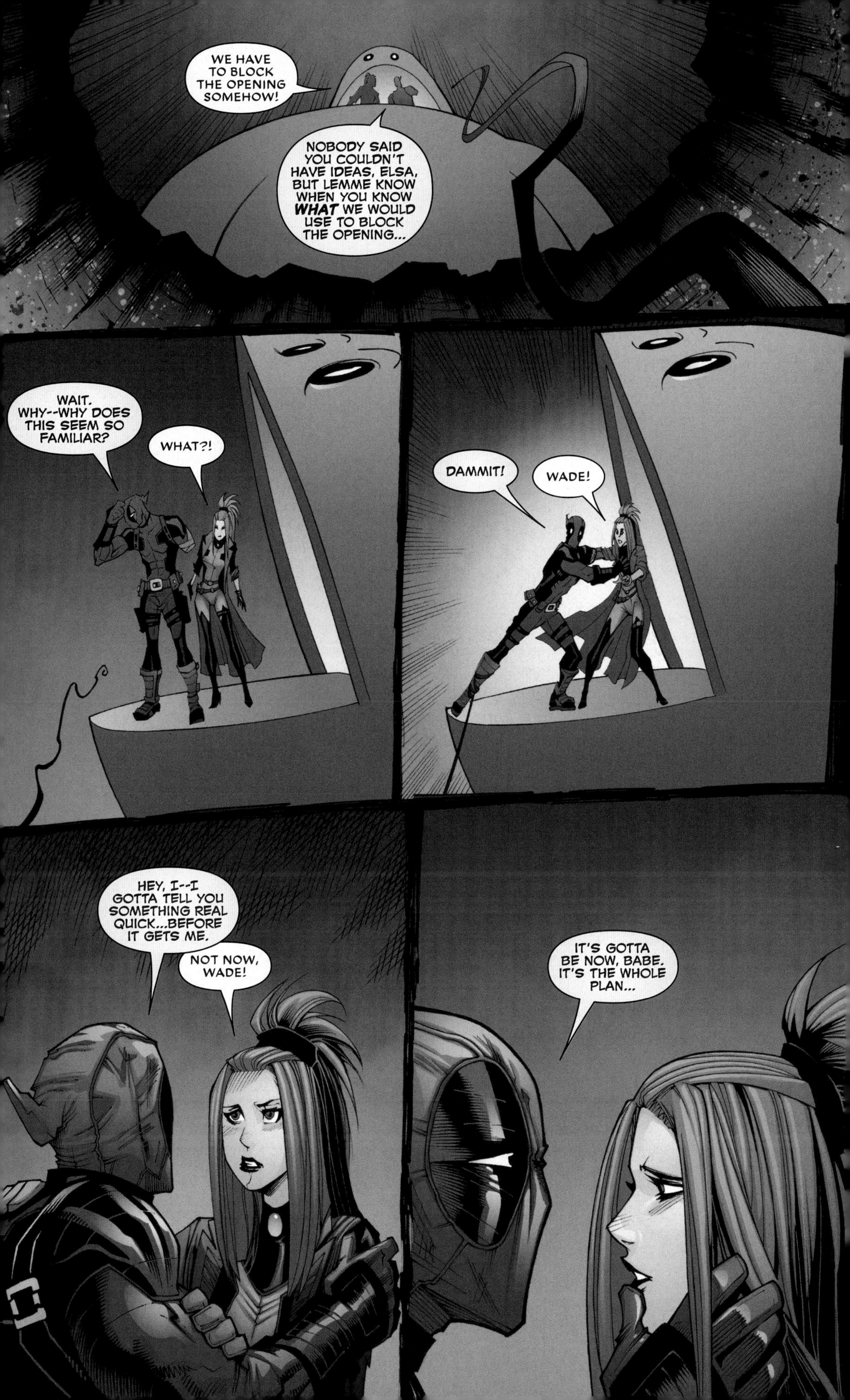
WE HAVE TO BLOCK THE OPENING SOMEHOW!
NOBODY SAID YOU COULDN'T HAVE IDEAS, ELSA, BUT LEMME KNOW WHEN YOU KNOW *WHAT* WE WOULD USE TO BLOCK THE OPENING...
WAIT. WHY--WHY DOES THIS SEEM SO FAMILIAR?
WHAT?!
DAMMIT!
WADE!
HEY, I--I GOTTA TELL YOU SOMETHING REAL QUICK...BEFORE IT GETS ME.
NOT NOW, WADE!
IT'S GOTTA BE NOW, BABE. IT'S THE WHOLE PLAN...

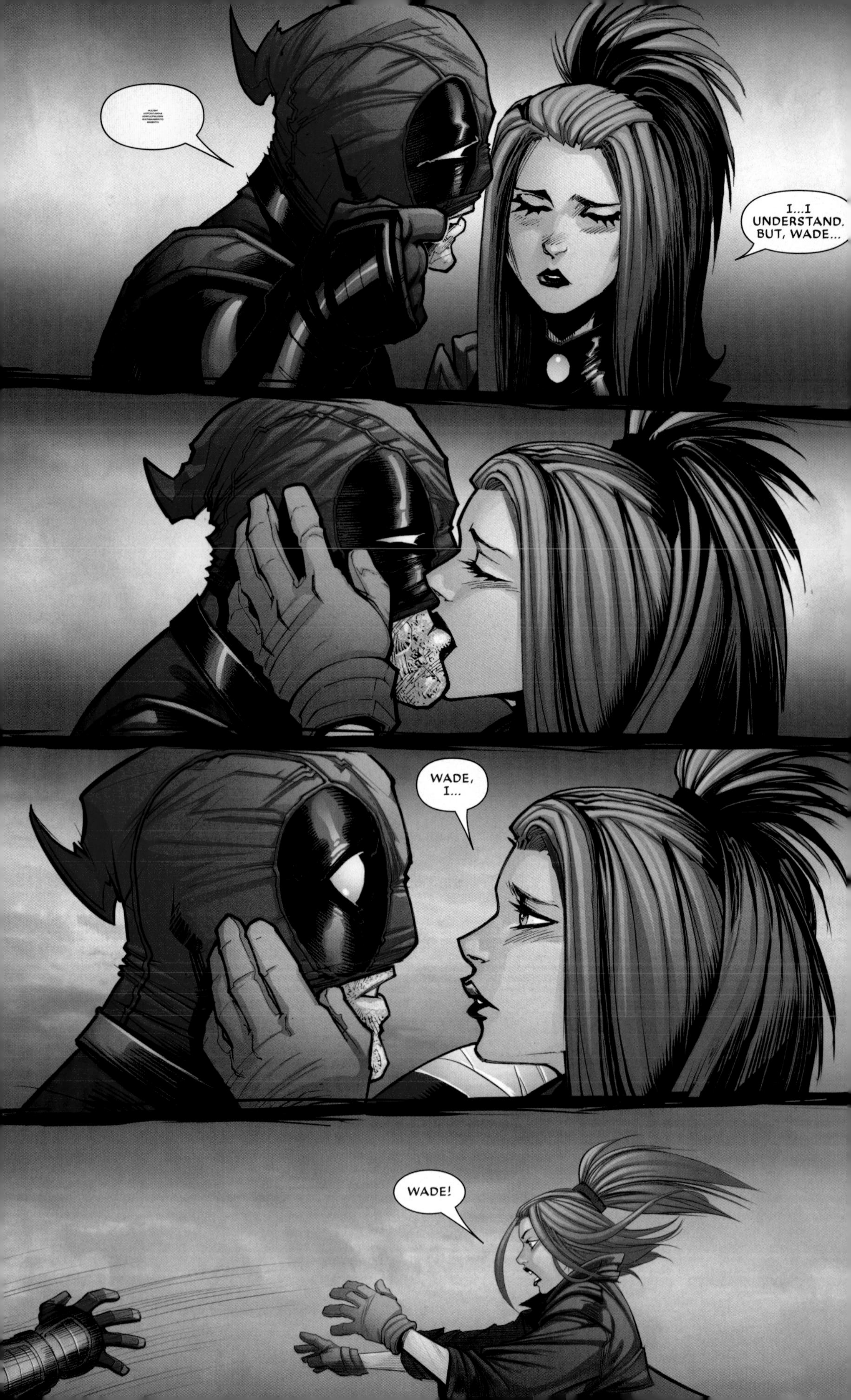
I...I UNDERSTAND. BUT, WADE...
WADE, I...
WADE!

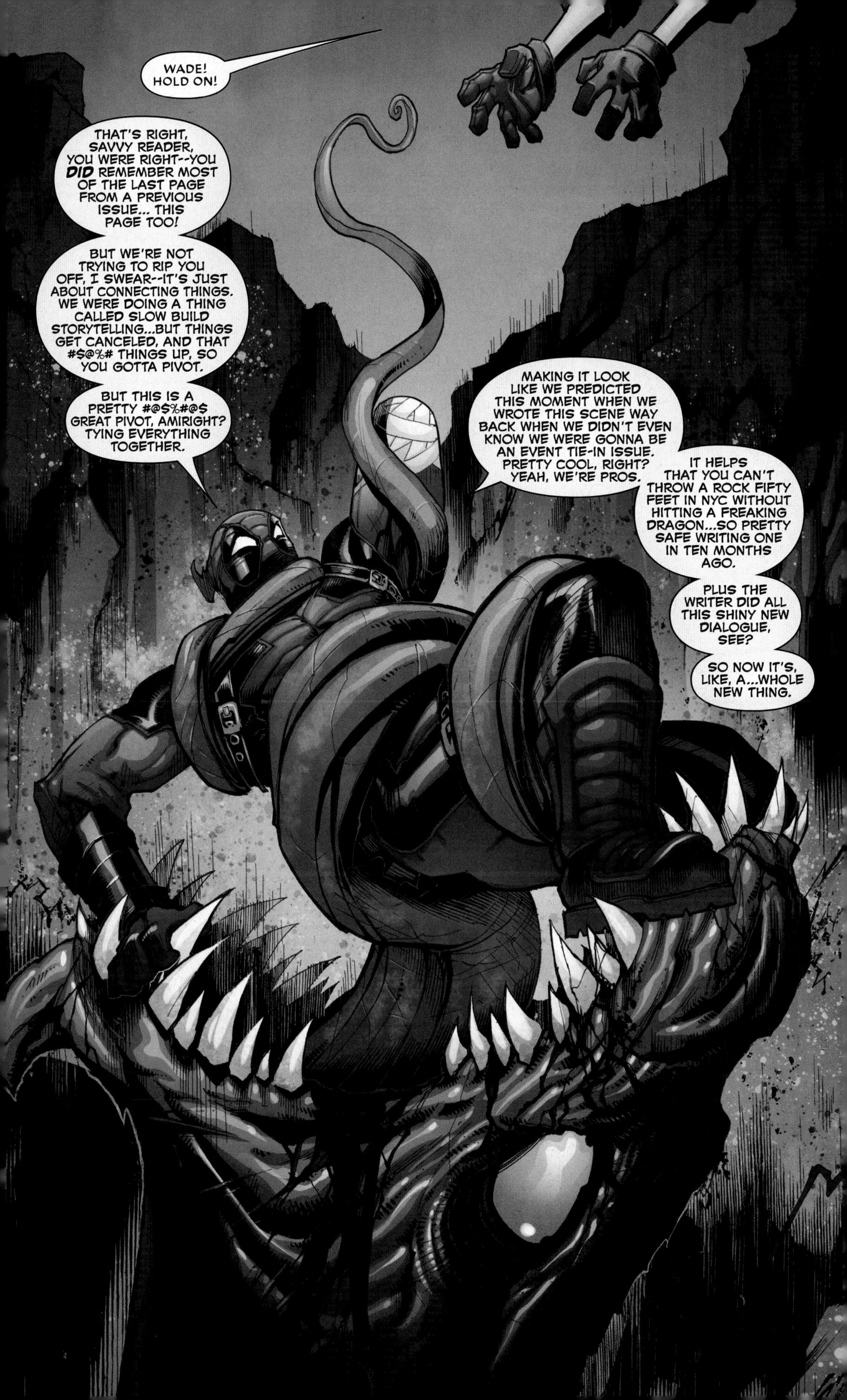
WADE! HOLD ON!
THAT'S RIGHT, SAVVY READER, YOU WERE RIGHT--YOU DID REMEMBER MOST OF THE LAST PAGE FROM A PREVIOUS ISSUE... THIS PAGE TOO!
BUT WE'RE NOT TRYING TO RIP YOU OFF, I SWEAR--IT'S JUST ABOUT CONNECTING THINGS. WE WERE DOING A THING CALLED SLOW BUILD STORYTELLING...BUT THINGS GET CANCELED, AND THAT #$@%# THINGS UP, SO YOU GOTTA PIVOT.
BUT THIS IS A PRETTY #@$%#@$ GREAT PIVOT, AMIRIGHT? TYING EVERYTHING TOGETHER.
MAKING IT LOOK LIKE WE PREDICTED THIS MOMENT WHEN WE WROTE THIS SCENE WAY BACK WHEN WE DIDN'T EVEN KNOW WE WERE GONNA BE AN EVENT TIE-IN ISSUE. PRETTY COOL, RIGHT? YEAH, WE'RE PROS.
IT HELPS THAT YOU CAN'T THROW A ROCK FIFTY FEET IN NYC WITHOUT HITTING A FREAKING DRAGON...SO PRETTY SAFE WRITING ONE IN TEN MONTHS AGO.
PLUS THE WRITER DID ALL THIS SHINY NEW DIALOGUE, SEE?
SO NOW IT'S, LIKE, A...WHOLE NEW THING.

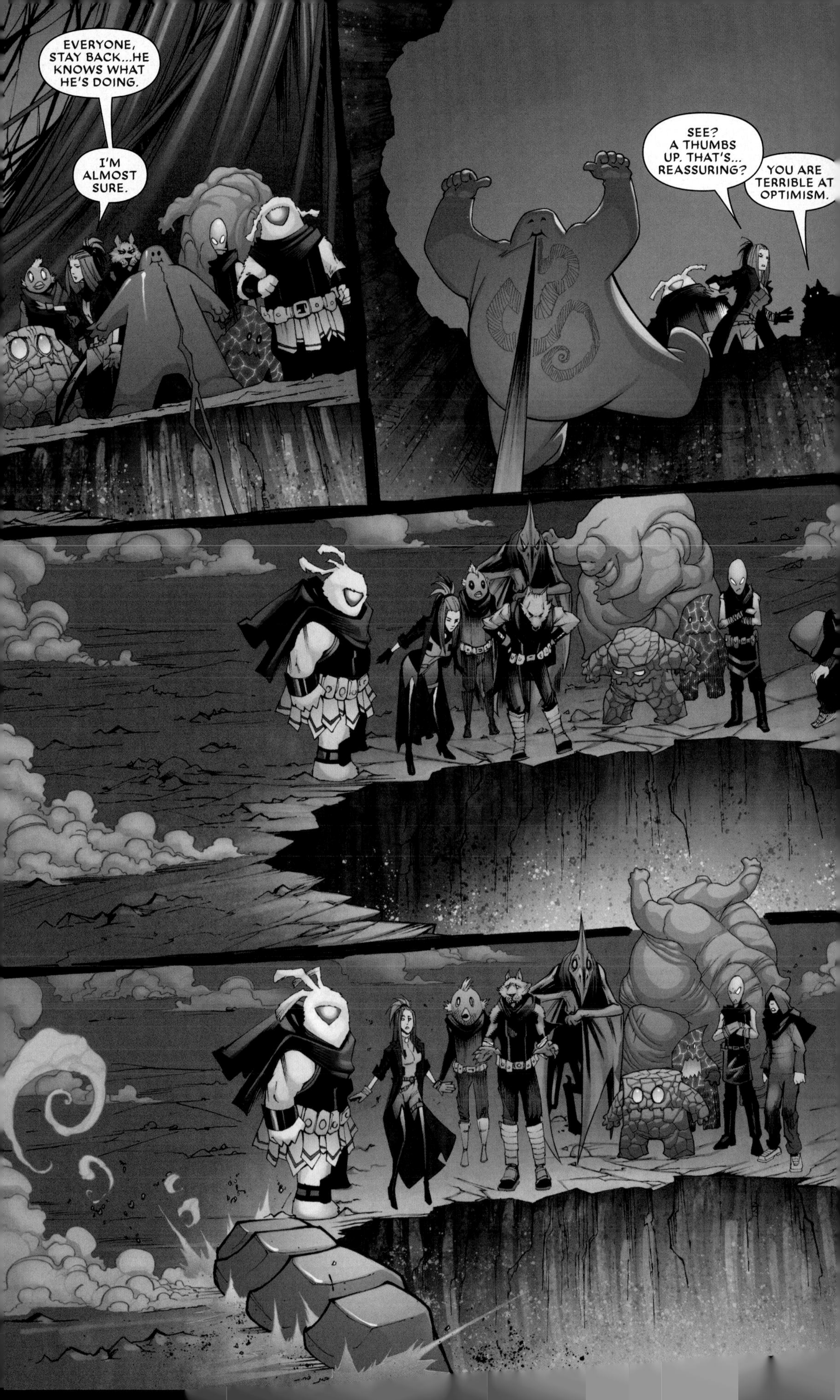
EVERYONE, STAY BACK...HE KNOWS WHAT HE'S DOING.
I'M ALMOST SURE.
SEE? A THUMBS UP. THAT'S... REASSURING?
YOU ARE TERRIBLE AT OPTIMISM.

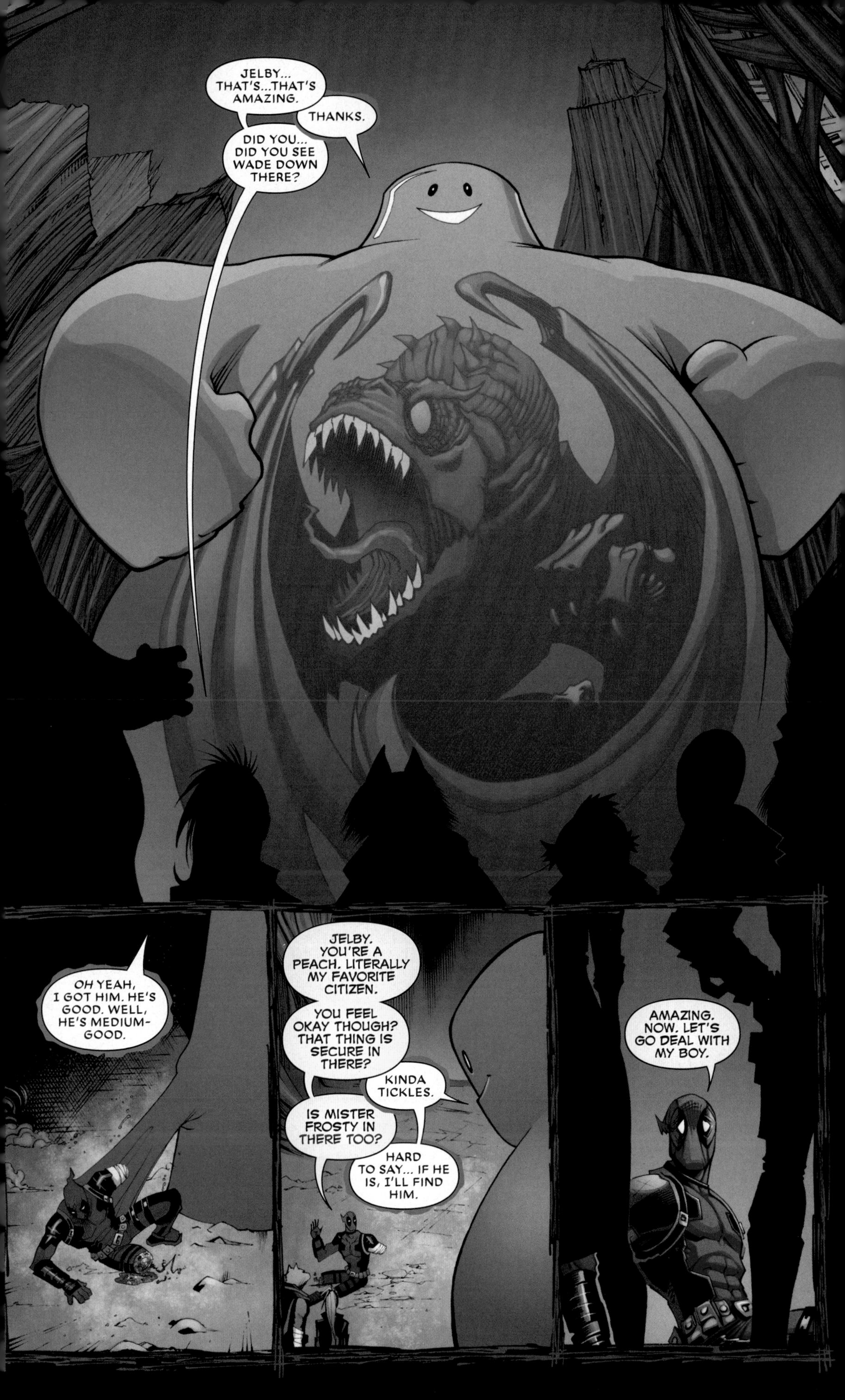
JELBY... THAT'S...THAT'S AMAZING.
THANKS.
DID YOU... DID YOU SEE WADE DOWN THERE?
OH YEAH, I GOT HIM. HE'S GOOD. WELL, HE'S MEDIUM-GOOD.
JELBY. YOU'RE A PEACH. LITERALLY MY FAVORITE CITIZEN.
YOU FEEL OKAY THOUGH? THAT THING IS SECURE IN THERE?
KINDA TICKLES.
IS MISTER FROSTY IN THERE TOO?
HARD TO SAY... IF HE IS, I'LL FIND HIM.
AMAZING. NOW. LET'S GO DEAL WITH MY BOY.

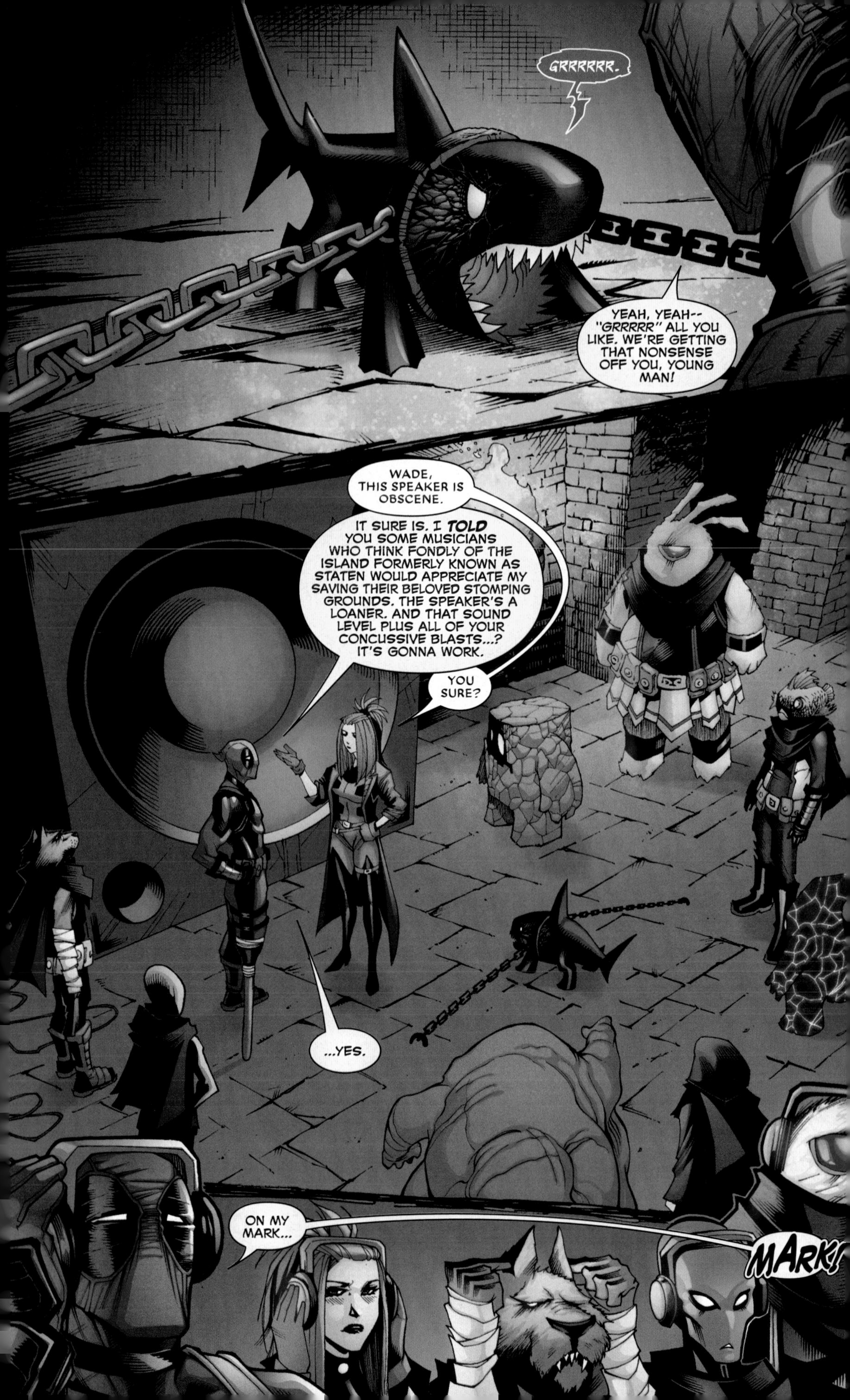
GRRRRRR.
YEAH, YEAH-- "GRRRRR" ALL YOU LIKE. WE'RE GETTING THAT NONSENSE OFF YOU, YOUNG MAN!
WADE, THIS SPEAKER IS OBSCENE.
IT SURE IS. I TOLD YOU SOME MUSICIANS WHO THINK FONDLY OF THE ISLAND FORMERLY KNOWN AS STATEN WOULD APPRECIATE MY SAVING THEIR BELOVED STOMPING GROUNDS. THE SPEAKER'S A LOANER. AND THAT SOUND LEVEL PLUS ALL OF YOUR CONCUSSIVE BLASTS...? IT'S GONNA WORK.
YOU SURE?
...YES.
ON MY MARK...
MARK!

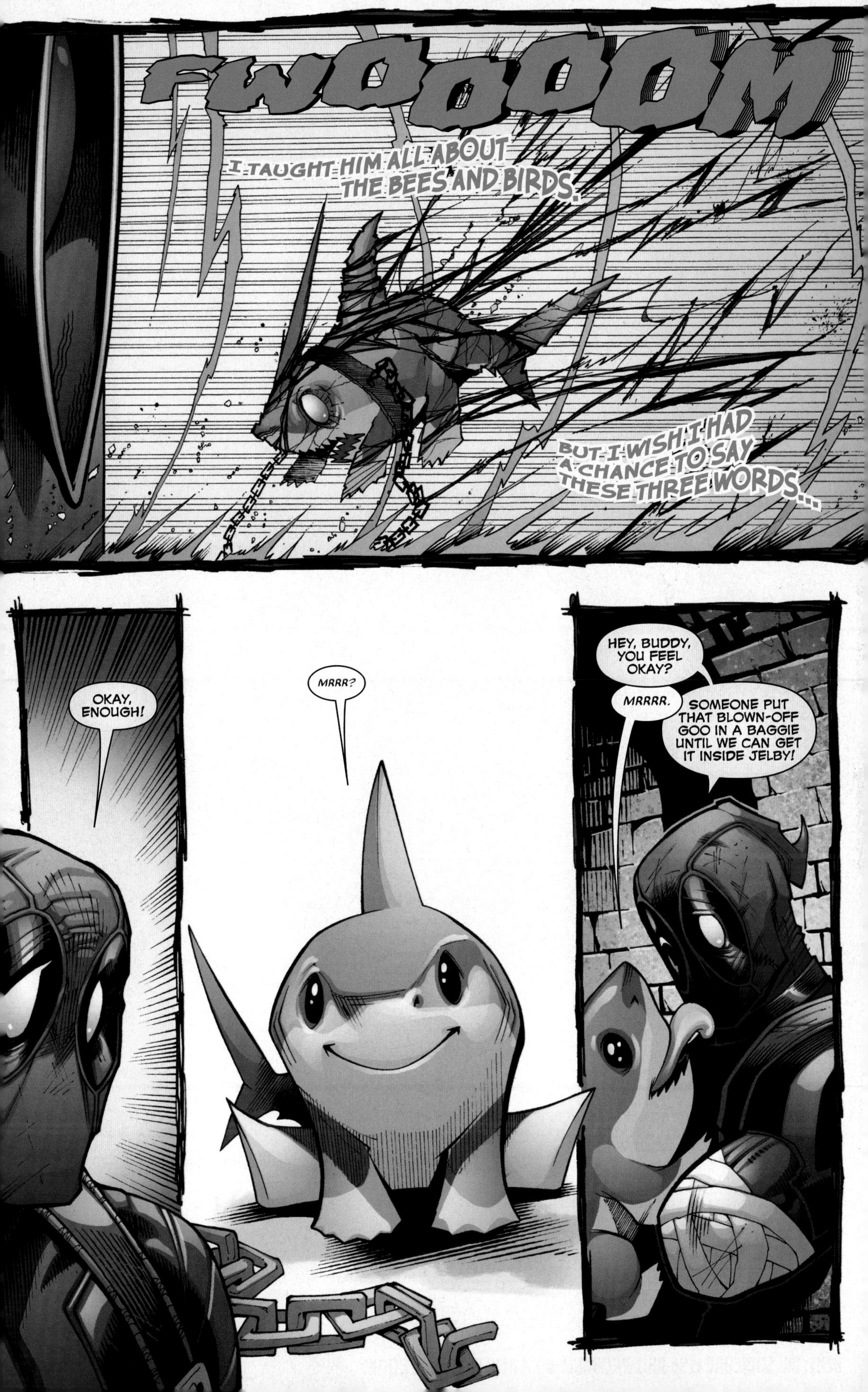
FWOOOOM
I TAUGHT HIM ALL ABOUT THE BEES AND BIRDS.
BUT I WISH I HAD A CHANCE TO SAY THESE THREE WORDS...
OKAY, ENOUGH!
MRRR?
HEY, BUDDY, YOU FEEL OKAY?
MRRRR.
SOMEONE PUT THAT BLOWN-OFF GOO IN A BAGGIE UNTIL WE CAN GET IT INSIDE JELBY!

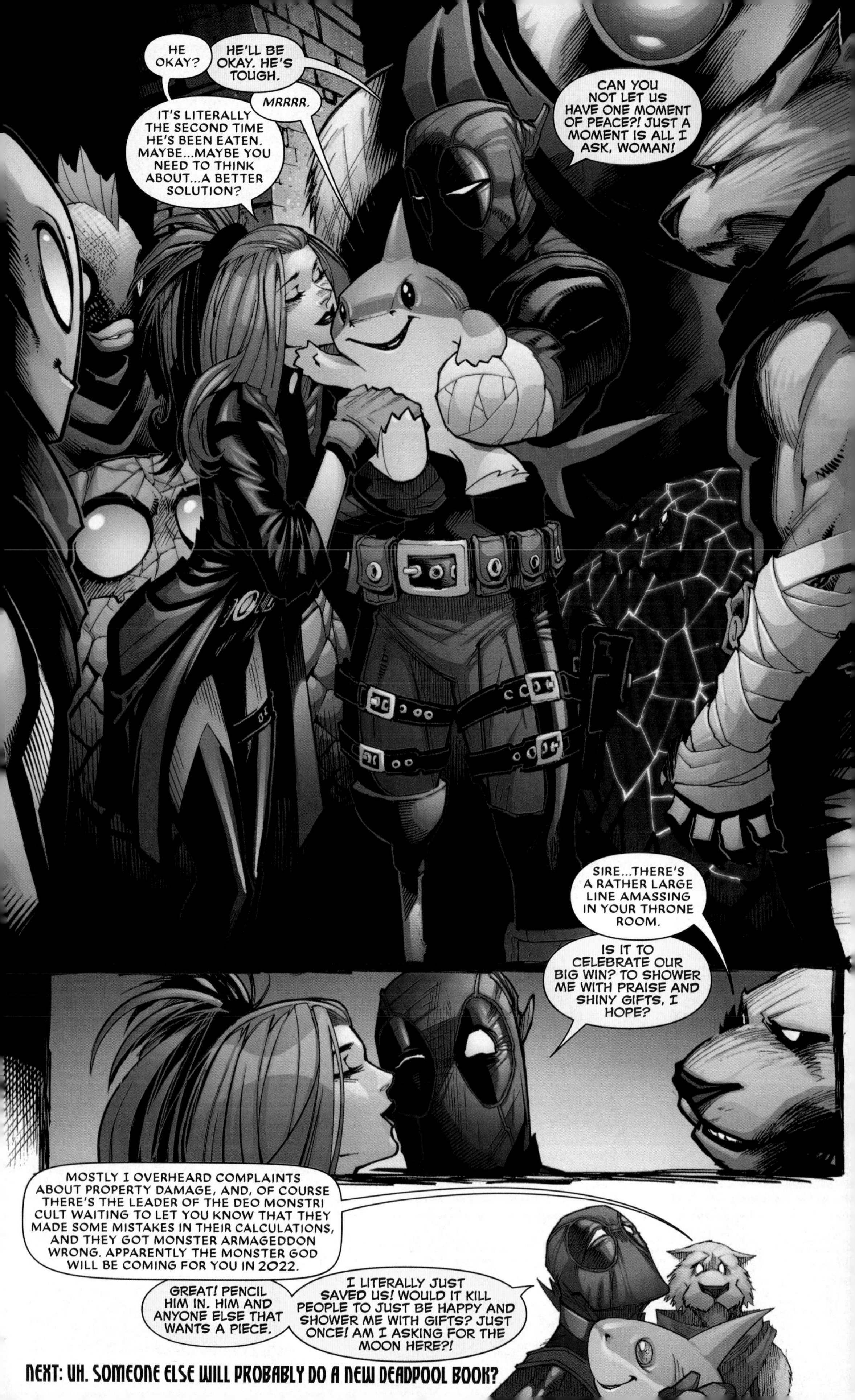
HE OKAY?
HE'LL BE OKAY. HE'S TOUGH.
MRRRR.
IT'S LITERALLY THE SECOND TIME HE'S BEEN EATEN. MAYBE...MAYBE YOU NEED TO THINK ABOUT...A BETTER SOLUTION?
CAN YOU NOT LET US HAVE ONE MOMENT OF PEACE?! JUST A MOMENT IS ALL I ASK, WOMAN!
SIRE...THERE'S A RATHER LARGE LINE AMASSING IN YOUR THRONE ROOM.
IS IT TO CELEBRATE OUR BIG WIN? TO SHOWER ME WITH PRAISE AND SHINY GIFTS, I HOPE?
MOSTLY I OVERHEARD COMPLAINTS ABOUT PROPERTY DAMAGE, AND, OF COURSE THERE'S THE LEADER OF THE DEO MONSTRI CULT WAITING TO LET YOU KNOW THAT THEY MADE SOME MISTAKES IN THEIR CALCULATIONS, AND THEY GOT MONSTER ARMAGEDDON WRONG. APPARENTLY THE MONSTER GOD WILL BE COMING FOR YOU IN 2022.
GREAT! PENCIL HIM IN. HIM AND ANYONE ELSE THAT WANTS A PIECE.
I LITERALLY JUST SAVED US! WOULD IT KILL PEOPLE TO JUST BE HAPPY AND SHOWER ME WITH GIFTS? JUST ONCE! AM I ASKING FOR THE MOON HERE?!
NEXT: UH. SOMEONE ELSE WILL PROBABLY DO A NEW DEADPOOL BOOK?

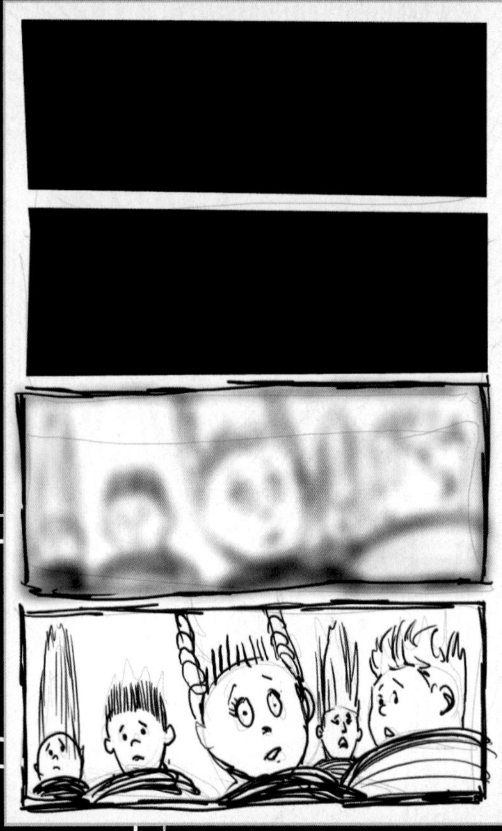

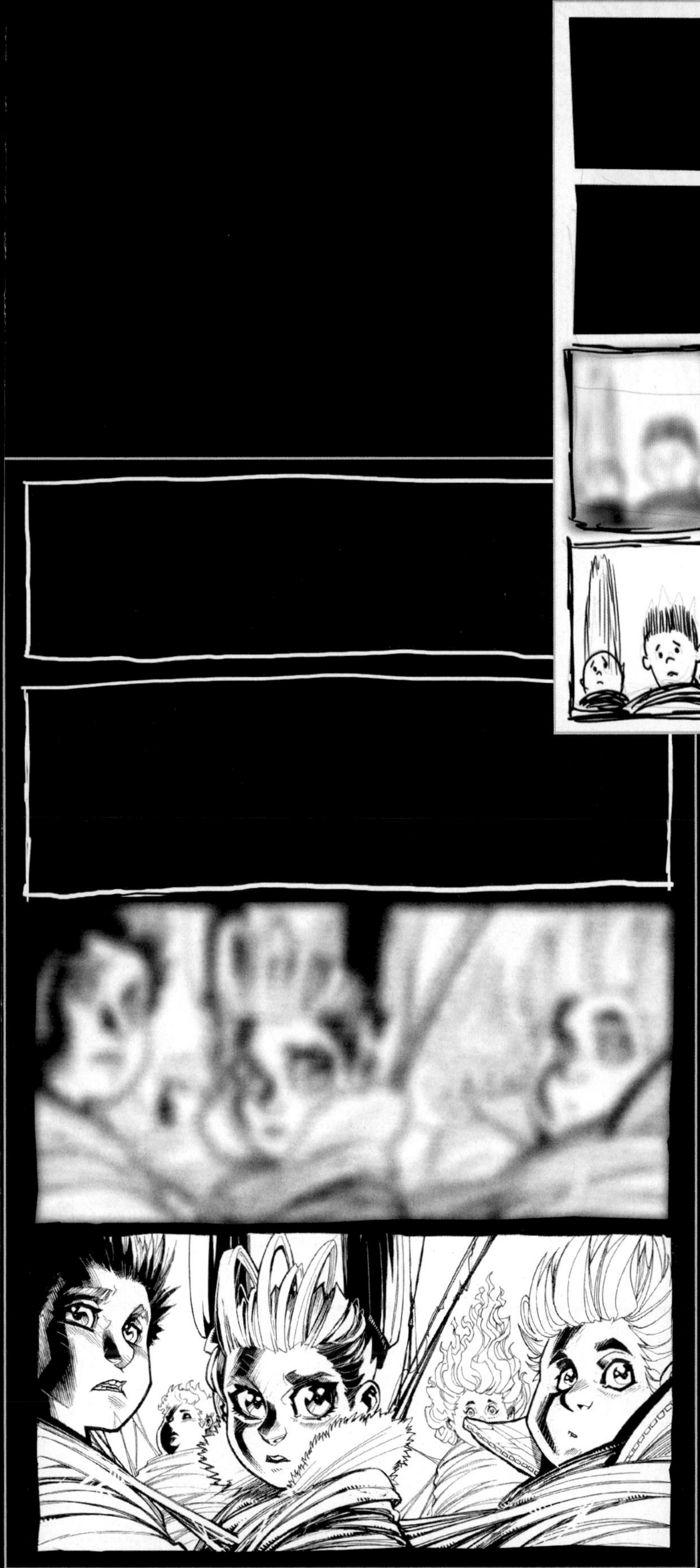

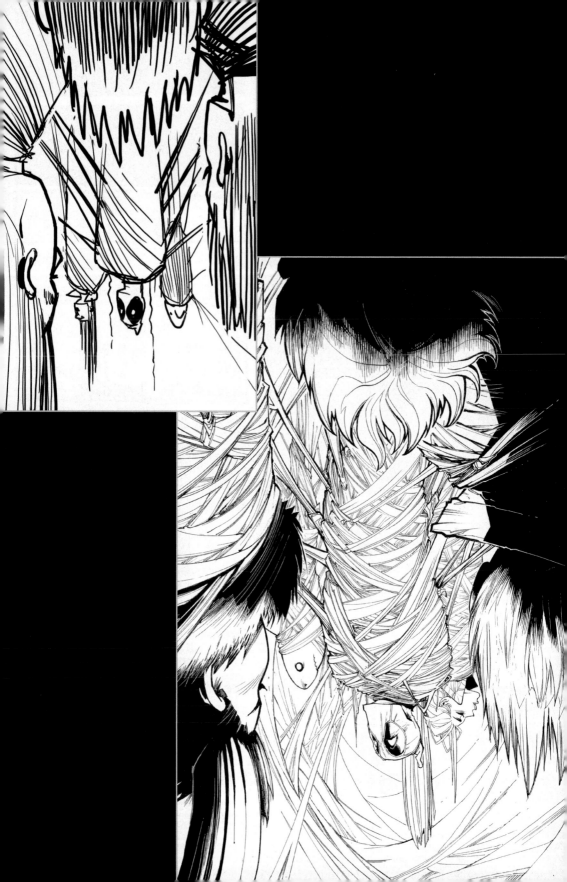

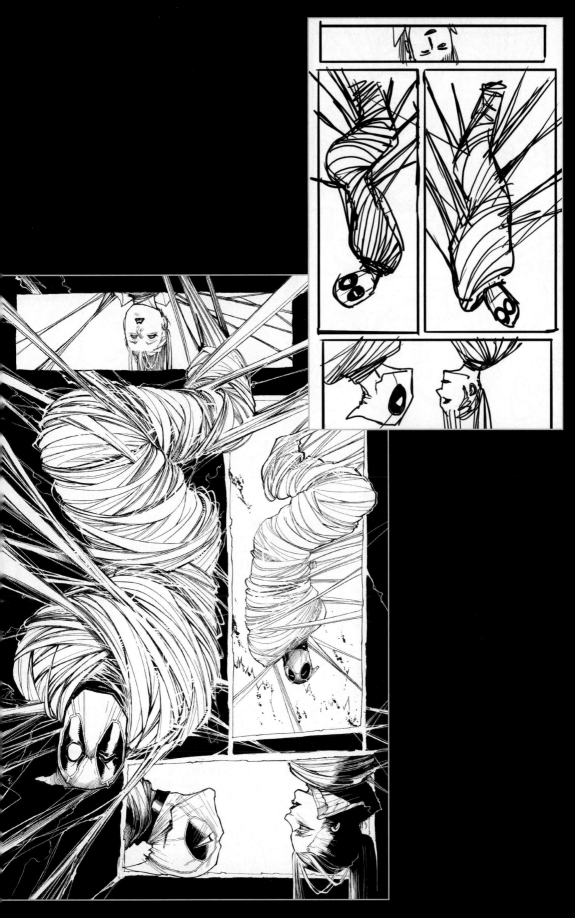

#8, Page 3 Art Process by
GERARDO SANDOVAL

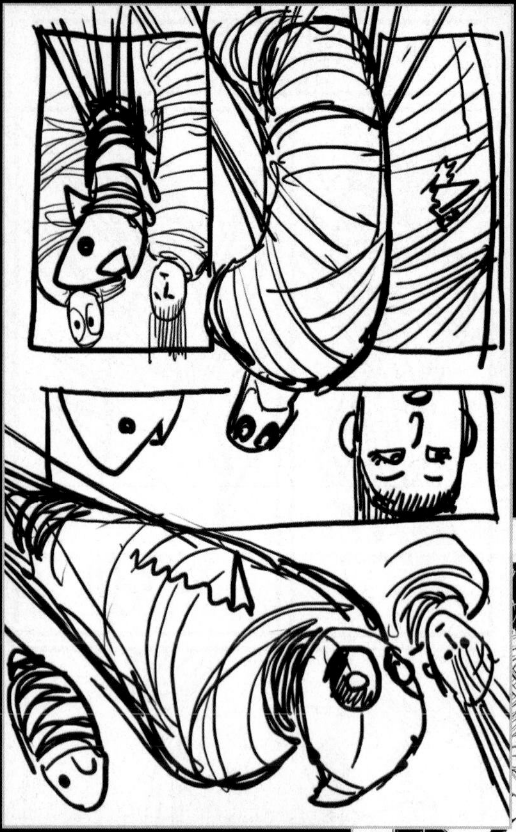

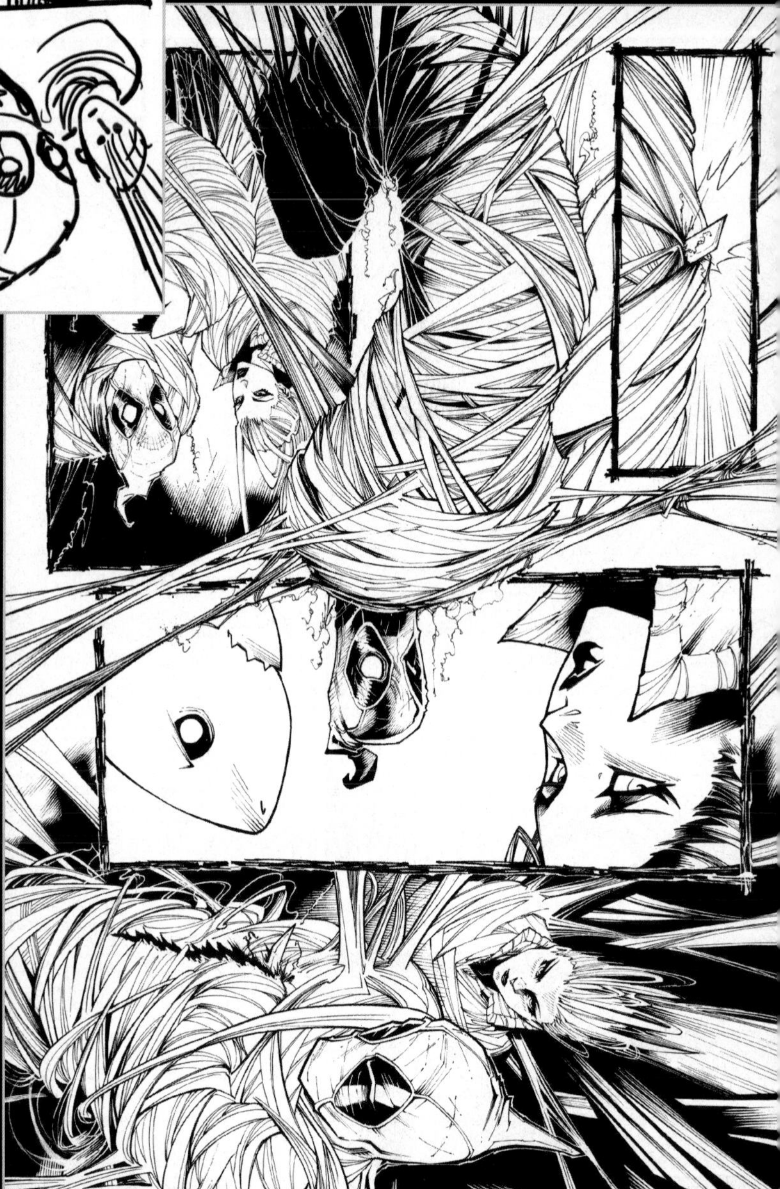

#8, Page 4 Art Process by

Gerardo Sandoval & Victor Nava

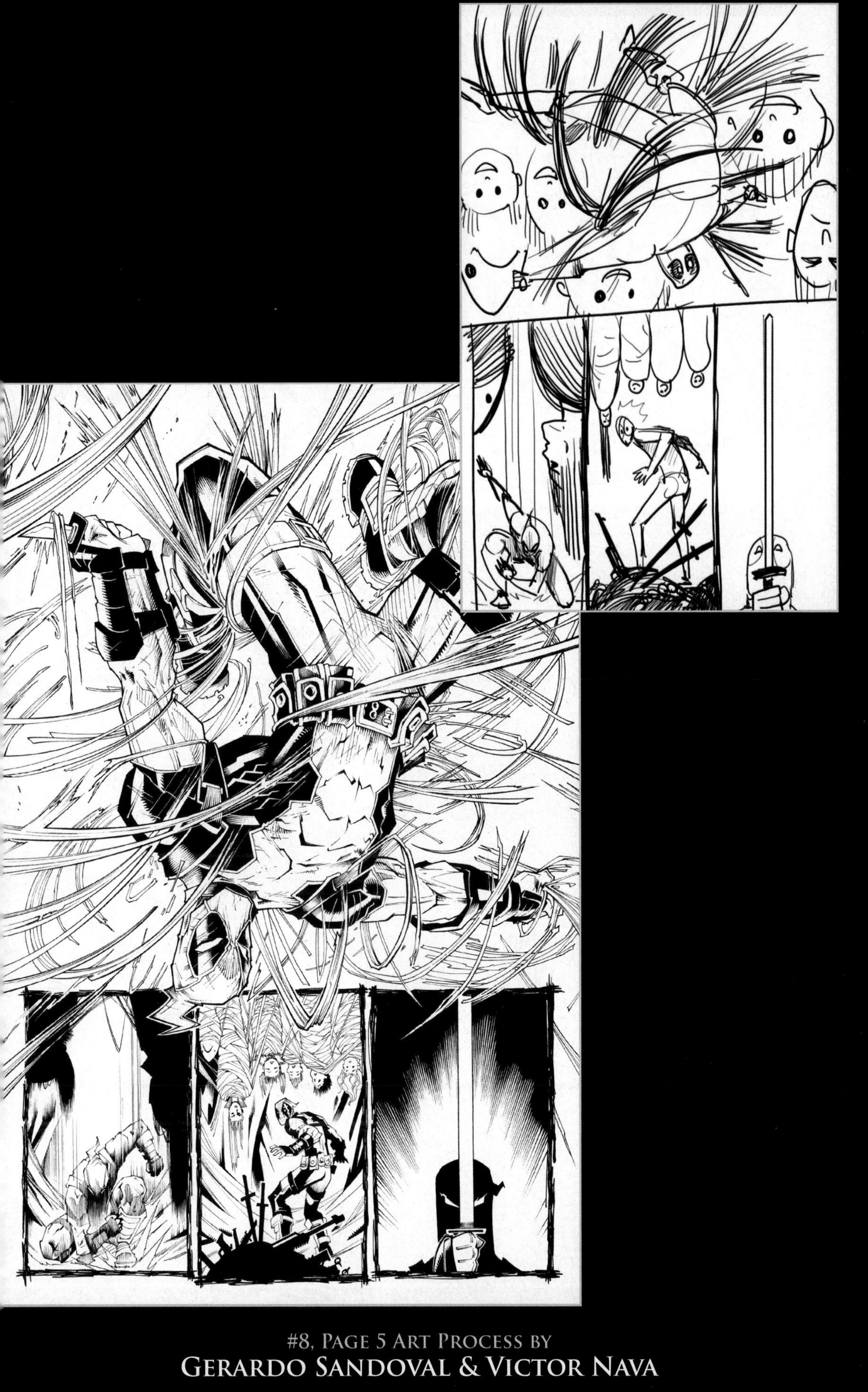

#8, Page 5 Art Process by
Gerardo Sandoval & Victor Nava

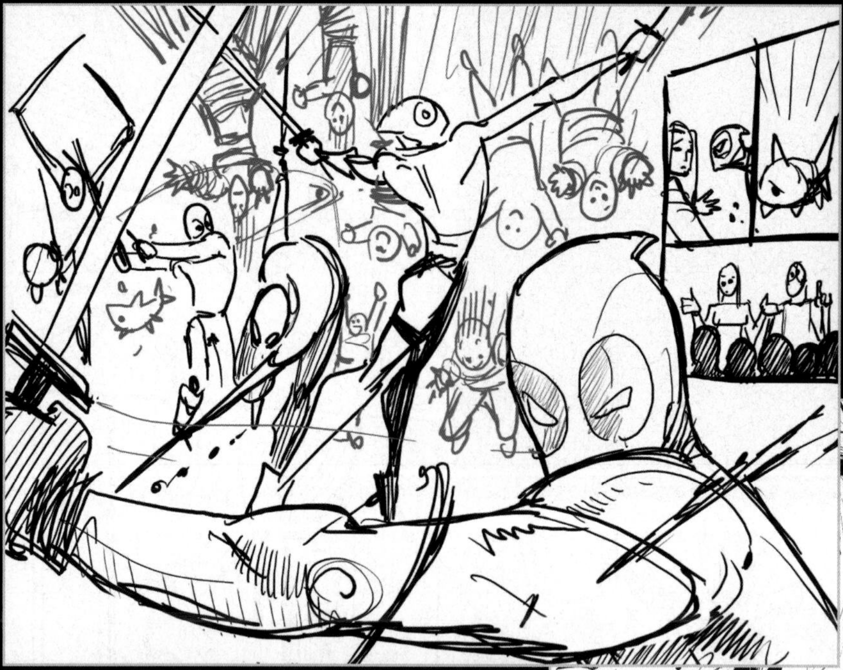

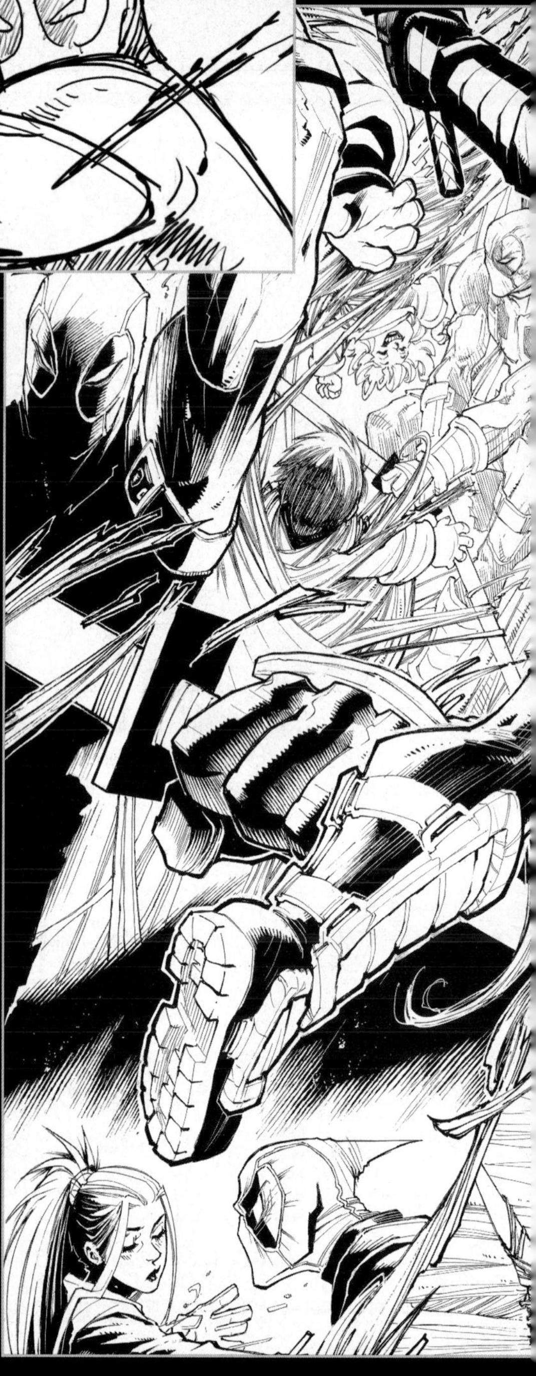

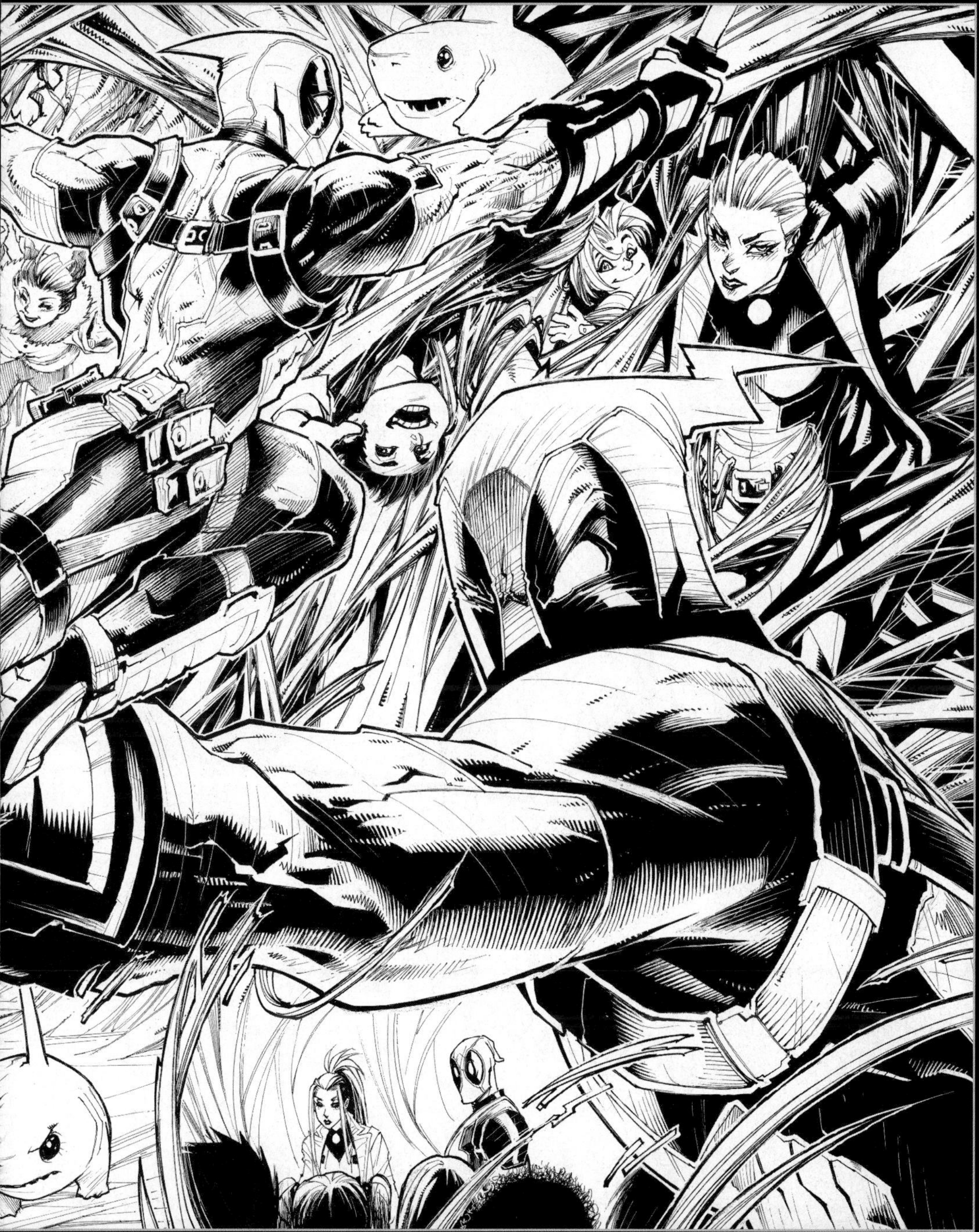

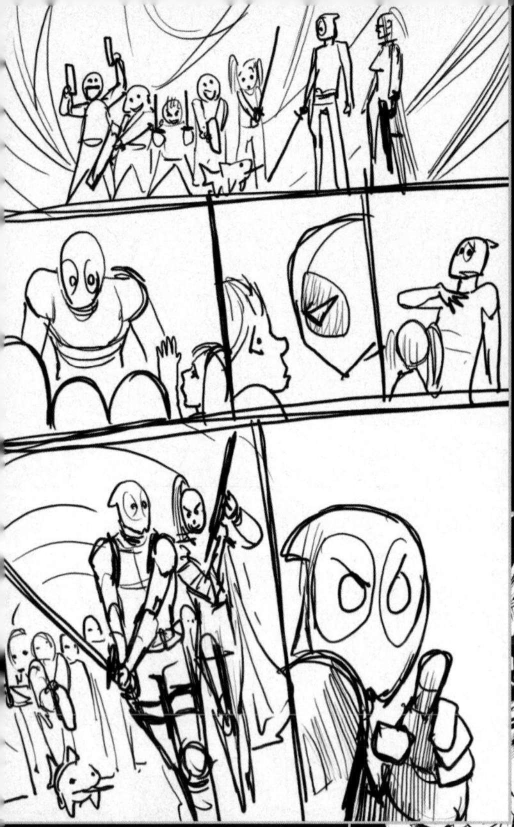
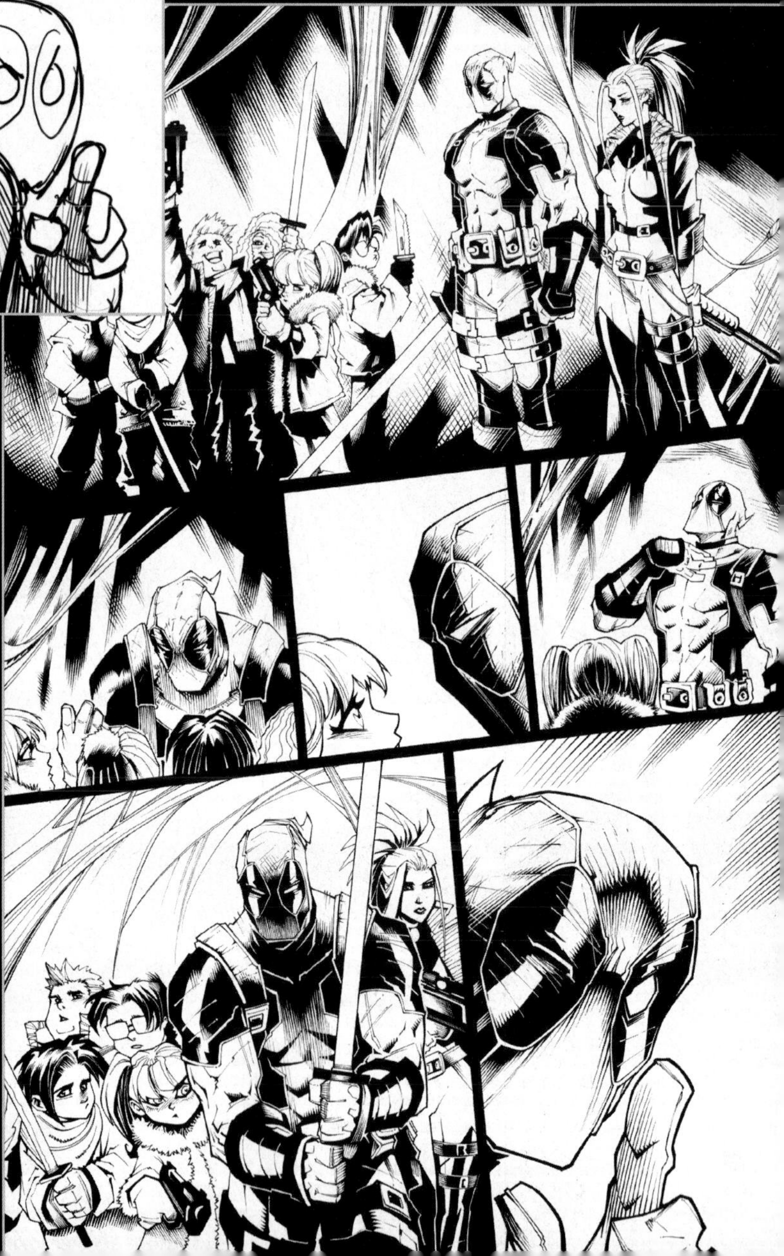

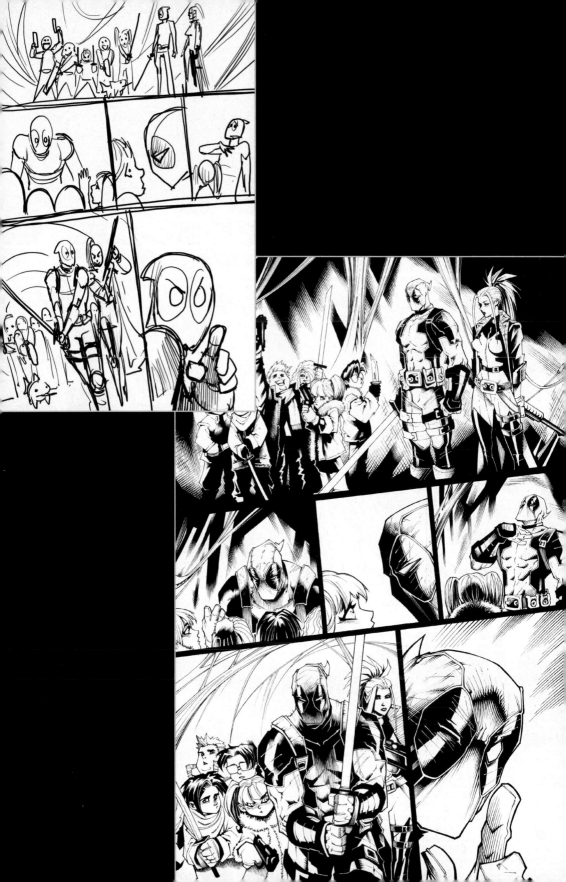

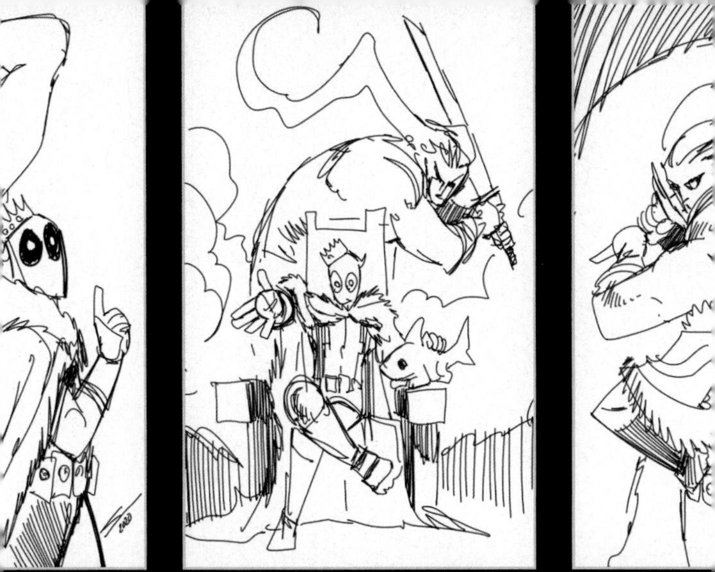

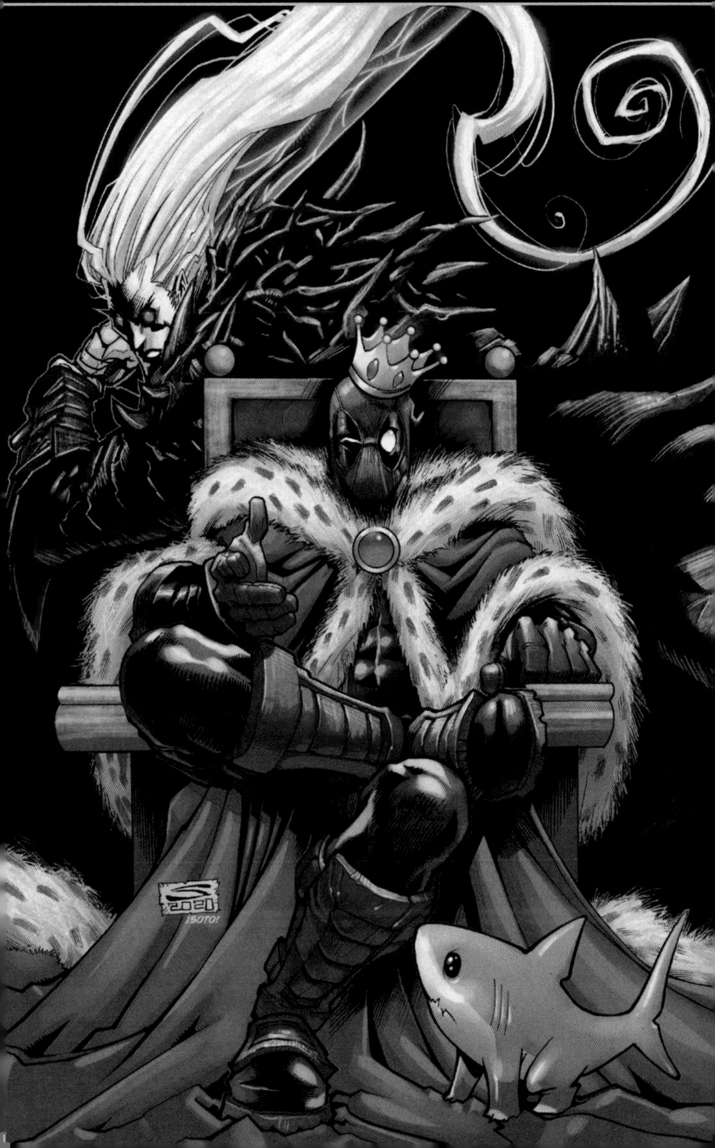

2020
¡SOTO!

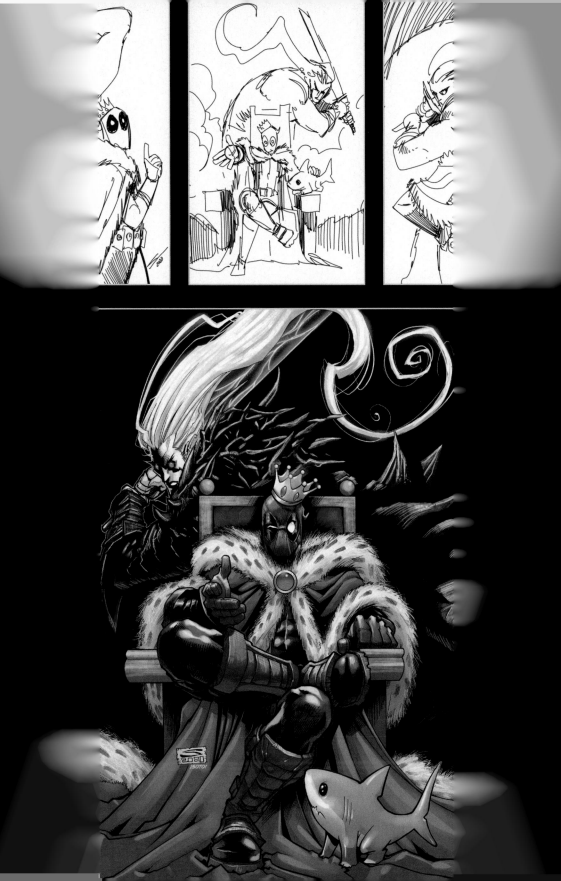